Studies in
(Pa

Gerald O'Nolan

Alpha Editions

This edition published in 2019

ISBN : 9789353955373

Design and Setting By
Alpha Editions
email - alphaedis@gmail.com

As per information held with us this book is in Public Domain.
This book is a reproduction of an important historical work.
Alpha Editions uses the best technology to reproduce historical work in the same manner it was first published to preserve its original nature. Any marks or number seen are left intentionally to preserve its true form.

STUDIES IN MODERN IRISH

Part I.

By

The Rev. GERALD Ó NOLAN, M.A., B.D.,

Professor of Irish,

ST. PATRICK'S COLLEGE,
MAYNOOTH.

Dom is dleact a peact do ṁoṁaḋ,
Dom is eol a rceol do rcaoileaḋ,
Liom is áil a cáil do cuiṁneaṁ,
Ór liom is cóir a glóir do niaṁaḋ.

(*Cf. Keating's Poems, XII, p.* 48)

[*Second edition revised.*]

THE EDUCATIONAL COMPANY OF IRELAND,
LIMITED, ... DUBLIN.

1920.

PREFACE.

In offering this book to the Irish public, the Author trusts that it will supply a long-felt want. The existing Grammars and Composition Books are quite inadequate for the purpose of giving the earnest student a thorough grasp of the niceties of Irish idiom, and the beauty of the language generally. It was at first intended to incorporate in the present work a treatise on Continuous Prose Composition, but it was found that such a proceeding would have made the volume inconveniently bulky. We hope before long to publish this Part II separately.

Our thanks are due to the Publishers and the Printers for their unfailing courtesy, and the expedition with which they have put the work through the Press.

⁊earóiᴅ Ó nuallá1n,
St. Patrick's College, Maynooth.

18th June, 1919.

CONTENTS:

	PAGE
CHAP. I.—THE VERB IS	1-49
Section I,—*Introductory*	1-4
II.—A.—*Classification.*—Direct Forms	4-7
Dependent Forms	7-8
B.—*Complex elliptical sentences*	
(Either *Classification or Identification*)	8-10
Exx. 1 and 2 (*Classification*)	11-12
C.—*Identification* :—	
Type I. VpPS.	12-13
Ex. 3 (Type I).	14
Type II. (Four Varieties) :—	
(*a*) VpSP.	15-18
Ex. 4 (Type II. a)	18-19
(*b*) VpS ná P.	19-20
Note on development of ná and aċ	20-22
(*c*) VpS aċ P.	23
Ex. 5 (Type IIc.)	23
Ex. 6 (Types IIb and IIc.)	24-25
(*d*) VpS maṗ P.	25
Ex. 7 (Type IId.)	25-26
Type III.—VpSP.	27-28
Ex. 8 (Type III.)	28-29

CONTENTS

	PAGE
Type IV.—PVpS.	29-31
Ex. 9 (Type IV.)	31-32
Type V.—PS.	32-33
Ex. 10 (Type V.)	33-34
Type VI.—SP.	34-35
Ex. 11 (Type VI.)	35
Type VII.—VPS.	35-37
Ex. 12 (Type VII.)	37
Type VIII.—VpPS.	38-40
Ex. 13 (Types VIII and VII.)	40
Type IX.—V*p*SP.	40-41
Type X.—SVpPs.	41
Note on Proper Names	41-43
Fundamental Rule of ⲓⲣ construction	44
Exceptions to so-called rule for insertion of pronoun before definite noun	44-47
Questions with Verb ⲓⲣ	47-49
Appendix	49
CHAP. II.—PROLEPSIS	50-87
1°. ⲟ̄, ⲓ̄, ⲓⲁⲩ, ⲉⲁⲩ	50
2°. ⲡⲟⲉ	50-51
3°. ⲡⲉ	51-52
4°. ⲡⲟ,	52
5°. ⲡⲁⲛ	52-53
6°. ⲉ̄ ⲡⲓⲛ	53
Ex. 14 (Prolepsis 1°-6°)	53-54
7°. ⲁ. (Three different uses)	54-55
First use	55-57
Ex. 15 (Proleptic ⲁ (1))	57-58
Second use	58-60
Ex. 16 (Proleptic ⲁ (2))	60-61
Third use	61-62
Ex. 17 (Proleptic ⲁ (3))	62-63

CONTENTS

	PAGE
8°. ɴá (however, notwithstanding, etc.)	63-64
Ex. 18 (Proleptic ᴀ : ᴅá)	64-66
9° Proportion Sentences	66-68
Ex. 19 (Proportion)	68
Exx. 20-23 (Proportion)	69-71
10° Proleptic ᴅe	72-73
Ex. 24 (Proleptic ᴅe)	73-74
Ex. 25 (ᴅe non-proleptic)	74-75
Ex. 26 (ᴅe Retrospective & Proleptic)	75
11°. ᴀcᴀ	75-76
Ex. 27 (Proleptic ᴀcᴀ)	77
12°. Other prepositional pronouns :—ᴀɪp, leɪr, uɪme, etc.	77-78
Ex. 28 (Proleptic prep. pronouns)	78
13°. Proleptic ᴀɪɴlᴀɪó	79-81
Exx. 29-34 (Proleptic ᴀɪɴlᴀɪó)	81-87
Remarks	87
CHAP. III.—RELATIVE PARTICLES	88-141
Section I. Direct Relatives :—	
1° ᴀ'	88-89
Exceptional uses for the oblique	89-92
2°. ᴅo'	93-94
3°. ᴀ ó'	94
4°. ? (The relative is understood)	94
Ex. 35 (Direct Relatives)	95-96
Ex. 36 (Superfluous use after ᴀɪɴlᴀɪó)	97
Ex. 37 (,, ,, ,, ,,)	97-98
Section II. The Oblique Relatives :—	
5°. ᴀⁿ ; ᴀp' (Genitive)	98
(Dative)	99
Ex. 38 Relatives ᴀⁿ and ᴀp	100
Ex. 39 (,, ,, ,, ,,)	100-101
6°. 50, 5up (Dative)	101
(Genitive)	102
Ex. 40 (Relatives 50 and 5up)	102-103
Ex. 41 (,, ,, ,, ,,)	103-104

CONTENTS

	PAGE
Note on expression of genitive relative	105
7°. n-ᴀ, n-ᴀp	105-106
Ex. 42 (n-ᴀ and n-ᴀp, Dative)	106
Ex. 43 (,, ,, ,, Genitive)	107
Remarks	108
Development of 50, 5up	108-111
Development of n-ᴀ, n-ᴀp	111-112
Further Remarks	112-113
The Relative in Scotch Gaelic	113-114
Section III. Double Relative Construction	114-116
Ex. 44 (Double Relative)	116-117
Exx. 45-49 (Double Relative)	118-125
Section IV.—Treble, Quadruple, Quintuple Relative Clauses	125-127
Ex. 50	127
Section V.—Double Relative.—Apparent exceptions and abnormal usages	128-133
Remarks	133-134
Section VI.—Negative Relatives	134-135
Section VII.—Comparative and Superlative Adjectives	136-137
Ex. 51 (Comparative and Superlative Adjectives.—Double Relative)	137-138
Section VIII.—Interrogative and Relative	138-140
Ex. 52 (Interrogative and Relative)	140-141
CHAP. IV.—THE VERBAL NOUN	142-153
Section I.—Ordinary uses in Nom., Gen., Dat., Accus.	142-147
Section II.—Subject and Object of Action expressed in Verbal Noun Phrase	147-148
Ex. 53 (Verbal Noun)	148-149
Ex. 54 (,, ,,)	149
Ex. 55 (Subject & Object expressed)	150-151
Remarks	151
Section III.—Verbal Noun in Passive Sense	151-152
Ex. 56 (Verbal Noun in Passive Sense)	152-153

CONTENTS

	PAGE
CHAP. V.—PARTITIVE ᴅe	154-156
Exx. 57-59 (Partitive ᴅe)	156-158
CHAP. VI.—NOUN PHRASES	158-162
Three kinds	158-159
A.—*The Bracketed Construction*	159
B.—*The Un-bracketed Construction*	160
C.—*Nouns used adverbially without preposition*	160
Ex. 60 (The Bracketed Construction)	160-161
Ex. 61 (The Un-bracketed Construction)	161-162
CHAP. VII.—PREPOSITIONAL PHRASES	163-192
Section I.—A.—*Substantival*	163
B.—*Adverbial*	163
C.—*Adjectival*	164
Ex. 63 (Prepositional Phrases)	165
Section II.—I. *Prepositions before Nouns*	166-172
(a) The preposition ap	166-176
(b) ,, , ᴀr	167
(c) ,, ,, cum	167
(d) ,, ,, ᴅo	168
(e) ,, ,, ᴅe	168-169
(f) ,, ,, ɪn	169
(g) ,, ,, le	169-171
(h) ,, ,, ó	171
(i) ,, ,, map	171
(l) ,, ,, óp	171
(m) ,, ,, pé	172
(n) , ,, pan	172
(o) ,, ,, um	172
II. *Prepositions after Nouns and Adjectives*	173-178
III. *Prepositions after Verbs*	178-187
Exx. 64-68 (Prepositions)	188-192
CHAP. VIII.—ELLIPSIS AND CHANGE OF CONSTRUCTION	193-196
Ex. 69 (Change of Construction)	196-197

CONTENTS

CHAP. IX.—CONTAMINATION AND OTHER PHENOMENA	..	198-208
A.—*Contamination*	.. ..	198-201
B.—*Other irregularities*	.. ..	201-204
C.—*Other cases of ellipsis*	..	204-208
CHAP. X.—MISCELLANEOUS	.. .. ..	209-223
A.—*Prepositional pronoun instead of Genitive or Nominative*		209
B.—*Introductory* "τά"	.. ..	209-210
Ex. 70 (Introductory "τά")	..	210-211
C.—ʒup *after* "ip minic"	.. ..	211-212
Ex. 71 (ip minic ʒup . .)	..	212
D.—*Accusative of Specification*	..	213
Ex, 72 (Accus. of Specification)	..	214
E.—*Accusative of Space and Time*	..	214-215
Ex. 73 (Accus. of Space and Time)		215
F.—Ꭺb *not inserted before vowel*	..	216
G.—*Aspiration after Genitive* "Ꭺ"	..	216-218
H.—*Sense Constructions*	.. ..	218-219
I.—*Absolute Constructions*	.. ..	219-220
L.—*The Subjunctive Mood*	.. ..	220-222
1°. *of purpose*		
2°. *optative*		
3°. *of indefinite time*		
4°. with "ʋá"		
5°. with "munᎪ"		
Ex. 74 (Subjunctive Mood)	..	222-223
CHAP. XI.—ACTIVE, PASSIVE, AUTONOMOUS, AND τᏜ CONSTRUCTIONS	.. .. ..	224-234
Ex. 75	.. .. ..	234-236
CHAP. XII.—REPETITION OF WORDS FOR SAKE OF CLEARNESS	.. ..	237-238
CHAP. XIII.—MISCELLANEOUS	.. .. ..	239-247
A.—*Fem. Adj. not inflected in dat. sing.*	..	239
B.—*Apposition*	.. .. ..	239-240
C.—*Dat. Gen. or Loc. instead of Nom.*		240-242
D.—*Change in Parts of Speech*	..	242-243
E.—*Loss of I.G.* "p"	.. ..	243-247

CONTENTS

xi

		PAGE
CHAP. XIV.—WORD FORMATION		248-274
A.—*Verbal Nouns*		248-252
B.—*Composition*		252-263
1°. Noun + Adjective		252
2°. Noun + Noun		252-253
3°. Adj. + Noun		253
4°. Adj. + Adj.		253
5ª. Adj. + Verb		253
6ª. Particle + Noun		253-254
7ᵘ. Particle + Adj.		254-255
8°. Preposition + Noun, Adj., Pron., or Verb		255-263
(a) The preposition ᴀᴅ		255
(b) ,, ,, ᴀᴘ		255-256
(c) ,, ,, ᴀɪċ-, ᴀɪᴜ́	256
(d) ,, ,, cé ᴅ-	
(e) ,, ,, cóṁ-	256-257
(f) ,, ,, ᴅí, ᴅe.	257-258
(g) ,, ,, eᴀċᴛᴀᵽ	258
(h) , ,, ess, as	258-259
(i) ,, ,, ᴢᴀn (O.I. cen)	
(l) ,, , ɪᴅɪᵽ, eᴀᴅᴀᵽ	259
(m) ,, , ᵽɪᴀᴜ́	
(n) ,, ,, ᵽó	259
(o) ,, ,, ᵽoᵽ	
(p) ,, , ᵽᵽɪċ	260
(r) ,, ,, ɪᴀᵽ, ɪᴀᵽm	
(s) ,, ,, ɪmb:, ɪm	261
(t) ,, ,, ɪn	261-262
(u) ,, ,, íoᵽ	
(v) ,, ,, ó, uᴀ, oᴜ́, uᴀᴜ́	
(w) ,, ,, óᵽ	262
(x) ,, ,, ᵽe-	
(y) ,, ,, ᵽo-	
(z) ,, ,, ᵽeᴀċ	
(j) ,, , ᴛᴀᵽ, ᴅᴀᵽ	263
(k) ,, ,, ᴛo-	
(q) ,, ,, ᴛᵽé	

CONTENTS

	PAGE
C.—*Suffixes* :—	
I. *Nominal Suffixes*	264-271
(*a*) Verbal Nouns	(248-252)
(*b*) From *adjectives*	264-266
(*c*) ,, *nouns*	266-270
(*d*) ,, *adverbs, prepositions of place, pronouns*	271
(*e*) ,, *verbs*	271
II. *Adjectival Suffixes* :	272-273
(*a*) From *verbs*	272
(*b*) ,, *numerals*	272
(*c*) ,, *nouns*	272-273
(*d*) ,, *prepositions*	273
(*e*) ,, *adjectives*	273
D. *Miscellaneous*	273-274
CHAP. XV.—CHANGE OF MEANING IN WORDS	275-286
I. Through association with particles, etc., in Composition	275-281
II. Through psychological and other causes	281-286

STUDIES IN MODERN IRISH

ABBREVIATIONS.

In addition to the usual Grammatical contractions :—

V = verb.
P = (material) predicate.
S = (,,) subject.
p = pronominal (formal) predicate.
s = pronominal (formal) subject.

1. Acts (Ɣníoṁaṗċa na n-Aṗpol), Canon O Leary.
2. Aeṗ. (Aeṗop a ċáınıɣ ɣo hĊıṗınn), Canon O Leary.
3. A.M.C. (Aislinge Meic Conglinne : The Vision of Mac Conglinne), Ed. Kuno Meyer.
4. B.K. (Stories from Keating).—Bergin.
5. Ḃṗ. (Ḃṗıcṗıu).—Canon O Leary.
6. C.Ḋ. (An Cṗaoṗ Ḋeaṁan).—Canon O Leary.
7. Ċ.S. (Na Ceıṫṗe Soıṗɣéıl).—Canon O Leary.
8. Caṫ. (Caṫılína).—Canon O Leary.
9. C. na nƔ. (Caṗaıḋ nan Ɣaıoheal).—Norman Mac Leod, D.D.
10. Cl. (An Cleaṗaıḋċ).—Canon O Leary.
11. Don. (Donlevy's Catechism, 1848).
12. D. (Manuel d'Irlandais Moyen).—G. Dottin (Paris).
13. D.S. (Na Daoine Sidhe is Uirsɣeulan eile).—Celtic Press, Glasgow.
14. Ḋonnċ. R. (Ḋonnċaḋ Ruaḋ Mac Conmaṗa).
15. D.I.L. (R.I.A.).—Dictionary of the Irish Language (Pub. by Royal Irish Academy).
16. eıṗ. (eıṗıṗṫ).—By Canon O Leary.
17. f.A. (fınnṡɣéalṫa na h-Aṗaıbe).—feaṗṗıɣuṗ fınn-béıl.
18. f.S. (fuınn na Smól).
19. Ɣ. (Ɣuaıṗe).—Canon O Leary.
20. Gl. (Old Irish Glosses).
21. Im. (Aıṫṗıṗ aṗ Ċṗíoṗṫ).—Canon O Leary.
22. K.T.B. (Keating's Ṫṗí Ḃıoṗ-ɣaoıṫe an Ḃáıṗ).
23. K.H.—Keating's History.
24. K.P.—Keating's Poems.

STUDIES IN MODERN IRISH

25. Luke (Gospel of St. Luke in na Ceitre Soirséil).—Canon O Leary.
26. L.O. (Laoi Oirín ar Tír na n-Óg).—Ed. Flannery.
27. MS.F. (mo Sgéal féin).—Canon O Leary.
28. Ml. (The Milan Glosses).
29. n. (niam).—Canon O Leary.
30. n. ng. (naoi ngábad an ſiolla duib).—míceál ó máille.
31. PH. (Passions and Homilies from the Leabar breac).—Ed. Atkinson.
32. PB. (Poetry of Badenoch).—Sinton.
33. Ser (Seanmóin ir trí pició).—Canon O Leary.
34. S.T. (Stories from the Táin).—Strachan.
35. S. (Séadna).—Canon O Leary.
36. Sg. (Sgot-Üualad).—Canon O Leary.
37. TBC (Táin bó Cuailgne).—Canon O Leary.
38. T.g. (Tadg gaba).—Doyle.
39. Thurn (Thurneysen). Th. Hb. (Thurneysen's Handbuch des Alt-Irischen).
40. John (Gospel of St. John in na Ceitre Soirséil).
41. Wb. (The Würzburg Glosses).
42. Z.C.P. (Zeitschrift für Celtische Philologie).

STUDIES IN MODERN IRISH.

CHAPTER I—THE VERB "ιp"

SECTION I.—INTRODUCTORY.

Every student of Irish knows that there are two verbs " to be " in the language—ιp and τά, and in a general way he understands the distinction between them. The principle that " ιp " must be used for " Classification " and " Identification," and " τά " for " Condition " sentences, is fairly clear and fairly comprehensive. But within the domain of " ιp " itself a great many errors are commonly taught, and a great deal of useful—nay, even essential, knowledge is left quite untouched. The result is that even good students rarely succeed in acquiring a really scientific grasp of this very remarkable verb, and are constantly liable to use it with extremely bad taste. My object in the following pages will be to give a clear and consistent account of the various uses in vogue in modern Irish, and to fill in the empty spaces, so as to provide the student with a more or less complete doctrine of the verb " ιp."

The older Grammars and Composition-books give the cast-iron rule that the order of words, with the verb ' ιp,' *must* be—Verb, Predicate, Subject. Indeed this rule appeared in print quite recently. It is of course erroneous, and leads to absurd conceptions of the language, ignoring, as it does, many of the most interesting, and certainly the most important types of identification. We shall see that neither in ' classification,' nor ' identification ' sentences, is it necessary that the Predicate (i.e the real or material Predicate) should occupy the specified place between the Verb and the Subject. What IS essential is, that the Subject should never stand—at least in non-interrogative sentences[1]—immediately after ' ɪꞃ ' ; and that when the material Predicate does *not*[2] come immediately after ' ɪꞃ ' a pronoun must be inserted to take its place, both in 'classification' and 'identification' sentences. And let it be observed that "Predicate" always means here *logical* Predicate. A great deal of nonsense has been talked and written about the distinction between the logical and the grammatical Predicate in connection with the verb ' ɪꞃ.' The verb ' ɪꞃ ' is in fact a *logical* copula, and its predicate is *always* the *logical* predicate. To say that the grammatical predicate with " ɪꞃ " in any sentence is really the logical subject lays one open to the suspicion of not understanding Irish speech at all. The difference between an English sentence and the supposed corresponding Irish one involves sometimes not only a peculiar turn of *expression*, but a peculiar turn of *thought*. It is to be hoped that we shall hear no more of the distinction between logical and grammatical predicate in connection with the verb ' ɪꞃ.' Such a distinction is simply non-existent. It is the very nature of the very ' ɪꞃ ' to be associated immediately with its predicate *either material or formal* (note this qualification). The whole history of the verb shows this ; it was from the beginning an unstressed verb,—the main stress of the sentence falling on the logical predicate, which followed it (either in the material, or pro-

---

[1]. For questions, see p. 47.
[2]. In Identification, type I, even when the predicate comes between the verb and the subject, the pronoun must be inserted in Modern Irish. (See p. 12, and for exceptions, pp. 44-47). This, however, is an anomaly, and due to a confusion of types. (See p. 44).

nominal form). The moment you separate it from its predicate (in either shape) that moment it ceases to have any power of predication or of indicating predication. Why, e.g., may you not answer the question—ᴀn leaḃaɾ é ɾin ?— by saying simply—" iɾ." Because ' iɾ ' by itself can predicate nothing ; you must join it to the predicate, and the predicate *must* be that which you *mean* to assert of the subject, it must be the *logical* predicate, the predicate in thought. Why may you not say—" iɾ é leaḃaɾ "—meaning " It is a book " ? Because the word é following ' iɾ ' *must* be the *logical* predicate if the sentence is to have any meaning at all, and as é here is the logical *subject*, the sentence so expressed has no meaning ; it is not bad Irish, it is simply nonsense, a mere senseless conglomeration of words. The same words *may* convey sense and meaning, but *only* if é is the logical predicate. E.g. if I say " iɾ é leaḃaɾ aᴄá ɾoiɾ láṁaiḃ aɡam ná ' Séaᴅna,' " that is intelligible, because é is the (temporary) logical predicate, " leaḃaɾ aᴄá ɾoiɾ láṁaiḃ aɡam " being the logical subject, and " Séaᴅna " the material, logical predicate. In the course of our investigations it will appear evident that this is the true doctrine of the verb ' iɾ.' With this verb we always *say what we mean*. No Irish speaker or writer ever indulged in the mental gymnastics attributed to him by the advocates of the distinction between the logical and the grammatical predicate (as applied here). In fact the distinction between ' iɾ ' and all other verbs in the language is that whereas all other verbs, including ᴄá, are predicates or part-predicates in themselves, they may be, and usually are, followed by their subjects ; ' iɾ ' on the other hand, being *in itself no predicate*, must, in order to have any sense at all, be immediately associated with its predicate, either in the material or pronominal form.

With these preliminary remarks we may proceed to the

discussion of classification and identification. Some authorities add a third use of the verb 'ιγ,' viz., ' emphasis.' But this is not a scientific division. As a matter of fact, the predicate must be either definite or indefinite in all cases, and so identification and classification comprise all the uses of the verb. It is of course òf practical importance to notice that 'ιγ' may be used to emphasise a particular element in a sentence. But then such an emphatic sentence involves either classification or identification, though sometimes it requires care to determine which. We shall examine the matter in detail later on.[1] Many of the ordinary types, both in classification and identification are emphatic in form. The sentences usually given under " emphasis " might perhaps be better designated as *complex* and *elliptical* cases either of classification or identification.[2]

§ 2.—A.—CLASSIFICATION.

The various types of predication may be summed up as follows :—

1°. VPS. Ιγ Leaδαγ é γιn. Ιγ αιnṁιδe capaLL. (Predicate is a noun).

2°. VPS. Ιγ maιċ é γιn. Ιγ oLc an peacaδ. (Predicate is an adjective).

3°. VPS. Ιγ bγeaჳ an Lá é. Ιγ maιċ an buacaιLL tú. Ιγ ჳunta an γeaγ é.

Ιγ oLc an aιmγιγ atá ann. (The subject involves a *relative clause* and is frequently elliptical, as in the first three examples given).

4°. (V)PS. Νί AιLL an Cuιm ιγ mó a tuჳαιδιγ uιγċι, aċ AιLL an Ṁαιγnéalaιჳ (n. nჳ. 4).

1. pp. 8-10.   2. See pp. 8-10.

STUDIES IN MODERN IRISH 5

 Iſ . . . Alba ſá h-ainm do'n chíc ſin (cf.
 K.H. II 374).
 Iſ Connla a bíod ag Mam aiſ. (n. 279).
 Éamonn a ataiſ (S. 20).
 (All (except the last,) nominal, as opposed to
 real, sentences. The predicate is a so-called
 proper name, but in reality, as used here,
 is a general term¹).

5°. VPS. Iſ dóig liom ná ciocfaid ſé. Iſ liom-ſa an
 leabaſ ſan.
 (The predicate is a prepositional phrase. In the
 second example liom- ſa is equivalent to
 ſud liom-ſa).

6°. PVpS. Leabaſ iſ ead é ſin. Ainmide iſ ead capall.
 (Emphatic form of 1°. Notice that, the real
 predicate coming *before* the verb, the pronoun
 ead must be inserted to take its place *after*
 the verb. The *meaning* of these emphatic
 forms is of course quite different to that of
 the unemphatic).

7°. PVpS. Maiṫ iſ ead é ſin, ⁊ ní h-olc. Olc iſ ead an
 peacad (emphatic form of 2°).

8°. PVpS. Olc iſ ead an aimſiſ atá ann.
 (Emphatic form of 3°. But notice that some
 forms under 3°. are never emphasised in ordinary language. Ordinarily one does not say
 breag iſ ead an lá é. The sentence is quite
 correct, but it is not usual).

9. PVpS. Alba iſ ead iſ ainm do'n chíc ſin.
 Finnbeannac iſ ead iſ ainm dó.
 (Emphatic form of 4° Notice that the pronoun
 inserted is ead (indefinite)).

 1. See note on Proper Names, pp. 41-43.

6 STUDIES IN MODERN IRISH

10°. PVpS. Liompa ip eað an Leaðap pan. (Emphatic form of 5°. Notice that the only emphatic form in use corresponding to — Ip ꝺóiṡ Liom ná ciocpaiꝺ pé — is an 'identification' not a 'classification' sentence. Ip é ip ꝺóiṡ Liom ná ciocpaiꝺ pé. (See Identification Type II a. p. 15), where, however, ꝺóiṡ Liom belongs to the *subject*.

11°. VPS. Cailín ꝺápꝺ ainm ꝺi ṡile na mꝺLác. Ip ainm ꝺó ꝺia, etc. (I give these a separate place because they have been misinterpreted. It has been said that in the first example 'ṡile na mꝺLác' (admitted as grammatical subject) is really the logical predicate. Of course it is not. It is logical subject, as it is the grammatical subject. If it were the logical predicate the proper Irish would be (and it is of course quite a common type (cf. classification type 4°.))—Cailín ṡup ṡile na mꝺLác aꝺ ainm ꝺí, or Cailín ṡupꝺ é ainm a ꝺí uipci (ná) ṡile na mꝺLác — (Identification). Both modes of expression are quite common over the whole range of Irish. Cf. PH 102. "*Filetus* din a ainm in descipuil-sin," where 'Filetus' is predicate. Cf. also PH 134. "*Gestus* din a ainm in latraind-sin."

12°. V(P)S. ꝺá mꝺa ná ꝺeaꝺ pé paṡálca poim pé aiṡe (S. 67). Here the predicate "puꝺ" is understood. This is no exception to the rule that the subject cannot stand immediately after 'ip' in non-interrogative sentences. The predicate is *felt* after ꝺa above, and *must* be understood in thought.

13°. SVP. Níl aoinne ir fearr a táinig ar ná mire (TBC. 6). Tabair do Dia an ní ir le Dia ⁊ coiméad agat féin an ní ir leat féin (Im. 82). (The subject is the relative particle a understood before ir). For 1st example see Double Relative (pp. 114-116).

14°. Fundamental part of predicate + VpS + remainder of predicate :—

Fir ab ead iad ná leogfad a gcroide ná a n-aigne dóib fanamaint ra baile. (This of course is an emphatic form of ir (ba) fir iad . .).

15°. SVPs. An teagarg ro a tugaim-re ní liom é. (ĊS. 245). (The material subject comes first. The sentence is rhetorically emphatic).

Dependent Forms.

1°. Deir ré gur leabar é rin. Ir deirim gur aimride capall. (For omission or insertion of ab before a predicate beginning with a vowel, see p. 21).
2°. Deirimre gurb olc an peacad. Ir dóig liom gur mait é rin.
3°. Nać dóig leat gur breag an lá é ?
4°. Tuigim nać aill an Tuim ir mó a tugaidír uirti, ać aill an Mlaipnéalaig.
5°. Deirim leat gur dóig liom ná tiocfaid ré.

N.B.—In the emphatic sentences 6°—10° there will be a *double* gur in the dependent form. It is really the first one that is logically pleonastic, but usage requires it. Notice that it is only when the *material* predicate precedes the verb, and the latter is followed by a *formal* (or pronominal) predicate

STUDIES IN MODERN IRISH

that the two ɡup's occur. It is only in this case that the subject is expressed after eaḋ.[1] Leaḃaр ıр eaḋ é. But in answer to the question—an leaḃaр é? we say ıр eaḋ (*Not* ıр eaḋ é).

6°. Deıр ré ɡuр leaḃaр ɡurḃ eaḋ é. Iр ʋeıṁın ɡuр aınṁıḋe ɡurḃ eaḋ capall.

7°. Deıрım-re ɡurḃ olc ɡurḃ eaḋ an peacaḋ.

8°. Iр ḋóıɡ lıom ɡurḃ olc ɡurḃ eaḋ an aımрıр aṫá ann.

9°. Iр рollur ɡuр Alba ɡurḃ eaḋ aḃ aınm ḋón ċріċ rın.

10°. Duḃaрt leır ɡuр lıomрa ɡurḃ eaḋ an leaḃaр рan.

With these contrast the following :—

Tá ré rocaıр am' aıɡne ɡuр am' рaɡarṫ ıр cearṫ ʋom mo рaoɡal a ċaıteaṁ (n. 29). (The direct form would be—ıр am' рaɡarṫ ıр cearṫ ʋom ... where the real predicate *follows* ıр).

Duḃaıрt ré ɡuр Caoılte aḃ'aınm ḋó. (n. 74), (Direct—ıр Caoılte aḃ'aınm ḋó).

But,—with two ɡuр-s—

Ceaр na ʋaoıne ɡuр naoṁ ɡurḃ eaḋ é. (ɡ. 35). (Dependent form of naoṁ aḃ eaḋ é).

Similarly—Aḃрaḋ na ḋıaıḋ rın ıр eaḋ ʋo h-ınnreaḋ ʋom **ɡuр** rраrаí ıaраınn **ɡurḃ eaḋ** na рlata рan. (M.S.F. 57).

Do cuıreaḋ na luıɡe oрtа ɡuр naṁaıʋ **ɡurḃ eaḋ** an рaɡarṫ (MSF. 115).

B.—COMPLEX ELLIPTICAL SENTENCES.

(Either classification or identification.)

In addition to the emphatic forms 6°—10° mentioned above there is a special group of sentences which are remarkable

---

1. A possible exception is the common expression ıр eaḋ рan. But here the рan may belong to the predicate.

not so much for their emphatic form, as for the complex nature of the expression. The thought is not expressed directly or in full, and one has to analyse it before dealing with such sentences.

Some of these sentences are clearly identification. E.g., ní ḃuit-ṡe iṡ cóiṗ é caraḋ liom is merely a short—but complex— way of stating the negative identification—ní tuṡa an té ṡuṗ cóiṗ ḋó é caraḋ liom. This fuller form sometimes occurs. Cf. S. 221.—ní hé ṡaċ aoinne ṡo ḋtairḃeáinṡinn an ṗáinne ṡin ḋó; instead of the elliptical—ní ḋo ṡaċ aoinne a tairḃeáinṡinn an ṗáinne ṡin; the short form is due to the influence of the ordinary classification sentence—ní cóiṗ ḃuit-ṡe é caraḋ liom. Such sentences may sometimes be still further emphasised. E.g., besides—iṡ ḋóṁ-ṡa iṡ ceaṗt é caraḋ leat, we have ḋóṁ-ṡa iṡ eaḋ iṡ ceaṗt é caraḋ leat. We have in fact three degrees of emphasis.—

(a) iṡ ceaṗt ḋóṁ-ṡa é caraḋ leat.
(b) (iṡ) ḋóṁṡa iṡ ceaṗt é caraḋ leat.
(c) Ḋóṁ-ṡa iṡ eaḋ iṡ ceaṗt é caraḋ leat.

In this last case (c) notice that eaḋ takes the place of ḋóṁ-ṡa. Otherwise it does not. E.g. in answering the question an ḋóṁ-ṡa . . . ? we do not say iṡ eaḋ, or ní heaḋ, but iṡ ḋuit, or ní ḋuit.

Other sentences are clearly classification. iṡ aṗ meirṡe a ḃí ṡé. iṡ aṗ buile ataoi. These merely convey the information (emphatically) that the person in question was in a state of intoxication, or is in a state of frenzy.

Others again may according to circumstances be either classification or identification. The question and answer— An aṗ an mbóṗḋ atá ṡé? iṡ aiṗ—may imply identification, the contrast being between *the* table and some other definite object. On the other hand the question and answer—An aiṗ atá ṡé anoiṡ? ní heaḋ, iṡ ṡé—imply classification, the contrast being not between THE chair and some other definite object, but between *a position* ON the chair and *a position* UNDER it. It is worthy of note that in answering a question the pronoun é can never stand for a propositional-phrase-predicate, no matter how definite its reference may be. Neither can é be used proleptically for a prepositional phrase when the latter follows the verb ' ιγ ' and *precedes the subject*. It can be used, however, and often is, to anticipate a prepositional-phrase-predicate when the latter *follows* the subject. E.g., ιγ é áιc n-a ραδαδαρ an uaιρ ριn ná ι δτεαṁαιρ. This shows that phrases like ι δτεαṁαιρ in such cases are quite definite. It is interesting to compare the use of so-called proper-name predicates in nominal (as opposed to real) sentences. E.g., An Séaδna ιγ aιnm δó? ιγ eaδ (where ' Séaδna ' is understood indefinitely, or as a general term.[1] But—ιγ é aιnm a δí aιρ ná Séaδna where Séaδna, understood definitely, is anticipated by é. So also nouns which ordinarily are indefinite can become definite in a certain type of identification.[2] E.g. ιγ ατρυξαδ ana ṁóρ é, nac eaδ? is classification. But ιγ é ρuδ é ná ατρυξαδ ana ṁóρ, is identification (of classes). Sentences like—ιγ é Séaδna an aιnm a δí aιρ (*they have appeared in print*) are just as bad Irish as—ιγ é aρ an mδóρδ ατá ρé.

Note that there are no emphatic forms in use corresponding to the types 11°—15°, Some of them are emphatic already. Unless we look (in the case of 11°) upon the sentence in which ζιLe na mδLát, etc., are logical predicates as more emphatic ways of making the statement (as in fact they are). They are not direct emphatic forms, because subject and predicate change places.

---

1. See note on Proper Names, pp. 41-43.   2. See p. 43.

Exercise I. (Classification).

Translate into idiomatic Irish :—

1°. *All that is high*[1] is not holy ; *nor*[2] all that is pleasant good ; *nor*[2] every desire pure ; *nor*[2] is everything that is dear to us pleasing to God.
2°. It is clear that Ireland was the name of that country. (Translate in both ways : emphatic and unemphatic).
3°. You say it is a man, but I say it is a horse.
4°. What I say is that it is not Irish at all ; it is English.
5°. Give to God what is His, and take to thyself what is thine.
6°. He says that " Séaona " is the title of the story.
7°. What can't be cured must be endured.
8°. My father says that Michael is *his*[3] second son's name.
9°. I think that Báb of the Liss was called Síle.
10°. I tell you it was " a Young Men's Society " they were.

Exercise II. (Classification, continued).

1°. He says that it is under *cover*[4] of darkness they do their work.
2°. Joseph, her husband, being a *just*[5] man, and not willing publicly to *expose*[6] her, was *minded*[7] to put her away privately.
3°. *They*[8] that were invited were not worthy.
4°. *That*[9] which is born *of*[10] the flesh is flesh, and that which is born of the spirit is spirit.
5°. A bad custom and the *neglect*[11] of our spiritual advance-

---

1. ʃac ápo.   2. ná ní . . .   3. Do not use possessive.   4. rsáċ.
5. píorsaonca.   6. Use marlaoú.   7. mian.   8. An muinntir.
9. An nroú.   10. ó.   11. Use neaṁ-ṡuim.

ment is a great *cause*[1] of our keeping so little guard upon our mouth.

6°. It is *truly*[2] a misery to live upon this earth at all.

7°. It is for this reason the prophet devoutly prays to be freed from the necessities of the body in this world.

8°. Then it is you will regret that you were so cold AND[3] careless.

9°. Nothing so defiles and entangles the heart of man as impure love to created things. (Say—It is impure love . . . that most . . .).

10°. All disquiet of heart and distraction of the senses arise from inordinate love and vain fear. (Say—It is out of . . . that . . . arise).

C.—Identification.—Type I VpPS.

1°. Sé an gníoṁ róganta ir gnátaċ le Riġ Cairil a ḋéanaṁ (C.D. 73).
    Subject = (an gníoṁ) ir gnátaċ le Riġ Caril a ḋéanaṁ.
    Predicate = an gníoṁ róganta.
    p (Temporary predicate) = é.
    In Old Irish the pronoun was frequently *not* inserted here. In fact there is clear indication that its use, in this type of sentence, is due to the influence of other types (notably II, III, IV). See pp. 15-31.

2°. 'Sé an t-uaḃar a tornuiġ an t-olc (Ser. 221).
    Subject = (an ruḋ) a tornuiġ an t-olc.
    Predicate = an t-uaḃar.
    Temporary predicate (p) = é.

---

1. ré nḋeara.   2. Express by emphatic form of sentence.
3. Repeat "so."

Notice the difference between the proleptic pronoun in Irish and in English. In the English—"It was pride that started the evil," the pronoun "it" stands for the subject. In Irish the pronoun é stands *not* for the subject but for the predicate. The introductory "it" (standing for the logical subject again) in English *classification* sentences is ordinarily not expressed in Irish at all : (It)'s a pity that he did not come,—ir truaġ nár táiniġ ré.

3°. Ir é an raoġal ro an t-eappac ⁊ ir é an raoġal eile an róġman (Serm. 54).
First subject = an t-eappac.
Second ,, = ,, róġman.
First predicate = an raoġal ro.
Second ,, = ,, raoġal eile.
Here we have the explanation of a parable. Notice that 'ir' often signifies "stands for, represents, means, is equivalent to." This meaning, however, it develops *from the context*.

4°. Ir é rud é ir éaġramlaiġe ⁊ ir tuatalaiġe ⁊ ir mó neam-tuirġint dár airiġear riam.
Subject = The *second* é. (The *first* é is temporary predicate).
Predicate = (an) rud ir éaġramlaiġe ... riam.
Notice the omission of article with rud, and the fact that only the fundamental noun of the predicate here precedes the subject. The subject *might* have been kept over till the end, thus — ir é rud ir éaġramlaiġe ... dár airiġear riam é.

5°. D'é a díceall féin i coimeád ar riubal an faid a mairr ré.

6°. Ní niad an muinntir a cáinear an lá déanac atá aġam a moladh indiu (SG. 45).

STUDIES IN MODERN IRISH

Exercise III.

Identification.—Type I.

1°. The man who stole the chalice was the one who found the key.
2°. He thinks it is the men themselves that are responsible for this ugly custom.
3°. I'm sorry I didn't take *your* advice from the beginning.
4°. Fasting will best prepare us for Christmas.
5°. It was pride that urged them to tell the lie.
6°. The wife that God had given him was responsible for *his*[1] sinning.
7°. It is *those*[2] who are lowly in this world are *most likely*[4] to be *high*[3] in the Kingdom of God.
8°. It is *those*[2] who get most who are always farthest from having enough.
9°. It isn't everyone I would give that ring to.
10°. It is the temptations and tribulations that show what progress one has made in righteousness.[5]
11°. If I love the world I rejoice at its prosperity, and am troubled at its adversity.
12°. If I love[6] the flesh my *imagination*[8] is *taken up with*[9] the things of the flesh.
13°. If I love[7] the spirit I delight[10] to think of spiritual things.
14°. It is not the poor man who has not a single word of English that is responsible

1. Do not use possessive. 2. an té. 3. uasal. 4. vóiċiże-ve
5. fíopaontaċt. 6. ip ionṁuin le . 7. ip áil le
8. maċtnaṁ. 9. Use tá. 10. ponn.

Identification.—Type II. (*Four varieties*).

(*a*) VpSP. Sometimes it was inconvenient, if not quite impossible, to place the predicate immediately after the verb. Moreover, for rhetorical purposes, the predicate was frequently reserved for the end of the sentence. This type is therefore very common even in the Old Irish period, and looms large in the Irish of every province down to the present day. As compared with type I, it throws some light on the construction of the verb 'ɪꞃ.' Type I is found frequently in Old Irish *without* the anticipatory pronoun, though there is a growing tendency to insert it, until at last—in Modern Irish—it is absolutely essential.[1] Type II on the other hand is NEVER found *without* the proleptic pronoun,—the obvious reason being that 'ɪꞃ' would otherwise be followed immediately by the *subject*. Some would-be authorities explain the pronoun here as part of the *subject*, and say it is inserted merely to separate 'ɪꞃ' from a definite noun. But why should this be necessary? (see p. 44). It was *not* necessary in type I in Old Irish, but it was, and is, in type II. We have a reasonable explanation of all the phenomena on the hypothesis that the subject must *not* follow ɪꞃ immediately: the pronoun is inserted here to take the place of the predicate, and render predication possible; it is inserted in type I on the analogy of types II, III and IV.

1°. 'Sé ɪꞃ mian ꞅɪꞃ an Eaglaɪꞅ ꞅeaꞃg Dé do ṁaoluġaḋ (Don. 282).

    Subject=(an ꞃuḋ) ɪꞃ mian ꞅɪꞃ an Eaglaɪꞅ
    Predicate=ꞅeaꞃg Dé do ṁaoluġaḋ
    Temporary predicate (p)=é

Literal meaning: The thing which the Church desires is *this*—to lessen God's anger.

---

1. For exceptions, see pp. 44-47.

2°. Séaṗd a ġnínn a leaṫ-ṫaoıḃ a ṫaḃaıṗṫ ṛa' nġaoıṫ
 (n. nġ.—14).
 Subject = (an ṗuḋ) a ġnínn.—Séaṗd='Sé (an) ṗuḋ
 Predicate = a leaṫ-ṫaoıḃ a ṫaḃaıṗṫ ṛa' nġaoıṫ.
 Temporary predicate é (in ṛéaṗd).
3°. 'Sé ḃuaḋ na ṛġéıṫe ṛın . . . an ṛeaṗ a ḃeaḋ aṛ a
 ṛġáṫ naċ ṛéıḋıṗ é ḃualaḋ, ḃıoḋ ná ḃeaḋ ann aċ
 ġaṗṛún ġan ṛéaṛóġ, nó ḃıoḋ ġo mḃeaḋ ṛé na
 ṛeanḋuıne.
 Here the cumbrous nature of the predicate makes
 it quite impossible to express the identification
 according to type I.
4°. Ḃ'é ḃ'ṛaḋa leıṛ ġo ṗaıḃ ṛé amuıġ (S. 39).
 Subject = (an ṗuḋ a) ḃ'ṛaḋa leıṛ.
 Predicate = ġo ṗaıḃ ṛé amuıġ. Here again the
 form of the predicate precludes the use of type I.
 Notice that, as in type I., we must frequently
 supply the fundamental noun of the *subject*. Observe
 also that the second ḃa introduces a classification
 sentence, the predicate being " ṛaḋa leıṛ," the
 subject being the relative particle a (or ḋo) understood before ḃa. It is very important to notice the
 difference in *meaning* between a *classification* like

$$\underbrace{\text{ḃ'é}}\ \underbrace{\text{ḃ'ṛaḋa leıṛ}}\ \underbrace{\text{ġo ṗaıḃ ṛé amuıġ.}}$$

and the *identification*—
	V	P	S
	Vp	S	P

$$\underbrace{\text{ḃ'é ḃ'ṛaḋa leıṛ}}\ \underbrace{\text{ġo ṗaıḃ ṛé amuıġ.}}$$

The passage referred to here is (S. p. 39) :—
 D'ayimshig Tayg a vata, agus do louir Míhál lesh
an sgueb. Heasiv Tayg a lár an tí. D'eirig an
sguab agus hug shí iaracht er é vuala idir an dá húil.
Ví an bata go mah agus an chuishli láidir, agus

ambasa chosin Tayg a cheaun agus a cheanácha, ach do vuel shí ins na cosiv é, agus do vuel shí ins na loraganuiv é, agus do vuel shí ins na glúiniv é, agus do vuel shí ins na cearhǎnuiv é, agus ins a droum, agus ins na hasnychuiv, a dreó ná feaduir shé er baul cad a ví ag imeacht er. Fé gheri do liúig shé an doras d'osguilt dò, agus gealuim 'oit gurav é b'ada lesh go roiv shé amùh.

Many a writer in describing such a scene would have said merely—"b'ḟaoa leiṟ go ṟaib ṟé amuiġ." Many do not seem to understand the difference between such pairs as ' b'ḟaoa leiṟ ' and ' b'é b'ḟaoa leiṟ.' Yet the difference is important. How often in reading certain Irish books has our taste been offended by the substitution of one such form for the other. In the above passage " b'ḟaoa leiṟ " would have been insufferably weak,—would in fact have been an anti-climax. " b'é b'ḟaoa leiṟ " on the other hand exactly suits the circumstances. The sentence identifies for us THE ONE THING which the poor ṟġuab-ridden Taoġ was longing for at the moment, viz. to be safely out of doors. This may seem a small point, but it is the uniform observance of these 'convenances' that distinguishes good writing, just as it is the habitual neglect of them that is at once the cause and the mark of mediocrity.

5°. b'é b'ḟaoa le ġaċ aoinne go mbeiòiṟ aġ teaċt a baile.
6°. na opuinġe . . . aġ aṟ ab é a n'Oia a mbolġ. (Don. 130) The people whose God is their belly. Subject = a n'oia. Predicate = a mbolġ.

Sentences like—Iṟ é a ḟao iṟ a ġeaṟṟ go . . . and iṟ é a toċt a tuiġeao belong here also. Sé mo ṫuaiṟim ná tiocṟaiò ṟé in aon coṟ anoiṟ belongs to

type II. rather than type I. This fact explains why
é is used (though tuairim is feminine). The é does
not refer directly to tuairim at all, but to the clause—
" ná tiocfaid ré . . . anoir.

Exercise IV.
Identification. Type IIa.

1°. The priest's business is to *pray*[1] to God for himself and all the people in a suppliant and humble manner.
2°. I long for the joy of peace.
3°. A person of the least intelligence ought to see that the people who have least sense in Ireland are those who have neither English nor Irish.
4°. My opinion is that the pair understood each other remarkably well.
5° Had I been in his place these are the three wishes I should have asked for—plenty of money in this world, a long and happy life, and eternal life thereafter.
6°. The reason why she broke it was that Séadna had promised that he would marry *her*.
7°. The queen's desire is to get plenty of badgers' milk to drink.
8°. I am longing exceedingly to possess that feat.
9°. The one desire of everyone was to be returning home.
10° The last state of man means the state he is in on leaving this world.
11°. The best thing you can do is to put that question to herself.

---

1. Beit ag cur a ġuiḋe suar.

12°. The long and the short of it is that he must go home at once.
13°. No man is secure in appearing abroad but he who would willingly lie hid at home.
14°. The number of them that did eat was 5,000 men, besides women and children.
15°. My meat is to do the will of Him that sent Me, that I may perfect His work.

Identification. Type IIb.

VpS ná P. The characteristic of this type is the particle ná which precedes the predicate. The force and origin of this ná will be explained later on. The *subject* is *in thick type* :—

1° 'Sé céad fud a bein ré ná a lám a cup na póca féacaint an paib an rpapán aige (S. 29).

2°. 'Sé céad fud eile a tug ré ré ndeara ná an sman ag taitneam ap an mealbóig i n-ionad na gealaige (S. 74).

3° Samluig ré gupb é fud a bí in ionad a cpoide aige ná map a bead cloc mór tpom (S. 90).

4° b'é cuma n-ap bein ré é ná le beit ag baint cainnte a méib (TBC. 201).

5°. b'iad dá ríg iad ran ná Concubap mac Neara 7 Feargur mac Róig (11. 82).

6°. tuig ré in' aigne gupb é fud Murcad ná annrgian diablaide (11. 104).

7°. b'iad beipt iad ran ná Maolmórda 7 Sitpic (11. 312).

8°. Ir iad neite iad ran ná deag-gnótact ra baile, fóplámar ceart amuig, raop-aigne i gcómairle, gan géille do coip ná do mian (Cat. 71).

9°. Ir é dion atá aip ná cleiti na n-éan ir áille dat (Eip. 54).

10°. b'é coinṡeall é ṗin ná poẋa a ṗéaḋ ḋ' ṗáġáilt aġ ḟeaṗṗġuṗ (eiṗ. 76).
11°. 1Sé ainm a ḃí aiṗ ná Séaḋna (S. 6).
12°. b'é neaṗt é ṗin ná neaṗt an Ċṗeiḋiṁ (11. 128).

All " ná " sentences are affirmative. The following one from Acts ix. 21 is *virtually* affirmative : " ṅaċ é ġnó a ṫuġ annṗo é ná ċun iaḋ ḋo ḃṗeiṫ leiṗ ġaḃṫa aġ ṫṗiall aṗ uaċtaṗánaiḃ na ṗaġaṗt ?" In sentences 1°, 2°, 3°, 4°, 9°, 11° the subject clearly contains a relative clause. In the others both the relative particle and the verb iṗ are understood. In 5°, e.g. " ḋá ṗiġ iaḋ ṗan " is equivalent to " an ḋá ṗiġ a iṗ iaḋṗan." In 6°, " ṗuḋ Muṗċaḋ " is equivalent to ".an ṗuḋ a ḃa Muṗċaḋ." (For omission of the pronoun here before the definite noun Muṗċaḋ, see p. 45-4°).

Ná in Sentences of Identification.

This particle *ná* is very widely used in Munster in sentences of the type *is é ainm a bhí air ná Séadna* (" Séadna," p. 6). The principal points to be noted in regard to its use are : (1) it introduces the material predicate ; (2) the predicate is strongly emphasized ; (3) the subject, taken in full, always contains a relative clause, though the relative particle need not appear explicitly ; or a genitive or possessive phrase, easily resolvable into a relative clause ; (4) while all *ná*-sentences are formally affirmative, *ná* gives them virtually the force of a rhetorical question, a negative sentence, or an exclusive comparative sentence. This points to the genesis of the construction.

I. The rhetorical question *annsan cé déarfadh ná gur dheaghdhuine é ?* is virtually equivalent to *is é déarfadh gach*

STUDIES IN MODERN IRISH

aoinne gur dheaghdhuine é, though the latter has less force and pointedness. If we assume that the negative *ná* in the former became associated with the expression of the predicate which it precedes, it is easy to understand how *ná* should have been gradually invected into the affirmative sentence. The resulting type, *is é déarfadh gach aoinne* **ná** *gur dheaghdhuine é*, thus acquires all the force of the rhetorical question.

II. Besides rhetorical questions we have rhetorical negations Thus *ní bhíodh fhios ag aoinne ná gur dhuine do mhuintir na tíre é* ("Niamh," p. 138) is virtually equivalent to *is é cheapadh gach aoinne gur dhuine do mhuintir na tíre é*. It was natural that the negative *ná* of the first form of expression should come to be used in the latter form as well. So, *ní deirim ná go bhfuil an ceart agat* is only a more emphatic way of saying *is é deirim go bhfuil an ceart agat*. A contamination of the affirmative form with the rhetorical-negative gives *is é deirim* **ná** *go bhfuil an ceart agat*.

III. This association with rhetorical questions and rhetorical negatives would of itself have been sufficient to account for the use of *ná* in affirmative sentences of identification, but the development was further promoted by another class of sentence, containing not the negative but the comparative *ná* (= *ioná*). Thus, the affirmative sentence with a superlative adjective *'sé cuma is fearr chun na h-oibre dhéanamh an Ghaedhilg do shaothrughadh ins na h-áiteannaibh 'ná bhfuil sí beo fós*, may be replaced by a negative with comparative *níl cuma is fearr chun na h-oibre dhéanamh ná an Ghaedhilg do shaothrughadh*, etc. ("Sgothbhualadh," p. 46). The interchange of the types 'this is the best' and 'no other is better than this' is helped by the fact that in Mod. Ir. there is no distinction in form between the comparative and the superlative. And here, as before, the affirmative sentence may be rendered more explicit and emphatic by introducing the particle *ná*: *is é cuma is fearr chun na h-oibre dhéanamh ná an Ghaedhilg do shaothrughadh*, etc. Thus two uses of the negative *ná* and one of the comparative *ná* have resulted in the affirmative *ná* of identification. In some districts *ach* (*acht*) is used in the same way. Its origin is similar. The rhetorical question and the rhetorical negation play a similar part in its development. Thus from *cad a dhéanfadh mac an chait ach luch a mharbhadh?* we may evolve an affirmative *is é rud a dhcineann mac an chait* ach *luch a mharbhadh*. Similarly such a negation as *nior dhein sé ach casadh agus imtheacht leis*, might be turned into an identification sentence : *is é rud a dhein sé* ach *casadh agus imtheacht leis*. Of course this similarity of meaning and development of *ach* and *ná* does not imply any phonetic connection between them.

The following further examples of rhetorical negative and exclusive comparative, sentences will help the student to realise how *ná* has been developed in sentences of Identity :

1°. Ní mirḋe a ráḋ ná go raiḃ ácar ar Colla (11. 244).

2°. Níor ḃfearra ḋuinn ruḋ a ḋéanfaimir ná an cuiḋ eile ḋ'ár raoġal a caiteaṁ i ḋceannta céile (T.G.)

3°. Ní raiḃ éinne ḃa ġéire ġá gcur go léir ruar cun na h-iḋḃirce rin a ḋéanaṁ ná mire.

4°. D'féiḋir nár ḃ'fearra ḋuit ruḋ a ḋéanfá ná an ruḋ a ḋein reirean (S. 66).

5°. Níorḃ' fearra ḋuit ruḋ a ḋéanfá anoir ná ḋul ⁊ grear a coḋla ḋuit féin (S. 69).

6°. Níorḃ' fearra ḋuit ruḋ a ḋéanfá ná cleaṁnar a ḋéanaṁ ḋó (S. 97).

7°. Ní ṁearraim ná go mbeaḋ ḋúil níor mó aġac ḋul ar aġaiḋ ra ḃfioraontact (Im. 19).

8°. Níl aon ruḋ ir mó a cuġann ráraṁ aigne ḋo'n ḋuine

ná a ċuirginc go bfuil ré ar aon coil le Dia na glóire (Im. 280).

9°. Níl aoinniḋ ir mó ċruaḋann croiḋe an ḋuine ⁊ a ḋeigleann amaċ é ó ġrárta Dé ná craor (Ser. 2).

Type IIc.

VpS aċ P.—The characteristic is that aċ (not ná) precedes the predicate.

It is not used by Canon O Leary, but his work contains copious examples of the rhetorical questions and rhetorical negations from which this use of aċ has developed.

Sé puḋ a ḋein ré aċ caraḋ ⁊ imteaċt an ḋorar amaċ. It will be useful to study the following examples :—

1° Le n-a linn rin cia ḃuailfeaḋ cúca an ḋorar irteaċ aċ an tinncéir món (S. 186).
2°. Le n-a linn rin cia ḃuailfeaḋ cúca irteaċ aċ Taḋg óg ó Cealla, ⁊ Conn ⁊ aċair Ċuinn (n. 259).
3°. Caḋ a ḋéanfaḋ rí aċ an puḋ atá ġeallta aici ó torac? (n. 313).
4° Cé ġeoḃaḋ tar an ḋorar aċ Séaḋna? (S. 89).
5°. Créaḋ ir iontuigte ar ro aċt naċ fuil cruć ar bit n-a mḃí an ḋuine aċ cruć n-a bfuil ré ro-ṁarḃta? (KTB. 10).
6°. Cár tug ré aġaiḋ aċ rotreo an ḃaill n-a raiḃ Donncaḋ? (n. 306).
7°. Níl ar riuḃal le ḋeiċ mḃliaḋnaiḃ aċ an t-ollṁú (SG. 138).
8°. Cé tiocfaḋ ⁊ tóġfaḋ an feirm aċ fear n-arḃ ainm ḋó Dóṁnall ó Duḃġáin? (MSF. 58).

Exercise V.

Re-write the above eight examples as formal identifications with the verb ir.

Exercise VI.
Identification. Types IIb and IIc.

1°. There is only one thing which keeps many back from *spiritual progress*[1] and fervent amendment of life, and that is *the apprehension of difficulty*,[2] or the labour which must be gone through in the conflict.
2°. Whilst I am kept in the prison of the body I acknowledge myself to need two things—food and light.
3°. You describe it as a trifling change, but in my opinion it's the sort of thing one calls a very big change.
4°. There are two things you would do well to avoid. They are ugly and hurtful to soul and body. The two things I mean are foolishness and evil-mindedness.
5°. The very first thing the messengers did was to ask if[3] he was Christ.
6°. The very first thing to be done was simply[4] to give the champion's portion to the best warrior.
7°. The manner of his coming was, if you please,[5] in a gentleman's suit.
8°. What brought me to talk to you now is simply this,[5] that I am in difficulties.
9°. The thought referred to was how little anyone expected that it was Cormac they'd be marrying in the end.
10°. There was one person who never thought of it, and that one was Cormac himself.
11°. I think there are only two people who understand him. These two are Fergus and Cúchulainn.
12°. The man they sent to do this work was *none other than*[5] Lonán.

1. Leaṟ a n-anama ḋéanaṁ ṟó ċṟuaiḋ.   3. Interrogative.
2. An oḃaiṟ a ḃeiṫ, ḋaṟ leo,
4. This is expressed by ná.
5. Expressed by ná.

13°. His food consisted *merely*[1] of locusts and wild honey.
14°. The act of injustice referred to was the insulting of a woman.
15°. The thought that occurred to him was that he had never tasted better food.

Identification. Type IId.

VpS mar P.—The characteristic of this type is that mar precedes the predicate. This mar is logically pleonastic, just as the word " because " sometimes is in English. We say, e.g., " he remained simply *because* he didn't wish to go," and influenced by this we say " the reason why he remained was (*because*) he didn't wish to go.

N.B.—Though cúir is fem. the pronoun used is é. This is quite regular because é refers directly, not to cúir, but to the predicate.

1°. 'Sé cúir ná h-éirteann rib-re le briatraib Dé mar ní h-ó Dia rib (Ser. 170).
2°. 'Sé cúir n-a bruil ran mar rin, mar, pé duine a bairteann, ir é Críort féin a deineann an bairte (Ser. 57).
3°. 'Sé cúir ná déanfad díogaltar oraib mar geall ar an earonóir rin, mar ní loingim mo glóire féin (Ser. 172).

Exercise VII. Type IId.

1°. The reason why this is so is that man's mind sinks down into outward things, and unless he quickly recover himself he willingly continues immersed in them.

---

1. Expressed by ná.

2°. Because thou hast yet too *inordinate*[1] a love for thyself, therefore art thou afraid to *resign*[2] thyself wholly *to* the will of others.

3°. This is the reason why there are found so few contemplative persons; because there are few that wholly sequester themselves from *transitory and created*[3] things.

4°. The reason that so *few*[4] become *illuminated*[5] and *internally free*[6] is because they do not know how to wholly[7] renounce themselves.

5°. The reason why you cannot speak Irish well is because you haven't learned it from oral instruction.

6°. I suppose it is because you think English 'respectable' that you have such little knowledge of, and esteem for, your own language.

7°. The only reason he can *advance for*[8] such conduct is that he doesn't know what he's doing.

8°. My principal reason for mentioning this matter now is that I have always felt it to be an Irishman's duty to help on the cause of his native language as much as he can.

9°. If there is one reason more than another to convince me that you are right, it is this—that "God helps those who help themselves."

10° The reason why so few people can write Irish well is that they do not study it in the proper way.

1. tomaᴅ.   2. fáġ . . . fé.   3. Cṛuċuiġṫe ᴅíombuana.
4. Oiṗeaᴅ.   5. Cóṁ beaġ ṛotuṛ aiġne (beaġ, because oiṗeaᴅ was used for "*few*").   6. Cóṁ beaġ ṛaoiṗṛe aiġne.   7. Amuiġ iṛ amaċ.   8. Cuiṛ ṛíoṛ le . . .

Identification Type III.

VpSP.—This is a very important type. It is quite common all along the ages, but it seems to have never been appreciated. As in type II (with which it has some affinity) the predicate comes at the end ; but the subject is different. In type II. the subject contains a relative clause (whether the relative be expressed or understood) or a genitive or possessive phrase which might easily be resolved into a relative clause. In type III. the subject is merely a noun with the definite article, and sometimes a demonstrative particle or an adjective. The reason for giving it as a special type is this,— because the same form of words might— in a different context— be a sentence of type I.—with entirely different construction and meaning. Take for instance the sentence— Sé an namaro an peacaḋ. If I have no context to guide me I cannot tell precisely what is the meaning. It *may be* a sentence of type I. (VpPS) implying that I am speaking of *sin* and asserting that sin is *the* enemy of man. But then it may also mean quite a different thing. In the context from which I have taken it (Ser. 238) it *does* mean quite a different thing. It is a sentence of this third type. The question was not about defining "sin," but about defining "the enemy" (previously mentioned). An namaro is clearly the subject, and an peacaḋ is just as clearly the predicate. To understand it any other way, is to misunderstand it, to miss the meaning of the passage entirely. Irish literature is full of this type, yet not a single writer on Irish Grammar—as far as I know— has ever called attention to it. It is of course more rhetorical than type one. In fact it is an abbreviated form of type II. Ir é an namaro an peacaḋ is virtually equivalent to—ir é ṗuḋ an namaro (ná) an peacaḋ. The words, too, are pronounced quite differently according to the meaning. If the sentence belongs to type I, it is spoken quickly with practically no pause from start to finish and of course the predicate "an namaiḋ" receives greater emphasis than the subject. If it belongs to type III, the utterance is slower, there being a distinct pause after é, and another after namaiḋ, and of course "an peacaḋ" will now receive the greater emphasis. Other examples :—

2°. . . . gurb í an iomáiġ úd an náduip ḋaonna (K.T.B. 3).

Here the context makes it quite clear that the subject is 'an iomáiġ úd' and that " an náduip ḋaonna " is predicate. Of course we are met here with the " bogey " of "*grammatical* predicate." But the distinction, as we have said already, is a myth,—as applied to the verb ' ir.' It seems to have arisen from the idea that type I. is the only possible type of predication. An absurd and disastrous idea !

3°. Sé an ceapḋ úd an náduip ḋaonna (K.T.B. 10).*

Sometimes there seems to be a mixture of types II. and III. in one sentence :—

4°. Ir é an corg go léir ⁊ an corg ir mó orainn . . . . ná ḋeinimíd aon iarracht ar ḋul ar ḃótar fiorḋaontaċta na naom (Im. 17).

Exercise VIII.

Identification. Type III.

1°. He is truly great who is great in charity,

2°. We ought to pay great attention to our Saviour's words :

---

* The proleptic pronoun, even in O.I., is frequently assimilated in gender to the subject, where the latter differs in gender from the predicate

because we understand that the Saviour is the Son of God.

3°. He spoke of rearing a noble castle; now this castle represents the actions of our lives.

4° The enemy means the devil, and night the time of temptation.

5° Spring means this present life, and autumn the next life. (Cf. Type I. Ex. 3, p. 13).

6°. That man is really wise who knows himself.

7°. The altar signifies *allegorically*[1] the human heart.

8°. The enemy is the devil, the harvest the fruits of grace in the human soul.

9°. Correct Irish is Irish with no taint of English upon it.

10°. Truth frequently signifies the one thing which you don't want to hear.

Type IV.

PVpS.—The predicate is brought forward to the beginning of the sentence for the sake of emphasis, or rhetorical effect. But observe that the proper pronoun must be inserted to take its place *after* the verb. Cf. the emphatic classification— leaḃar iſ eaḋ é. Proverbial and sententious sayings are often cast in this mould. The pronoun is here retrospective.

1°. Toraċ an uilc iſ é iſ uſa do corg. Predicate = toraċ an uilc.
    Subject = (an cuid de'n olc) iſ uſa do corg.
              P   V p   S

2°. An bás a ceapaſ do'n éan iſ é iſ tſuig ḃáiſ dom féin (Aeſ. II. 11). Here again we must supply the

---

1. So ṗáirċiallaċ.

fundamental noun of the subject—ᴀn ꞅuᴅ. Note (as in example 1°) that the 2nd 'iꞅ' has for subject the relative particle ᴀ (understood).

3°. Nᴀ ᵹioLLᴀí cuꞅuiꞅ iꞅ iᴀᴅ bᴀ ṁó ᴀ ċuᴀiᴅ ᴀᵹ ꞅuic nᴀ ꞅáꞅ
       P   V p   S
(N. 89).

Here with the subject, when we analyse it, we must supply " nᴀ ᴅᴀoine " or some such antecedent to the relative particle understood with bᴀ ṁó.

This type is very common in Old and Middle Irish, as it is in Modern Irish. E.g., Wb. 21c5 Crist didiu is si inchathir ; ind noib ata ellachti hi Crist ithé cives. In such cases, where the subject noun and the predicate are of different gender, the retrospective pronoun is assimilated to the gender of the subject noun.

4°. ᵹoꞅmꝑLᴀiċ ⁊ 111ᴀṁ iꞅ iᴀᴅ ᴀ bí ᴀnn (11. 166) Supply " nᴀ ᴅᴀoine " as antecedent to the relative " a " in the subject.
       P   V p   S

       P   V p S

5°. CLᴀnn nᴀ ꞅiᵹċe ⁊ nᴀ n-uᴀꞅᴀL iꞅ iᴀᴅ ᴀ ċᴀᵹᴀᴅ (11. 10). See previous remark.

6°. ᴀn ꞅoc-ċleᴀꞅ iꞅ é ᴀ bí ᴀꞅ ꞅiubᴀL ᴀcᴀ, Supply 'ᴀn ꞅuᴅ' or some such words in subject.
       P   Vp   S

Ordinarily the unemphasised pronouns é, í, iᴀᴅ are not used by themselves as predicates. When they appear to be so used it will be found that they refer back to the material predicate, mentioned in the preceding clause or sentence. E.g. :

S. 29.—Agur ir é a bí go breag ceann ⁊ go breag trom
(Referring to "an rpapán" previously mentioned.)

S. 59.—Ir dóiċ liom gur Síle b'ainm do báb an leara, ⁊ gurb í ba roga leir.
(Referring back to "báb an leara.")

S. 68.—Nuair d'éirig Siubán ar maidin, ir í a bí go cuirreaċ.
(Referring back to "Siubán.")

SG. 92.—Agur ir é ir tuirge riteann ón gcómrac.
(Referring to "an gadar meatta" mentioned by previous speaker.)

7⁰. An t-uabar ir é cuireann duine ag rormad le n-a cómarrain (Ser. 13).

Exercise IX.
Identification. Type IV.

1⁰ It's the people who know least that talk most.
2⁰. The hardest people to set talking are *those*[1] who know Irish best.
3°. It was *none other than*[2] the barefooted woman.
4⁰ It was the high character of that action that destroyed me.
5⁰ The worst people are those who don't know a single word of Irish.
6° The very thing that is a credit to them is the one they want to disown.
7⁰. It is his own *affairs*[3] that are worrying him, not those of Irish or Ireland.

1. An té.   2. Expressed by rhetorical form of sentence.
3. Singular.

8°. What I have asked must be done.
9°. As soon as they were near him they recognized him. It was St. Caillin.
10°. It is our *liberties*[1]—our very *lives*[1]—that are in danger.
11°. What he coveted most was friendship with the young. Their minds were *impressionable*[2] and *changeable*,[3] and it was not difficult to inveigle them.[4]
12°. Oftentimes they that are *better in men's judgment*[5] fall lowest, because of their too great confidence.
13°. The saints that are highest in the sight of God are the least in their own eyes.
14°. The higher a person is advanced in spirit the heavier crosses shall he often meet with.
15°. That thing most readily comes to my mind which naturally delights me, or which through custom is pleasing to me.
16°. I beg for the peace of thy children who are fed by thee in the light of thy consolation.
17°. The stone which the builders rejected the same is become the head of the corner.
18°. He that shall endure unto the end, he shall be saved.
19°. He that believeth,[6] and is baptized[6], shall be saved; but he that believeth[6] not shall be condemned.
20°. He that is lesser among you all, he is the greater.

Identification. Type V.

PS.—The predicate and subject are simply juxtaposed without the verb. If the verb (with, of course, the necessary pronoun) is placed *before* the predicate we reduce the sentence

---

1. Singular. 2. boṡ. 3. ṡuaṡaċ. 4. This sentence must be joined to the preceding one, because it gives *his* reason. 5. Iṗ aoiṗoe cáiL. 6. Future tense.

STUDIES IN MODERN IRISH 33

to type I; if placed *after* the predicate we have type IV. Proverbs are often expressed in this form.

1°. An pud ıſ annaṁ ıſ ıongantac (proverb). Notice that once more we must supply the fundamental noun of the subject; further that the main verb is wanting, and that each of the two verbs expressed is relative (the particle being understood).

2°. Topac an uılc ıſ uſa do coſg (proverb).

3°. Niaṁ a caıteaḋ na ceıſteana go léıſ a ḟſeagaıſt dó. (n. 278).

4°. Goſmſlaıt an céad duıne do ḃuaıl uıme.

It will be noticed that if above sentences are made dependent they must take the form of type I or of type IV. *Questions* like cad é an puḋ é ſın? belong here (p. 48).

Exercise X.

Type V.

1°. My father was the first person I met on entering the house.
2°. It is hardest to check evil when it has run its course. (Cf. Ex. 2 above).
3°. The fear of God is the beginning of wisdom.
4°. What surprised me most was *the excellence*[2] of his performance.

2. A ḟeaḃaſ.

5°. It's the people who have least sense that talk most.
6°. We like best what pleases us best.
7°. We *ought* always *to do*[1] the thing that is most beneficial to us.
8° One *naturally*[2] likes a nice person.
9°. The heaviest weapon is the most profitable.
10°. The highest chair suits the tallest person best.
11°-20°. (Re-write above sentences in the dependent form).

Type VI.

SP. Subject and predicate juxtaposed, without the verb. As type V is an abbreviated variety of type I or type IV, so this type is an abbreviated variety of type II. Sentences of this kind frequently look like classification sentences and are not seldom misunderstood.

1°. Eagla Dé cúip na heagna. This sentence *may* belong to type V if it is understood to define what is the beginning of wisdom,--if it means that to begin to be truly wise we must fear God. But it *might* mean in the mind of a speaker that we are defining "the fear of God." It would in this case belong here, and would be equivalent to an abbreviated form of—1p é puo eagla Dé na cúip na heagna (type II). Cf. the relation of type III to type II.

   S   P

2. Típ gan teanga típ gan anam. Here we are obviously defining típ gan teanga. At first sight it looks like classification, but a little thought will show us that típ gan teanga means not any individual land, but that class or kind of land which is gan teanga; so that we have here not the classification of an individual, but the identification of classes. The

---

1. 1p inoéanta.   2. nío nac iongna.

sentence is a brief way of saying-- Sé puḋ ṫiṗ ꝝan ceanꝝa ná ṫiṗ ꝝan anam.

3. Móinach Casil comdas rí (M. of Cashel is a just king). (From an O. I. poem in LL., p. 149a, published in " Miscellanea Hibernica " (Kuno Meyer). Studies in Language and Literature (University of Illinois), Vol. II, No. 4).

Exercise XI.
Type VI.

1°. A man's enemies are those of his own household.
2°. The life of a language is the speaking of it.
3° A man of no property is no good.
4° A fire without heat is no use.
5°. Rain followed by fine weather never causes a wilderness.
6°. A language that has no poetry has no literature.
7°-12°. (*Re-write above sentences in dependent form.*)

This 6th type is quite common from the oldest times. E.g. (P.H. 187) Tu-ssa Dia, mei-se duine ; tusu tigerna, mei-se mog.

Proverbs are often expressed in this way :—Obaiṗ ꝝan biaḋ ꝝan páꝝ, obaiṗ ꝝan ꝼonn ꝝan ꝼiaḋaċ aiṗ. As type V, when it becomes dependent, is reduced to type I or type IV, so this present type takes the form of type II. Notice that in sentences 3°-6° above the fundamental noun of the subject must be repeated in the predicate.

Type VII.

VPS. The predicate is either—
1°. A pronoun of the 1st or 2nd pers. sing. or plur.

STUDIES IN MODERN IRISH

    2°. A pronoun of the 3rd pers.+ṫeo, ṫin, ṫiú𝐝
        (ṫo, ṫan, ṫú𝐝).
    3°. Any pronoun + ṫéin.

1°. (Iṫ) Ṁiṫe ʒeaṫóiɒ ó Ṅuallàin.
2°. Ɒeiṫ ṫé ʒuṫb é ṫin paoṫaiʒ ó Cealla.
3°. Aċ iṫ miṫe a baiṫt é (S. 18).
4°. Aiṫiú, a Ṡéaɒna an tu ṫan ? (S. 34).
5° B'é ṫéin aṫ𝐝-ollaṁ Ulaɒ.

It has been maintained that in a sentence like "Ṁiṫe an báṫ" in answer to the question Cia tuṫa? Ṁiṫe must be the logical subject. With this we cannot agree, *unless the sentence be understood as an example of type VI.* . If the verb is expressed immediately before miṫe then miṫe *must* be the logical predicate. It is no argument to compare such a sentence with English, and say that in the English " I " is the logical subject. This is only an attempt to bring Irish into line with English. It is sheer " anglicisation " of the language. The whole history of the verb ' iṫ ' shows it is impossible to predicate anything by means of it unless it be joined immediately to its logical predicate (at least in the pronominal form). On any other hypothesis we cannot explain the invariable presence of the pronoun in types II, III, and IV and its frequent absence in type I in Old Irish. Furthermore, when miṫe, etc., are logical subjects in the Irish mind the sentence takes quite a different form (type VIII). The use of the proleptic prepositional pronouns—(see p. 78) and certain relative constructions—(see p. 108) are further evidence that the subject must *not* come immediately ᴀfter ιf in non-interrogative sentences. The Grammars and Composition Books are absolutely wrong on this point. They lead us to suppose that when any of the words mentioned as predicates in this type constitute one of the terms of 'identity,' they *must* be predicates (logical or *grammatical !*) in the Irish sentence. This is entirely misleading as will appear from the next type (VIII).

Exercise XII.
Type VII.

1°. You're the queerest man I ever met.
2°. If thou seek thyself thou wilt indeed find thyself, but to thine own ruin.
3°. We ourselves are responsible for the game going against us.
4°. You want Tomás ó Cealla, do you ? Here he is. No, I'm wrong. That is he, over there.
5°. These are the friends, mother, I was talking to you about, yesterday.
6°. I was the first person to speak Irish in the house.
7°. I tell you it was I who did it, not you.
8°. You said first that you were his mother, and then that it was you who baptized him.
9°. Ye are the salt of the earth. Ye are the light of the world.
10°. It is they who bear witness concerning me.
11°. I am the bread of life. I am the light of the world.
12°. I know him because I am from him and he hath sent me.

Type VIII.

VpPS. The only difference between this and type I lies in the subject. Here the subject is a pronoun of the 1st or 2nd person, or a pronoun of the third person strengthened by a demonstrative. A priori there is no reason why such words should not be used as subjects, and it is difficult to understand how the idea arose that they cannot be so used. Because a posteriori there is abundant proof that they not only *may* be so used, but that they *must* be if it is necessary to express the meaning ; if there is a strong desire (for any reason whatsoever) to keep them definitely as *subjects* in our minds. The following examples will show that such necessity or such desire frequently exists :—

1°. 'Sí cainnt an tSlánuigteora féin i rin. Here it was the writer's desire to predicate "cainnt an tSlánuigteora féin" of the words in question (denoted by i rin).

2°. Sé mo corp é reo. Here it was imperative, owing to the special circumstances, (the words being *factitive*), to express it in this way. All previous translations of these words of Consecration are unsatisfactory, if not absolutely wrong. An attempt has been made to save the theological aspect of the language by saying that in "ir é reo mo corp-ra" the é is proleptic, (standing for the predicate mo corp-ra) and reo is subject. Against this, however, is the fact that é reo are too closely connected to be thus separated, and the further fact that instead of é reo, é rin in such sentences the modern language frequently substitutes rio é, rin é, where the theory cannot be applied. The emphatic particle above is out of place also. The real meaning of ir é reo mo corp-ra is

STUDIES IN MODERN IRISH

that it states where the body of Christ is to be found,—viz., *in the object denoted by* "**é ṟeo**." It insinuates therefore that Christ's Body is NOWHERE ELSE ; But Christ's Body is in Heaven, and also in every consecrated particle throughout the world. Theologically and linguistically it is quite untenable as a translation of the Words of Consecration. On the other hand 1ṟ é mo ċoṟp é ṟeo, states of the object in question (denoted by é ṟeo) that it is " Christ's " Body. It neither states nor insinuates anything about Christ's Body being, or *not* being, anywhere else. It means exactly what was wanted. Where the é and the ṟeo (or ṟın) are actually separated in the sentence, they are separated in thought also, é standing for the predicate, and ṟeo (or ṟın) for the subject. E.g.,

(Dott. II 13).—is e Crist Mac Dé sin.
(PH. 268).—ni he m'étach féin seo itir.

3°. 'Sí mo ċuıḋ ḟola, ṟa' cıomna nua, í ṟeo. The same remarks apply here as above.

4°. 1ṟ ıaḋ ḋo ḃṟıaṫṟa-ṟa ıaḋ-ṟo, a Ċṟíoṟc, ḃíoḋ naċ ın-aon am amáın a ḋuḃṟaḋ ıaḋ (Im. 235).

5°. An é ṟın an cáṟca ḋuḃ ? Ní hé, aċ ṟın é é (type VII). Here we are looking for an cáṟca ḋuḃ, and the answer given is the proper one).

An é an cáṟca ḋuḃ é ṟın ? (type VIII). Ní hé, ṟé an cáṟca bán é. (Here we were *not* looking for an cáṟca ḋuḃ, but only for the colour of the card pointed at. To transpose the answers would be to misunderstand the questions).

6°. Ḃṟéıṫṟe Cṟíoṟc ıaḋ ṟan (Im. 1).

7°. Ɣo ḟíoṟ ḋoḃ' é Mac Ḋé é ṟın (C.S. 83).

8°. Naċ é mac Ióṟeıp é ṟeo ? (C.S. 150).

9°. Maois ⁊ eliar iad ran (C.S. 169).
10°. Ir é reo an páiḋ gan aṁpar. Dubairt cuille acu: Ir é an Criort é reo (C.S. 246).
(Here we have VII and VIII combined.)
11°. Adeir se ina letrechaib fein curabb é tigerna na tigerna ⁊ rí na ríg é féin (G.M., ZCP II, 268).
12°. Féaċ, mo Ḋia tu, mo ċuiḋ an traogal tu (Im. 168).

Exercise XIII.
Type VIII (and VII).

1°. Is that the book you wanted yesterday? (VII) No· This is it, here.
2°. Is this the pen I gave you this day week? (VIII) No. It's the one you had in your hand this morning.
3°. These are Thy words, O Christ, the eternal Truth, though not delivered at one time nor written in one place.
4°. Is this the white box? (VIII) No, it's the black one.
5°. ,, ,, ,, ,, ,, ? (VII) No, there it is yonder.
6°. This must be our business to strive to overcome ourselves and daily to gain strength against ourselves, and to grow better.
7°. I chose them out of the world; they were not beforehand with me, to choose Me.
8°. I imparted to them extraordinary comforts, gave them perseverance and crowned their patience.
9°. And they put over His head His cause written: " This is Jesus King of the Jews."
10°. I gave testimony that this is the Son of God.

Type IX.

VpSP. The peculiarity is in the proleptic pronoun, which is eaḋ here (as distinguished from types II and III (é, í, iaḋ).

STUDIES IN MODERN IRISH 41

The pronoun eaḋ (originally neuter) is specialised in Modern Irish to take the place of an indefinite predicate whether masc., fem. or (originally) neuter, in classification. In the present type we have a survival of the Old Irish use of eaḋ to anticipate a definite predicate (like the others). Nowadays it is found mostly in poetry, and occasionally in folk lore. In Keating, of course, it is quite common. Examples :

1°. 'Seaḋ ḃuḃaiṗt ṕí—éirt liom ꞅo ꞅoil (L.O. 260).
2°. iS eaḋ ḃo póṅꞅaḃ na h-Aꞅꞅtail ꞅmuaineaḋ aꞅ an mḃáꞅ (KTB. 5).
3°. iꞅ eaḋ ciałuiꞅeaꞅ an taoḃ toiꞅ ḃo'n aitóiꞅ, oiꞅteaꞅ, .i. toꞅać aoiꞅe an ḃuine (KTB. 6).
4°. iꞅ eaḋ aḃuḃaiꞅt, 'ní taḃaiꞅ ḃuine uaiḋ an niḋ naċ ḃí aiꞅe (KTB. 8).

Type X.

SVpPs. The real subject comes first, and a pronoun comes in at the end referring back to it. (Cf. Classification, type XV).

An t-apáṅ a taḃaꞅꞅaḋ-ꞅa uaim iꞅ é mo ċuiḋ ꞅeoła ꞅéin é cun ḃeata an ḋoṁain (Ċ.S. 242).

NOTE.—Sometimes we find identification and classification in the same sentence :—

1°. Ḃeiꞅ cuiḋ acu ꞅuꞅḃ é ieꞅemiaꞅ é (Identification) nó ḃuine ḃe ꞅna ꞅáiḋiḃ (ĊS 45) (classification).
2°. Ní ꞅeoil ꞅ ꞅuil a ḃ'ꞅoillꞅiꞅ ḃuit-ꞅe ꞅin (classification aċ m' Ataiꞅ-ꞅe atá inꞅ na ꞅlataiꞅ (identification of the type PS, only the S is understood from the preceding clause) (Ċ.S. 45).

Note on Proper Names.

In " Séaḋna," p. 20, we read the following :—
Síle.—Coꞅaꞅ a Ċáit ! Caḋ é an ainm atá aiꞅ ?

Cáit.—Tá Éamonn.
Peig.—Agur Éamonn a atair.

Here the sentence (ir) Éamonn a atair is a classification sentence like the others in type 4° (Classification, p. 5). All these examples show clearly that words which at first sight are Proper Names, are in reality sometimes true general terms, considered logically. This fact has been overlooked, and students have been led astray on the point. It was stated, in a book published some years ago, that " the rule requiring *a definite noun* to be separated from ir by a personal pronoun is subject to exception, viz. : (*a*) where the sentence gives a name or title and ná is not used, e.g., ADubairt ré ṡup Páoparg ainm a ṁic ; aoubairt ré ṡup 'Oún Ṡaṗbán oo bí ar an mbaile rin ruaṁ. (*b*) In such sentences as Seumur ó hAonṡura oo-riṡne an claioe rin amurṡ where a proper name is emphasised ir is suppressed."

Now, neither of these cases is an exception to the rule in question. The example (*b*) is not, because, as the writer himself remarked, " ir is suppressed." If ir is suppressed of course there is no question of the Rule at all ; if there is no ' ir ' the rule can neither be observed nor broken ; the sentence is ' diversa materia.' The examples given under (*a*) are more serious. The nouns in question—Páoparg and 'Oún Ṡaṗbán are NOT DEFINITE NOUNS AT ALL, and so the examples again fall altogether outside the scope of the rule. Words like Páoparg, etc., have an entirely different force when predicated of a person or place or thing, and when predicated merely of *the name* of a person, place or thing. When I say ' This man's NAME is Páoparg ' " Páoparg " is used in what logicians call its ' suppositio materialis.' But when I say " This MAN is Páoparg," " Páoparg" is used in its ' suppositio realis ' and the sentence means either " This man is an individual bearing the name Páoparg " or

STUDIES IN MODERN IRISH

he is "*the* special individual" to whom alone "páopaiṡ," in the sense I now attach to it, belongs. All these distinctions are clearly marked in Irish.

We can distinguish *four* uses of such terms :—

1° Sé páopaiṡ a bí ann.
2°. Ꝺeiр ré ṡuр páopaiṡ é riúo, Leiр.
3°. Sé ainm atá aiр ná páopaiṡ.
4°. Ꝺeiр ré ṡuр páopaiṡ ir ainm oó.

In 1° and 2° páopaiṡ is used in its 'real supposition,' but in 1° only is it a true proper name, a true individual term, a true definite noun. In 2° it is really a general term equivalent to "*a person bearing the name* páopaiṡ." In 3° and 4° the 'supposition' is material, whilst in 3° the term is definite but in 4° quite general. 1° and 3° are therefore identification sentences, 2° and 4° are merely classification. 1° and 2° are *real* sentences, 3° and 4° are merely 'nominal' sentences. Compared with these two 'nominal' sentences there are two 'real' sentences which will throw light on the situation. These are, e.g., { 3a. Ir é puo é ná atpuṡao ana-móр.
and { 4a. Ir atpuṡao ana-móр é.

4*a*. means simply that the matter in question is 'a great change,' a thing that comes under that heading, one of the several things or occurrences to which we should give that name. 3*a*. means more than this. The subject is no longer it (é) but 'the *kind of thing* that "*it*" is' (an puo ir é). The predicate is no longer merely 'a great change' but 'THE KIND OF THING which we call a great change' (for this is the real meaning of "atpuṡao ana-móр" in 3*a*). We are no longer *classifying* the *individual occurrence ;* we are identifying 'the class to which that occurrence is conceived as belonging' with 'the class we describe as atpuṡao ana-móр." To put it another way—3*a* considered logically expresses the generic judgment S is P., while 4*a* represents the form "this S is P."

In regard to "the rule requiring a definite noun to be separated from ιγ by a personal pronoun" it is time to remark that there IS NO SUCH RULE AT ALL! In Old Irish, even in type I, there *was* no such rule. In type I the presence of the pronoun—though necessary according to present-day usage—is due to a misunderstanding, a confusion of types. It is inserted in order to assimilate type I to types II, III, and IV, not in order to separate 'ιγ' from a definite noun. THAT was NEVER necessary. The real rule was, and is *that the subject must not stand immediately after* ιγ. That is the real reason why the pronoun is used in types II, III, IV. The *definite* character of the following noun *has nothing whatever to do with it*, as is seen from type I in O.I. where the pronoun was seldom used (and then, as we have said, owing to a misconception); and also from the fact that the insertion of a pronoun is *equally necessary* in classification sentences of a certain kind even when the following noun is indefinite (if it is the SUBJECT). We must say, e.g., ainmιδe ιγ eαδ capall. This eαδ is as necessary, and *for precisely the same reason* (viz., to separate ιγ and the subject) as é, í or ιαδ are necessary in types II, III and IV. In type I the presence of the pronoun is an anomaly.

We have said that the alleged exceptions to the rule as quoted on p. 42 are not exceptions at all. If we admit the Rule in that un-emended form, we find there are *real* exceptions to it in Modern Irish. (In the emended form given above there is ABSOLUTELY NO EXCEPTION.)

1°. An occasional example like that in Keating's poems (I)

> ξιδ eαδρα ceανξα ιγ γeανδα
> ξιδ laιδeαn ιγ léιξeαnnca.

This is merely an archaism.

2°. Where certain definite expressions have taken on an

adverbial signification. E.g., ir dóċa gur an faid a ḃí an dealḃar air a ḋein ré é.

One must say, however, b'é faid an turuir a cuir tuirre orm. (*Not* in order to separate ir from a definite noun, but by assimilation to types II, III and IV).

Similar exceptions are—an iomad, anoir, induu, etc. Ir anoir é (C.S. 233).

3°. When the predicate is a prepositional phrase, even though *definite* in sense,—*unless it comes last in the sentence* :—

Ir idteaṁair a ḃiodar an uair rin.

But—Ir é áit n-a raḃadar an uair rin ná i dteaṁair.

This last qualification applies also to the phrases mentioned under exception 2°. E.g., Ir dóċa gur bé uair a ḋein ré é ná an faid a ḃí an dealḃar air. In these cases if the pronoun were not used the subject would follow ir immediately. That is *never* allowable. (For questions, see pp. 47-48).

4°. The chief exception is *in relative* ir *sentences* when the relative particle (generally understood) is *subject* to the ir.

(a) . . . gurb é iora ir Críort ann (Acts xviii. 5).

(b) Ir ead ir Dia ann, Spioraid ríopuiḋe (Don. 40).

(c) Ir é ir míḋeaṁain nó Uprnaig na Meanmna ann, ḃreatnuġaḋ dúċractac 7rl. (Don. 394).

(d) Do rgríoḃaḋ an méid reo ionur go gcreidfeaḋ riḃ gurb é iora ir Críort mac Dé ann.

When, however, the relative particle (expressed or understood) is genitive, accusative, or dative the pronoun is inserted in the ordinary way :—

(a) Níl aoinne ó ḃaoġal ag teaċt or cóṁair daoine aċ an té gurbé a ḋúil ḃeit in aonar (Im. 36).

(b) Tá marcaigeaċt fuaire ag duine an faid ir é gpárta Dé atá gá iomċar. (The Relative understood before

ir is dative; direct instead of oblique in temporal
clause. See p. 89). Agur **nuair ir é Dia** a bíonn
ag iomčap ouine . . . cao é an iongna ná motui-
zeann an ouine rin ualač. (Rel. dat.—The Subject
of ir is "an té a bíonn ag iomčap ouine)(Im. 77).

(c) Cačoin a Cruinneočao mo maċtnaṁ go h-iomlán
ionnac-ra, iotreo . . . ná motóčao mé féin in aon
čop, ač Tura aṁáin ap cuma **nač é gač aoinne** a
tuigeann (Im. 141). (Neg. rel. accus. governed
by tuigeann. Subject of ir = an té (understood)
a tuigeann. Predicate = gač aoinne).

(d) An té **nač é Dia** a bíonn or cómair a fúl aige ní oea-
cair huaireaṁ a čup air le rocailín tromaioeačta
(Im. 191). (Rel. is genitive. Subject of 'ir' =
(an té) a bíonn or cómair a fúl aige. Predicate =
Dia.

(e) Ir reipbtean mór 7 ir pian mór oo'n Críortaíoe
fíoraonta a beit air beit ag fpeagairt oo gač
oualgur oá mbaineann le ná'oúp an ouine ar an
raogal ro, **nuair ir é puo ba miαn leir féin ná**
beit rgarta leo (Im. 43). Rel. is dat. Direct for
oblique in temporal clause. See p. 89. Here (and
in example [a]) as the predicate is at the *end*, the
insertion of the pronoun is absolutely necessary.
All the other examples = type I.

(f) **nuair ir é an rí féin** ir mó atá cionntač cá bruil
leigear le ragáil ar an olc? (Eir. 14). Rel. dat.
Direct for oblique. (See p. 89).

(g) Daoine a bíonn ag gabáil timčeall i gcómnuíoe 7
nač é an cruaotan a o' fuiling íora Críort a bíonn
uata ač gač aon puo oá míne. (Rel. dat.—if relative
at all). (Im. 165).

(h) Tabarran ouit rolur aigne 7 eolur cóm faoa 7 ir é

STUDIES IN MODERN IRISH 47

do leaṗ é. (Im. 287). (Rel. dat. Direct for oblique in temporal clause. See p. 89).

(1) Ní ṁaċtnuiġeann riḃ eonur maṗ iṗ é ḃuṗ leaṗ aon duine aṁáin d' ḟaġáil ḃáiṗ ċaṗ ċeann an ṗobuil ⁊ ġan an cinéal ġo léiṗ do ḋul aṗ ceal (C.S. 259). (Dat. Rel. Direct for oblique in modal clause; p. 90).

Rarely, when the relative clause is negative though the relative is subject to the verb iṗ, the pronoun is expressed:—

ḃí a lán neiċe náṗḃ é an lá aṗ áilneaċt aġainn (SG. 135).

The insertion of the pronoun here is merely a reminiscence of the common expressions—puḋ naċ é, puḋ náṗḃ é, where é *must* be used because the material predicate is suppressed. We may therefore look upon the above sentence as peculiar, not in the use of é, but in the repetition of the material predicate. Early exx. of omission of pronoun :—P.H. 130 Cid he *is airchindech na n-apstal*. P.H. 130 :—Co n-id he Crist *is rig ⁊ is brethem na n-uli dúl*.

NOTE 1.—In Donlevy 44 An Dia an t-Ataiṗ? is correct. An é Dia an t-Ataiṗ would seem to imply *only one person* in God.

Similarly, Ser. 180—Iṗ Dia áṗ Slánuiġċeoiṗ. Here the direct reference is to the divine *nature*. Dia means *a* person of *divine* nature. (There are *three* such Persons).

NOTE 2.—We have said frequently that the great rule of iṗ construction is "*that the subject must not follow* iṗ *immediately*."

It is this rule which necessitates the insertion of the pronoun in types II, III, IV, VIII and IX of Identification, and in certain kinds of Classification (types 6, 7, 8, 9, 10, pp. 5, 6). Up to the present we have not considered questions. Questions of course are peculiar. (*I am speaking of What and Who questions. Questions like*—An é Tomáṗ ó Ceallaiġ do bí ann? SUGGEST *a predicate and follow the ordinary rules*). In the first place there is no real predication, properly so called. The essence of such a question is that it asks for, not gives, a predicate. The interrogative takes the place of the predicate, and comes first, and as a rule 'ir' is not expressed. It is to be noted that where 'ir' does follow cad or cia it is not the principal verb at all. We have two kinds of question therefore to discuss :—1° Cad é an puv é rin? Here we have simply juxtaposition of predicate and subject (type V, pp 32-33), the verb being understood. There is therefore no question of the above rule being violated here. In cia h é rin?, if we look upon h- as the lenited r of 'ir' we may consider this question as coming under the next catagory.

2°. Cia ir Críorc ann? Cad ir bris do'n focal ran?

Cad ir ciall leir an scainnt reo? Cad ir ainm duic? etc., etc. All these are elliptical. The verb 'ir' which is heard is not the principal verb of the question at all (this is not expressed) and the words following this ir constitute its *predicate* in every case, the subject being the relative particle understood. E.g., the meaning of the question Cad ir ainm duic? is made clear by the following analysis :—

Subject = (an ainm a ir) ainm duic
Predicate = Cad?
Subject of the 'ir' expressed = a
Predicate of the 'ir' expressed = ainm dom.
ainm du t.

In form it is exactly the same as the answer :—pádraig ir ainm dom.

It would seem therefore to be universally true that wherever the verb ir appears it must *never* be followed immediately by its subject. This is not equivalent to saying that it must always be followed by its (*material*) predicate. (That is the mistake made by many writers on Irish Grammar). The material predicate may come first (*before* the verb) or after it, and before the subject, or at the very end, after verb and subject.

APPENDIX.

We may add here some early examples of the various types of Identification :—

I. P.H. 134.—Indissid Lucás co n-id he in dara latrand nama do.s.gní a écnach-sum.
II. ,, 131.—Co n-id hí cet aním for a r-hiadad iffern iarum arím Júdáis.
,, 202.—Is hí mo chomarli dúib co ro-chara cách uaib araile mar ro-charus-sa sib-se.
,, 163.—Bid he a hainnim tégdais ernaigthe ⁊ etarguide dar cend beo ⁊ marb.
III. ,, 139.—Is e imorro in forcometus tanaise co ro-p is in cetna mís na bliadna celebarthar.
,, 209.—Is he in brécaire in tí thadbanus sechtair do dóinib a beith maith ⁊ sé olc ar-medón.
IV. ,, 132.—Demun tra do-dechaid ann-sin do thoirmesc in cesta, cid he is auctor oc aslach in césta remi.
,, 53.—Dia uli-cumachtach is e bus liaig dam.
,, 202.—Ísu Crist mac Dé bíí . . is e ro-raid na briathra-sa.
VII. ,, 131.—In tu-sa rig na n-Iúdaide ?
,, 136.—dénaid tindenus co ro-p sib toisech innises bethaid do'n doman.
,, 227.—is tu mo choimdiu, is tu mo Dia.
,, 199.—uair is í sin aimser i-n ro-aithin in coimdiu in timna sin dó.
VIII. ,, 134.—Ma-sa mac Dé tú.
,, 146.—Is e Crist mac Dé sin.
IX. ,, 132.—is ed atbert Piláit friu . . .
,, 60.—co n-id ed tra tanic ass fuil ⁊ fín (and *passim*).

CHAPTER II.

Prolepsis.

In most languages certain words come, in the course of time, to be used PROLEPTICALLY, i.e., in anticipation of certain other parts of the sentence occurring later on. In Irish, pronouns and prepositional pronouns are so used, and the detailed study of this phenomenon is absolutely necessary for anyone who wishes to obtain a scientific grasp of the language. This detailed study will occupy the present chapter.

é, í, iad
ead

I. (a) The first group of words which are used proleptically comprises the pronouns é, í, iad, ead. We have already met them, standing in anticipation of the *predicate* in Types I, II, III, VIII, IX and X of Identification ; (b) Sometimes also, in " What ? ' and " Who ?" questions, the pronouns é, í, iad anticipate the *subject*, e.g., Cad é an rud é rin? where é anticipates the subject—an rud (ir) é rin ; (c) Occasionally, outside of 'ir' sentences, we find the pronoun é used proleptically :—

1°. bí átar orta é beit le rád aca
go breacadar an rí.

2°. tá ceirt 7 ceann-fé orm é breit am beataid orm

go gcaitfinn teact as tmall ort-ra
as lorg airsid ar iaract (S. 48).

Cf. the use of proleptic a (1), p. 55.

II. sidé.

rud é.

1°. **sidé** an freagra a tugad orta :—**muna** n-iompuigid rib 7 beit ar nór leanbaí

STUDIES IN MODERN IRISH 51

beaga ní ragaid rib irteac i rigeact na
brlaicear. (Im. 231).
2°. Sidé ir mó a coirgeann rólár ó Dia ar
teact cúgat, a deacaract leat iompáil cun
úrnuigte. (Im. 150).
III. Sé.
1°. Cuireann Sé átar orm
tú beit cóṁ mait ir taoi.
2°. Do cuir Sé iongna orm
a ṗeabar do bein ré an gnó.
3° Ná ḟuil Sé cóṁ mait agat
tairbe na rgillinge úd d'ṗágáil mar
atá ré? (S. 14).

This proleptic use of ré serves to explain certain
sentences in which the logical connection between
the two portions is, at first sight, not very clearly
expressed. From the first two examples just given
we can also say—

1a. Tá átar orm tu beit cóṁ mait ir taoi.
2a. Bí iongna orm a ṗeabar do bein ré an gnó.

So we frequently find such constructions as the
following :—

4°. Ní raib uain aige cuiṁneaṁ ar cad ba
ceart dó a déanaṁ (S. 46), which may be most
easily explained by a reference to the proleptic ré
in—ní raib Sé d'uain aige . . . (See p. 154).

5°. Tá náire orm teact cun cainnte leat (S. 48).
This can hardly be explained as apposition,
because náire here clearly means " the FEELING of
shame," not the *cause* of that feeling, though in a
different kind of sentence náire is used in this
sense also—ir mór an náire duit é. Once more
a reference to the proleptic Sé in—cuireann ré

náire orm . . . explains the relation of effect and cause between "cá náire orm" and "ceacc cun cainnce leac."

6°. bí iongna orca é gá fiaffuide (S. 63). The same remarks apply here.

7°. If air a bí an iongna nuair a fuair ré ná iaib Séavna ag ceacc (S. 72). Here we find suggested another explanation of the apparently loose construction in question. It often happens that part of the thought, as originally expressed, is omitted, the shortcomings of the remainder being made up for by the recollection of the full expression. In the course of time, however, people accept the shortened expression without *recollection* and without question. Here, e.g., if we omit the words "nuair a fuair ré" we shall have—

If air a bí an iongna . . . ná raib Séavna ag ceacc.

IV. SO.
1°. Ac cuireav SO buairc orc,

San cu beic cóm maic ná cóm haireac orc féin 7 ba ceart vo vuine vémóibeac a beic i reirbír vé? (Im. 224).

2°. Cav a tug SO vóm-ra

mácair mo cígearna vo ceacc ag triall orm? (C.S. 140).

3°. Co n-id so dethbir dún a thoga sech cach lá aire-sin (P.H. 139).

V. SAN.

Ordinarily the distinction between ro, rivé, é rev on the one hand, and ran, rin é, é rin, on the other, is that the former refer to what comes after, and the latter to what has gone before. Occasionally, however, we find ᵃn used proleptically :—

Ná cuimir ꞃan de maꞃla aꞃ aꞃ nglóiꞃe
 ꞃo dteictimír ón ꞃcꞃoiꞃ. (Im. 224).

VI. é sin. See previous remarks (V).

1°. Cad é sin dó ꞃan
 Cad a béanꞃaid an Aꞃd-Ríꞃeact? (N. 296).

2°. Cad é sin dúinne
 Cia'cu tátaꞃ ꞃocaiꞃ aiꞃ nó ná ꞃuilteaꞃ? (N. 315).

3° Like proleptic é, it may anticipate the 1st or 2nd person :
 Cad é sin dúinne
 tuꞃa, a íoꞃa, a ṁic Dé? (C.S. 21).

4°. So strong is this *proleptic* tendency of é ꞃin n such questions, that even when its real reference has gone before it, a word " ꞃin " is added at the end to satisfy this tendency (cf. proleptic de, p. 72)
 Aꞃuꞃ máꞃ ꞃioꞃ é, a ꞃiꞃtiꞃiꞃ, cad é sin d'aoinne eile sin?

Exercise XIV.
Prolepsis (I-VI).

1°. It is not permissible for anyone to return evil for evil.
2°. May we not as well tackle the combat now?
3°. I was often *on the point*[1] of asking you what was wrong with you.
4°. Before he had time to return the war started.
5°. He was utterly incapable of coming to a decision as to which of them would please him best.

1. táiniꞃ ꞃé cun mo béil.

6°. I have definitely made up my mind that I ought to spend my life *in the priesthood*.[1]
7°. There is this much difference in the matter. Michael was an honest man, whereas " the gentleman " was a villain.
8°. Let thy concern be that thou dost not carry thyself so well and so circumspectly as it becomes a servant of God and a devout religious man.
9°. What is it, to such a one as that, what Cathal will do?
10°. ,, ,, ,, to me how *he* ill treats himself ?
11° What need we concern ourselves about questions of philosophy ?
12° What concern is it of yours, whether I shall be alive or not, after my head is cut off ?
13°. What is this or that to thee ? Do thou follow Me.
14° What is it to thee whether this man be such or such, or that man do or say this or the other ?
15°. What do I care how you treat one another ?

Prolepsis (continued).

VII. ᴀ.

This is by far the most important of all proleptic words. For the sake of clearness we had better consider it under three separate headings :—

I. It is used before *a verbal noun* to anticipate the *object* (when this is a phrase or clause which cannot be inflected) of the act in question (whether the verbal noun is of the ordinary type, or another sort really implying action, e.g., burdeacar).

II. It is used before a noun denoting *quality, quantity, time, intensity, meaning*, and similar notions, to anticipate *the action itself*, or a noun, which is not a noun of action at all ; or a pronoun.

---

1. This is emphatic.

STUDIES IN MODERN IRISH

III. It is used before a noun denoting *quality, condition*, etc., to anticipate a "tá" clause.

Examples.

I. 1°. Ir upur a aitne ar maoite do meanman deapóile t'inntinne (BK. 61).

2°. Bí rí tréir a domáil do Siubán 50 raib a croide dá ṁníoṁ le buaipt (S. 110).

3°. Bí buile ar ṁicil rotaob a rád 50 mbead sé de pláinéid ar Séadna 50 dtug ré 5eallaṁaint pórta do Sadb (S. 116).

Observe how the sentence is built up by two proleptic words. The sentence in (S. 247)—ṅuair a bí ré in a-am rtaid d'eipizeadar cun imtiġte a baile—is hardly an example of prolepsis, as rtaid is genitive, and "am-rtaid" is simply qualified by a. Cf. also MSF., 141.—in' am rtaid. It may be a survival of the old usage, according to which proleptic a in such cases was followed by a genitive in apposition. E.g., a uathmaire ind fir (S.T.); a masse in chuirp (Gl.). The only other instances of a genitive, in apposition to this proleptic a, in the best modern writers, are with the phrases a lán and a tuille. These are sometimes followed by partitive de: a beag and a móp and a ṁalaipt are generally followed by this partitive de. The phrase in am ṁaipb na hoidče may be another instance, but it is also possible that there is no "a" here at all. In "ar a bpeabap de ġníoṁartaib" (MSF., 44) the a is not proleptic at all.

4°. Táinig ré or cómair na Seanaide fé deire ag geapán, niar 'd 'ead, go rabtar gá crád le h-acrann ; ⁊ é gá leogaint air

Sur ceartuig uaid é góin do glanad (Cat. 35).

As the English " it " corresponding to this " a " does not appear in English as a rule, the student must be careful to use the Irish " a." Unfortunately there is a tendency in some places to give it up. When the object of the action is expressed by a genitive noun then (outside the few cases mentioned above) proleptic a is not used. But in all other instances (with the restriction to be mentioned just now) the true Irish idiom requires proleptic a.

Some verbal nouns, however,— especially leogaint, bagairt, aitint—occasionally dispense with it :—

Bí rí ag bagairt oirmra ranamaint léi (S. 19). This may easily be explained as elliptical, and equivalent to—

Bí rí ag bagairt orm-ra (⁊ gá rad liom) ranamaint léi.

So—do b'fuirirte aitint air go raid rúil aige . . . (br. 24) may be a case of " a " getting lost between the two words, like " a " in tá tior agam. Similarly after a word ending in a vowel :

Már mait leatra leogaint do Mardán ⁊ do Suaire beit ag magad fút, níl bac ort ann (g. 77). D'feadrai leogaint dó radarc fagáil ar árt (n. 112)].

Other examples are not so easily explained away :

STUDIES IN MODERN IRISH

E.g.—Ní misde liom leogaint duit beit ag imirt do cuid cleas ar duine éigin eile (S. 38).

Some earlier examples of proleptic ᴀ :—

5°. Is cóir dúinn a smuaineaḋ 7 a creideaḋ go daingion gur ab éigin dúinn go cinnte bás d'fagail (Don. 174).

6°. Creud ciallaigeas a ṗáḋ gur cóir do'n doilgeas so a beit inmeodónaċ ? (Don. 246).

7°. Is féidir dó a taḋairt fá deara gur tuill ré díogaltas dé (Don. 252).

Exercise XV.

Proleptic ᴀ (I).

1°. I am inclined to *probe*[1] that question to the root until I succeed in solving it sooner or later.
2°. On the *contrary*[2] you ought to think worse of yourself than anyone else does, and to see that no one is weaker than yourself.
3°. I had to promise her that I would marry her daughter.
4°. It's a great shame for them to pretend they don't eat much, whereas they have the king robbed.
5°. I should never cease to regret my being married to a fool.
6°. I must tell my mother and consult her as to the best course to pursue.
7°. Tell me exactly what it is you blame for the untoward turn which the game has taken.
8°. It is not easy to suppose that the inhabitants will allow the bull to be taken from them.

1. Leanaṁaint siar ar . . .   2. Is aṁlaiḋ.

9°. One could not easily discern whether she *thought*[1] less of her riches or her reputation.
10°. *He pitied*[2] their hard plight, and proceeded to ask them what escape from the difficulty they hoped for.
11°. He told the messengers to pretend that they were quite sympathetic towards the conspiracy.
12°. Thanks be to Thee that Thou hast not spared me in my evil-doing.
13°. I thank Thee, o God, that I am not as the rest of men.
14°. He thought to convince us, rightly or wrongly, that his was the true version of the story.

Prolepsis (continued).

VII II. 1°. Bí iongna a gcroibe orca a feabar do beineadar an gnó (S. 183).

This sentence is elliptical. It means "They were surprised at the excellence OF IT (viz. the way in) which they accomplished the business. This is one of the instances in which the direct relative is used where logically we should have expected the oblique. See p. 91

2° Ar tugair ré ndeara a cruinne ⁊ a feabar a coimeád ré é, ón uile duine d'ár labair leir.

Here again the direct relative is used for the oblique.

When the noun following proleptic a ends in a vowel the relative particle need not appear at all:

---

1. Use beann.   2. There is a difference in meaning between
a) ba ċruaġ leir   . (b) bí ċruaġ aige do   and (c) do bein ré
ċruaġ de

3°. muna mbeaḋ a ġlice
   Cuiṗ Séaḋna cúpṗaí an Cleamnaiṗ 1
   mbéalaiḃ na nḋaoine (S. 148).

When another noun follows the noun of quality (quantity, etc.) after a that noun will NOT be in the genitive case.

4°. 'neoṗaiḋ ṗé ḋóiḃ a luiġeaḋ
   Aiṗṡeaḋ a ḃí aġaṫṗa ṫá beaġán aimṗiṗe
   ó ṗoin ann (S. 157).

5°. Caḋ é a ḃṗíġ
   Aon Laoċ amáin am' Coinniḃ-ṗe anoiṗ?

That this is the true modern construction is shown by the practice of the best writers and speakers; and also by the fact that *all* the personal pronouns mé, tú, é, í, ṗinn, ṗiḃ, iaḋ, are freely used as the " terms " of this proleptic " a," and used, not of course in the genitive, but in the nom. FORM.

We find ourselves, therefore, in total disagreement with some remarks on this construction which appeared in a recent book. In the phrase " ḋa méiḋ ṗaiḋḃṗiṗ " the word ṗaiḋḃṗiṗ had been previously parsed as nom. plural (!). It was then stated to be gen. sing., and the nom. usage explained as due to careless speech. But then what of ḋa ġéiṗe é, ṗiḃ, ṗinn, iaḋ, etc.? It is rather a sweeping statement to put all these down to careless speech. We explain the matter quite differently. In such cases the noun or pronoun is used absolutely (see p. 220) in the nom. *form* (though of course sometimes it is logically accusative). The genitive is never used in the modern language by the best speakers and writers (outside the cases already mentioned, p. 55). When inferior writers use the genitive it is due either to ignorance, or a self-conscious working out of the case in defiance of the best usage. The fact that in Old Irish the genitive WAS frequently used in apposition, proves nothing in regard to the modern language. The use of the pronouns é, í, etc., after proleptic ᴀ shows conclusively that the old construction has changed.

Exercise XVI.

Proleptic ᴀ (II).

1°. What is man in thy sight?
2°. *It is most extraordinary*[1] how *very easily*[2] we believe sometimes the thing that pleases us.
3°. They wondered much how badly he did it.
4°. They were quite satisfied with the way they had escaped.
5°. He wondered that he was so little tired *though*[3] the hill was so steep.
6°. There's no knowing how soon he might need him again.
7°. What does Connor's treachery signify compared with this one?
8°. Had they not brought her away with them thus quickly they *would undoubtedly*[4] have had her dead.
9°. I think he was surprised at the way some of them understood *what was said.*[5]

---

1. ɴíl ᴀon τρeo ᴀċ . . .   2. Express *superlative* by *two nouns* of kindred meaning.   3. Aζuρ.   4. Express *certainty* of event by using *past* tense indicative.   5. An ċᴀınnτ.

STUDIES IN MODERN IRISH 61

10°. I will let them know how little money you have and how much you need more.
11°. I was told to inform you that your father is delighted at the way you succeeded.
12°. What matters here a little pain,—when Heaven is won all toil is gain?
13°. I am naturally pleased at the difficulty *you find*[1] in falling out with me.
14° There is one thing strikes me very forcibly—*it is so easy*[2] to make a fool of oneself without knowing it.
15°. He told me he didn't care how soon I went away.
16°. I thought he might have concealed from me the extent of his anger *against*[3] me.
17°. I can't tell you how loth I am to go home again.
18° Did I ever tell you how beautifully I tricked the trickster?
19°. How often one's misdeeds recoil " to plague the inventor "!
20°. Isn't it extraordinary how hard some people find it to be civil to their friends?

Prolepsis (continued).

VII (III) 1°. . . . ionʒna oṗta a ḟaıḋ ataım uata (TBC. 252).
2°. Caḋ é an beann a ḃeaḋ aıge rıúḋ aṗ uırʒe te, aʒuṗ a teo ata an aıt aṗ a ḋtaınıʒ ṗé? (S. 113).
3°. Ḃi ionʒna oṗm, ⁊ a ḟuaıṗe a ḃi an aımsır, é beıt amuıʒ ṗé'n rṗéıṗ ınaun coṗ.
4°. Occasionally proleptic a (especially when

1. Use le.   2. Use proleptic a.   3. Cum.

followed by another proleptic ᴀ) takes partitive
ᴅᴇ :—ᴀ ʟᴜɪʒᴇᴀᴅ ᴅᴀ́ ᴘ̇ɪᴏꜱ ᴀ ʙɪ́ ᴀʒ ᴀɴ ʀᴀʒᴀʀᴛ ᴅᴏċᴛ
úᴅ ʒᴜʀʙ ᴀʀ ʙ̇ʀɪʒɪᴅ ɴᴀᴏṁᴛᴀ ʙᴀ ċᴇᴀʀᴛ ᴅᴏ́ ᴀ
ʙᴜɪʀᴅᴇᴀċᴀʀ ᴀ ʙᴇɪᴛ ᴀɪʒᴇ . . . (MSF., 159). This
of course is not a case of ᴀ anticipating a "ᴛᴀ́"
clause. Here the (second) ᴀ anticipates the ʒᴜʀ
clause.

It is of course ʟᴜɪʒᴇᴀᴅ that causes the use of
the partitive ᴅᴇ. Cf. ʙᴇᴀʒᴀ́ɴ ᴀʀᴀ́ɪɴ ; but ʙᴇᴀʒᴀ́ɴ
ᴅᴇ'ɴ ᴀʀᴀ́ɴ ᴀʙ 'ᴘᴇᴀʀʀ ᴀ ʙɪ́ in Éɪʀɪɴɴ.

Notice again that in the first three instances
the direct relative is used instead of the oblique
(See p. 91).

In order to be quite familiar with these Constructions (VII, ɪɪ and ɪɪɪ) it is necessary to know the abstract nouns corresponding to all ordinary adjectives. It is worthy of note also that, where there are several abstracts corresponding to one adjective, only one of them can be used in proleptic ᴀ constructions. E.g., corresponding to ᴍᴀɪᴛ we have three nouns ᴍᴀɪᴛᴇ, ᴍᴀɪᴛᴇᴀʀ, ᴘᴇᴀʙᴀʀ. Corresponding to ꜰᴜᴀʀ we have ꜰᴜᴀċᴛ and ꜰᴜᴀɪʀᴇ. Corresponding to ᴛᴇ we have ᴛᴇᴏ and ᴛᴇᴀʀ. In proleptic-ᴀ constructions only ᴘᴇᴀʙᴀʀ, ꜰᴜᴀɪʀᴇ, ᴛᴇᴏ are to be used.

Exercise XVII.

1º. I was quite surprised that I was so near home at such an early hour.
2º. I was not as tired as I thought I should be, considering that the day was so hot.
3º. I don't think I'll go out at all to-day, it is so cold.

STUDIES IN MODERN IRISH

4°. I hardly knew him he had grown so tall.
5°. I was glad to be so far away from that man during the journey.
6°. *He was wondering*¹ all the time at the depth of the hole.
7°. His one topic was how slippery the law is.
8°. One would have thought, the entrance to the cave was so narrow, that he could never have got in or out.
9°. I thought it must be near evening the sun was so low in the sky.
10°. He told me quite calmly by how little I had missed him.

Proleptic " ᴀ " (continued).

VIII. ᴅá (translating—however, notwithstanding, for all that, in spite of, etc.).

This of course is merely an extension of proleptic á, with the preposition ᴅe, (or ᴅo) attached to it. Proleptic usages are naturally posterior, in point of time, to retrospective usages. We may therefore see the starting-point of this ᴅá idiom (if we may call it so) in such cases as—

í ꞡcᴀc ᴅá cpuime, i n-éiꞡin ᴅ'á ꞡéipe, i ppéipliꞡ ᴅá ᴅéine.

From this it is an easy stage to—

ᴅá cpuime cᴀc, ᴅá ꞡéipe éiꞡin, ᴅá ᴅéine ppéipliꞡ.

It will be noticed that proleptic " á " always causes aspiration irrespective of the gender and number of the noun to which it logically refers (For this cf. p. 217). We have seen already that it can anticipate 1st and 2nd as well as 3rd person

---

1. Use ionꞡn ᴅéᴀnᴀih ᴅe.

Examples :—

1°. Dá ṡarcaċt é tá ḋeaṙṁaḋ ḋéanta aiġe (n. 150).

2°. Dá feaḃar ṗí bíonn ḋroċ-ḋuine éiġin ar a ti (f.á.).

3°. Dá ġéire a ċaḃrṗá tuairim ré'n ġcainnt ḃeaḋ rí reaċt mile ón ḋtuairim (S).

4°. Dá feaḃar a ḃí an bia ɼ ḋá ṁéiḋ ġreann ɼ rult a ḃí or cionn an ḃiḋ ḃí an rmaoineaṁ ran irtiġ acu ġo léir (S. 225).

It will be observed that two of the three uses of proleptic a (pp. 54, 55) are still visible here; 1°, 2°, and 3° e.g., are instances of the second use; and 4° of the third. The Connaught use of a double ḋá may be due to a confusion with the conjunction ḋá in such a sentence as—ḋá feaḃar ḋá mḃei eɼ ní ċuiġrá ġo ḃrát é: "If you were ever so good you could never understand it"; or with partitive ḋe and the compound relative in—ḋá olcar cuiḋ ḋá raiḃ ann. Cf. Ní fuair hí do chogad da mét da ndernaid na diaidh (ZCP. II, 256, G.M.). Stokes inadequately translates :—" he got it not by the war which he carried on to obtain it "; rather—
" by any of the wars however great that he carried on, etc."

Exercise XVIII.

(Proleptic A : Dá . . .).

1°. I assure you there are people in the world who haven't been roused out of their slumber yet in spite of all the noise that is going on around them.

2°. I have spent only a short portion of my life, but for all that, it has been *considerably*¹ worried of late.
3°. Sharp as the two of us are we have made a mistake.
4. Notwithstanding all our haste we failed to overtake them until we reached the city.
5°. Young though he was he was persuaded that the girl wasn't very well pleased with the business.
6°. Though they knew only very little they knew enough to tell them that it was not *genuine*² Irish that was in these books.
7° Though she was very shrewd that quality could not fail to be blinded by her *self-importance*.³
8° He was listening eagerly for the sound of carriage-wheels in spite of all the fun and noise that were going on around him.
9°. No matter how carefully I guard it someone will come and sit in it.
10°. His eyes may have been very sleepy, but he observed his master's look all the same.
11°. Though he looked long and eagerly her face kept growing in brightness, and her eyes in nobility and lovableness.
12°. He twisted his mouth to laugh in spite of all his trouble and the soreness that he felt.
13°. I tell you that, small though you are, you are no child.
14°. You'll admit that though the ice looks attractive it is rather dangerous.
15°. Though it's very cold I mean to go out for a while.
16°. Though the day was broiling I couldn't refrain from going out into the air.

1. ɡo ᴍᴀɪᴛ.   2. ceaᴘᴛ.   3. móp-ċúıp.

17°. No matter how long you study Irish you'll never come to an end of its wonders.

18° Though the poor man was quite near the water he couldn't *even*[1] taste it.

19°. In spite of all your cleverness you were unable to solve my riddle.

20°. Though the day be long the night will come some time.

IX. Proleptic ᴀ (continued).
Proportion.

In early Irish proportion was expressed in various ways :—

(a) P.H. 155.—Cech méit is moo in onoir i mbi nech is i sin méit is guasacht dó ⁊ is coir dó imecla ⁊ faitchius ⁊ rá-imchomét.

(b) P.H. 156.—áithiu cech delg is ou ; i.e., ʋᴊ óıɼᴄ ʋeıʟɼ ıɼ eᴀʋ ıɼ ɼéıɲe.

(c) P.H. 155.—na slébti is ardi and, it iat sin is guasachtaigi loiscter-sum ó shaignénu.

(d) P.H. 54.—in méit ba glan a chorp ó lubra is e méit ba glana a ainmm ó peccdaib.

(e) 1ɼ dóigh léo san cach mét d'olc do gebatt isin inad sin curab móidi an anoiɼ thall é (ꞅ.m. ZCP. II, 246).

(f) An duine is mó mharbus do dhaeinib acu issé is mó anɼ́ir díb sın uile (Ibid, 254).

Modern Irish uses the much more convenient mould ʋᴀ ... ıɼ eᴀʋ ıɼ ... It is interesting to notice the stages of development :—

1°. First there is what we may call the "mathematical" stage :—

Ɗᴀ ɼᴀıʋ ᴀ ɼᴀꞅᴀm ᴀɼ ᴀꞅᴀıʋ ıɼ eᴀʋ ıɼ ꞅıoɼɼᴀ ƀeımıʋ ʋo'n ƀᴀıʟe.

---

1. oıɼeᴀʋ ᴀꞅuɼ.

Here we are measuring mathematical quantities, and the measurement is exact. ᵼᵽ еаᴆ is equivalent to ᵼᵽ ᴆе'n ᵽаıᴆ céаᴆnа ᴆíᵽеаć. Notice also that the clause "а ᵽаȝам аᵽ аȝаıᴆ" is taken absolutely (logically *accusative*, if you like) and the meaning of the whole is—"(Consider) (the distance) that we advance in all its length (ᴆа ᵽаıᴆ) [all this is a complex adverb qualifying the main statement which follows]—it is by the same length exactly we shall be nearer home."

2°. In the second stage we are still measuring mathematical quantities, but the measurement is no longer exact. Becoming accustomed to the language mould ᴆа . . . ᵼᵽ еаᴆ ᵼᵽ . . . we don't look carefully into detail, and the result is a mathematical flaw.—

ᴆа ᵽаıᴆ аn lá ᵼᵽ еаᴆ ᵼᵽ ȝıоᵽᵽа аn оıᴆće.

Taken literally this means—"Consider the day *in all its length*—then it is *by exactly the same length* the night is shortened." This is not true, unless we take ᵽаıᴆ to mean the *increase* in length (after the equinox). This of course is what we do, but we do not worry about the exactitude of the expression.

3° In this stage we simply use the mould ᴆа . ᵼᵽ еаᴆ ᵼᵽ . . . to express all observed proportions, no matter whether the measurement is mathematically accurate or not, or whether even the thing measured and the measure are of the same nature.

ᴆа ᵽаıᴆ а leоȝᵽаᵽ ın аıᵽȝe léı é ᵼᵽ еаᴆ ᵼᵽ ᴆаnа leаnᵽаıᴆ ᵽı ᴆе (S. 119).

Here we measure "increase in boldness" by hours and days and weeks. But it is accurate enough for the purpose of such comparisons.

Examples:—

1°. ᴆа péıᴆе а h-оlcаᵽ é ᵼᵽ еаᴆ ᵼᵽ ᵽеаᵽᵽ é.

2°. Ir dóċa dá méid é an mian gurab eaḋ ir mó é an gníoṁ (S. 110).

3°. Dá faid a rgaoilṫear leo ir eaḋ ir ura an láṁ-uaċtair fagáil orta ra deire.

It is clear that we have here a construction based once more on proleptic " A."

Exercise XIX.

Proportion.

1°. The more and better thou knowest the more heavy will be thy judgment, unless thy life be also more holy.
2°. The more a man is united within himself the more and higher things doth he understand.
3°. The more humble a man is in himself the more wise will he be in all things.
4°. The longer a man is negligent in resisting, the weaker he daily becomes in himself.
5°. The more thoroughly a man considers himself the more he grieves.
6°. The more a man desires to be spiritual the more this present life becomes distasteful to him.
7°. The more the flesh is brought down by affliction the more the spirit is strengthened by inward grace.
8°. The greater things a man is able to bear for God the more acceptable to Him he believes himself to be.
9°. The more thou withdrawest thyself from all comfort in created things the greater consolation will thou find in Me.
10°. The more difficult it is to me the easier it is to you.

STUDIES IN MODERN IRISH

Exercise XX.
Proportion (continued).

1°. The purer the eye of your intention with the more constancy may you pass through these divers storms.
2°. The sooner you effect this the better it will be for you.
3°. The more you withdraw yourself from all earthly comfort the nearer you draw to God.
4°. The lower you descend into yourself the higher you ascend to God.
5°. The more a man dies to himself by contempt of himself the more speedily grace comes.
6°. The less talk he is allowed to *indulge in*[1] the better.
7°. The more I think of it the more I wonder at it.
8°. The more she reflected on these two things the more utterly she failed to *reconcile*[2] them.
9°. The sooner the battle was fought the better, they believed, it would be.
10°. They said that the sooner he was ordained priest the better.

Exercise XXI.
Proportion (continued).

1°. The more important the business, the more, I suppose, there will be to pay for it.
2°. The more of them come now the less danger there is of their ever coming to you again.
3°. It seems to me he understood perfectly that the less they feared death the better they would fight.
4°. The more clearly she grasped the fact the less indi-

---

1. ᴅéanaṁ.   2. ᴛaḃairᴛ ᴅá ċéile

cation she gave that she understood it or anything of the kind.

5°. The more firmly he became persuaded of this the more energetically did he strive by every effort to consolidate his forces.

6°. Did you observe that the more it *was struck*¹ the brighter *it shone*² ?

7°. If it must be had the sooner one sets out to find it the sooner it will be got.

8° That is a very good idea of yours. The sooner it is *carried*³ out the better.

9°. I think the less we say about the matter the better.

10°. It is my firm conviction that the laugh against us will increase in proportion to the earnestness of our attempt at self-defence.

Exercise XXII.

1°. Least said is soonest mended.

2° The firmness of people's belief in this matter will be in exact proportion to the energy of your denial.

3° These girls are so good at teaching Irish that the sooner they are set to teach it the better.

4°. The place had a peculiar fascination for me ; the more I looked at it the more beautiful it appeared to me.

5°. The higher the saints are in glory the greater is their humility, and the nearer and dearer they are to God.

6°. All are agreed that the sooner he is given carte blanche the sooner will the power of the enemy be annihilated.

7°. The greater the knowledge and intelligence and mental ballast of the public the mightier and nobler is their power, and the more fully is that power exercised,

---

1. Imperfect. 2. Imperfect. 3. cuıp ı ngníoṁ.

8°. The deeper one reflects on such a matter as this the stronger hold it gets on one's heart.
9°. I think the sooner the matter is told to all whom it may concern the better it will be for all.
10°. Though he questioned them well, the matter for all that became more complicated, and it was all the harder for him to make any guess at the villain's identity.

Exercise XXIII.

1°. She had persuaded Brian that her dearest wish was that he should live long, because the longer he lived the longer Murchadh would be kept out of the High Kingship.
2°. The weaker the enemy thinks we are, the less likely it is that he will have large forces to meet us.
3° There are some people and when they see a work done, the better it is done the less they understand it.
4°. The more he charged them the more they published it and the more they wondered at it.
5°. The sooner Irishmen begin to learn their own language the better.
6°. A man will write Irish well in proportion to the accuracy of his knowledge of it.
7°. The more haste the worse speed.
8°. The more the merrier.
9°. The higher the tree the worse the fall; the greater the sanctity the worse the sin.
10°. The deeper the well the sweeter the water; the greater the humility the higher the sanctity.

Prolepsis (continued).

X. ᴅe. Proleptic ᴅe is found as early as the O. I. Glosses. It is used chiefly with comparatives, but often without them, e.g.—

1°. Mór mirᴅe ᴅeirim a ᴅéanam ᴅe
    Go nᴅéanfaidir gaeᴅil alban ᴅo ḃirgiú (n. 271).
2°. Ná ᴅein iongna ᴅe
    Go nᴅubaṫ leaṫ : ní fuláir riḃ a ḃreiṫ an ṫarna huair (C.S. 229).

With Comparatives :—

3°. Is fearrᴅe dia no ᴅeoċ é caiteam go réiᴅ.

This is the *comparative* way of expressing the proportion Dá péiᴅe (a h-iṫṫean nó) a hóltar é is eaᴅ is fearr é.

4°. Ní feaᴅar an fearrᴅe iaᴅ AR ṫugas ᴅóiḃ (S. 56).

Notice that iaᴅ is subject to the verb is ; while fearrᴅe is predicate. As ᴅe anticipates "ar ṫugar ᴅóiḃ " this also pertains to the predicate.

Sometimes " ᴅe " is not proleptic, but merely *retrospective* :—

Dá mbeaᴅ méiḃ cóm h-onóireaċ leis ᴅob' fuaraiᴅe é
Sometimes it is both. (Cf. é rin. p. 53) :—

5°. Má ḃaineann sé roinnṫ ġáiri asainn is fearrᴅe sinn é.

According as we change arainn here in number and person we shall have at the end—

Is fearrᴅe	mé	é	The final é never changes ; it is the term which the proleptic ᴅe anticipates, and like ᴅe itself it refers back to má . . . . arainn.
,,	,,	ṫu	é
,,	,,	é	é
,,	,,	í	é
,,	,,	riḃ	é
,,	,,	iaᴅ	é

PH. 112.—Ní LUGATI dognid sum forcetul in popuil IN NÍ-SIN.

KH II, 98.—ir móroe meapaim an céaopaio pin vo beit pipinneac gupab i laignib vo bí ppiom-longpopt éipeamóin.

6°. 1p ap peoil naoirdean vo biacav leip na Déipib i ionnup gupab luacaide vo páppav é (KH II, 316). NOTE.—De has become petrified in two words móroe and mipde (meapa-de). Sometimes the -de has no appreciable force, especially with móroe. With mirde we can frequently trace the proleptic nature of de. E.g., ní mipde buic bul a baile láitpeac, can be expanded into ní meapaide buic an sgéal (Real Subject) bul a baile (the " term" which De refers to). Practically however, one may neglect the prolepsis and take mirde buic as predicate, and bul a baile as SUBJECT.

Exercise XXIV.
Proleptic de.

1°. It is easy to understand that the danger is all the greater the less it is *appreciated*.[1]
2°. Don't you think a man is the more likely to have success in his worldly affairs when he does his best to fulfil his religious obligations?
3°. I desire to hear it all the more *since you tell me this*.[2]
4°. His heart is all the heavier and his grief all the greater for all the fun and pleasure that surround him.
5°. We thought the change would shorten her life.
6°. I am quite convinced that she is no better of a single hour she spends in that woman's company.

1. tuig.   2. Verbal noun.

7°. Perhaps the prayers will be offered all the more earnestly if the message is sent round from you.
8°. I shall be able to form a judgment on that point all the better if I see what you can do.
9°. Perhaps you will understand that any help I might give you would be enhanced by the fact that I have a personal grievance against your enemy.
10°. I should be all the more likely to manage this affair properly if I were free from the mental disturbance incident to public contentions.
11°. He told them he had acted in this manner in order that their mutual loyalty might be all the greater, because, *they were all involved in the same secret.*[1]
12°. He deprived them of all the horses in order that the men's courage might be all the greater because, in the peril that faced them, they were all on the same level.
13°. Sometimes it improves us if other people see our bad qualities and find fault with them.

Exercise XXV.

ᴅe non-proleptic.

1°. This point is appreciated : that if something could be done to delay the enemy there would be all the greater likelihood of our being thoroughly ready for them.
2°. If we execute heavy slaughter on them now they will be all the less anxious to come again.
3°. Yours is the true version as far as my side of the wrong is concerned ; I think it all the more likely, therefore

---

1. Use ᴀṗ ᴀ ċéıle to bring out the idea.

that you have the true version as regards the other side also.
4°. They didn't use much expiratory force in producing the sound in order that their voice might last all the longer.
5°. It appeared to him that, if matters went no further with them, it would be all the easier.
6°. I accept these words with pleasure from your lips, in order that I may obtain a firmer grasp of them in my heart.

Exercise XXVI.

(ᴅe Retrospective and Proleptic).

1° Had you been as straight in your lifetime as you are in death your life would have been all the longer.
2°. She acted in this manner lest she should be anticipated, and receive thereby a smaller offering.
3°. If a man reveal his secret to his wife his life is thereby shortened.
4°. Other days he is so frightful that anyone looking at him would be none the better of it.
5°. Many a man is in a hurry to secure a comfortable berth near royalty,—but his life is none the longer for it, when he obtains his wish.

Prolepsis (continued).

XI. ᴀcᴀ.
1°. Ciᴀ 'Cᴀ ir ꝼeᴀꝶꝶ leᴀᴄ ꝶᴀeᴅilꝶ nó ḃéᴀꝶlᴀ?
Note that the subject of 'ir' (understood) here is— (ᴀn ceᴀnn) ir ꝼeᴀꝶꝶ leᴀᴄ; and the predicate ciᴀ' cᴀ;

but as aca stands proleptically for "ᵹaeḃilᵹ nó béaṗla" these words also are part of the predicate. The 'iṗ which appears is of course not the principal verb.

2°. Ciá'ca
    tátaṗ ṗocaiṗ aiṗ nó ná ṗuilteaṗ.

In alternatives of this kind introduced by verbs it is worthy of note that the affirmative verb is used in the direct form, while the negative is always in the dependent form.

3°. Cia 'cu
    an ċaṫaoiṗ nó an ṁin nó an t-uḃall ba ḋeaṗ? (S., p. 6).

Subject = (an ṗuḋ) ba ḋeaṗ. Predicate cia 'cu (an ċaṫaoiṗ, etc.). Notice that the nominative form of the noun is used (just as with proleptic a the nom. form (not gen.) is used).

When the English "whether" introduces a *substantival* clause it is to be translated by cia 'cu (when there is an alternative; when there is no alternative offered "whether" is simply the interrogative " an "), when "whether" introduces an *adverbial* clause it is to be translated by pé 'cu.

I don't know whether he will come or not = { ní ṗeaḋaṗ cia 'cu tiocṗaiḋ ṗé nó ná tiocṗaiḋ.

So { iṗ cuma liom cia 'cu tiocṗaiḋ ṗé nó ná tiocṗaiḋ.

I wonder whether he has done it yet = ní ṗeaḋaṗ aṗ ḋein ṗé ṗóṗ é.

Whether he comes or not I will stay = pé 'cu tiocṗaiḋ ṗé nó ná tiocṗaiḋ ṗanṗaḋ-ṗa.

Exercise XXVII.

Proleptic ᴀcᴀ.

1°. Whether he used these words or not I shall act in the matter as I please.
2°. As a matter of fact I don't remember at all whether he used them or not.
3°. People like that don't care whether their action is justifiable[1] or not.
4°. Whether she had any hold upon him *by promise*[2] or not up to the present, she can no longer pretend that she has now, or that she ever had.
5°. Whoever is condemned on *a capital charge*,[3] whether it be from his own confession, or from *evidence produced against him*,[4] must, according to the customs of our ancestors, be put to death.
6°. Consider whether it is *my honour*[5] or *your own interests*[6] you want most.
7°. I don't care whether the enemy succeed in beating us or not.
8°. Whether they do or not we shall be in a sorry plight.
9°. He was asked whether he would prefer to be put to death by hanging or crucifixion.
10°. It matters little to a man whether he dies this way or that, as long as he dies.

Prolepsis (continued).

XII Other prepositional pronouns: ᴀιρ, Leιρ, uιme, etc.
    1°. Ďíoρ ᴀϛ bρᴀċ ᴀ1R

                         ϛo mbeιċeᴀ-ρᴀ ᴀnnρo ρómᴀm.

1. Use cúιρ.   2. Genitive.   3. Coιρ ɓáιρ.   4. ḃ ḟᴀϛáιl ᴀmᴀċ ᴀιρ.   5. Onóιρ ⱴóṁ-ρᴀ.   6. Cᴀιρɓe úιτ ρéιn.

2°. Ní ṗaiḃ aon ċoinne aġam leis, 7 a ḟeaḃar a ṫuiġ
ré an oḃair,
ġo ḋteipṗeaḋ air mar ḋo ṫeip.

3° Is uime ċeana ṗuġ Dia an ḋaor-ḃreaṫ ṡo ar
na ḋaoiniḃ,
ṫré ċaill a ċána ḋo'n ċéaḋ aṫair ó'r ḟáraḋar
(KTB.).

4°. Is uime ḋo ṫánaġ isteaċ ran uair reo,
ċun t'onóra-ṡa (Im. 157).

This use of uime in the last two sentences and of
amlaiḋ (p. 79) is further proof that our theory of type II
Identification, and of the verb 'is' in general, is the
only tenable one—(see p. 36).

Exercise XXVIII.

1°. I was expecting to see him here to-morrow.
2°. I never *thought*[1] that he would treat me as badly as he did.
3°. *This is the reason*[2] he acted in that way,—he wanted to impress you with his importance.
4°. *Can it be that*[3] you were expecting me to come so soon?
5°. I was unable to *make any guess as to*[4] who the villain was.
6°. My *purpose*[5] in coming was to set you free.
7°. If it was to anger me you did it, you have laboured in vain.
8°. I have made up my mind to go home at once.
9°. My object in learning Irish was to acquit myself as befits an Irishman.
10°. The reason why one talks Irish is to show the world that one *is* Irish.

1. Use coinne.   2. Use uime.   3. An amlaiḋ . . . ?
4. Aon tuairim a ṫaḃairt ḋó.   5. Cuiġe.

STUDIES IN MODERN IRISH

XIII. Amlaiḋ.

1°. ɪſ Amlaiḋ a ḃí náiɼe aiɼ ɼómam-ɼa.

Observe that the subject of the verb 'ɪſ' is here understood. The full expression would be (and it is sometimes used)— ɪſ Amlaiḋ maɼ a ḃí an ſséal aɪse ḃí náɪſe aɪſ ɼómam-ɼa.

Like many other proleptic words amlaiḋ is sometimes used in a purely retrospective way :—

Ouḃaſc leiɼ é ḋéanam 5o meaɼ, ⁊ ɪſ Amlaiḋ ḋo ḃein.

As the proleptic uses are very important, and reflect various meanings in English, we think it useful to append here those different meanings :—

1°. On the contrary; whereas. (Removal of wrong impression).
2°. The result was (is, will be, would be, etc.) Perhaps. In that case. Surely. (The unexpected, or the undesired).
3°. He found, etc. (Descriptive).
4°. The fact is; if the truth be told; to tell the truth; as a matter of fact; in such a plight; of course (Descriptive, with suggested explanation).
5°. Can it be? Is it possible? You don't mean to tell me? Then? (reasoning).
6°. (With negative). Not that . . . but. (Apologetic or satirical).
7°. Really (in reference to a *doubt*).
8°. (With negative). Surely not; I don't suppose it possible; not exactly. (Negative form of the interrogative 5°—Surprise, indignation, hurt feelings, satire, rejection of possible explanation, suggested only to be rejected).

80 STUDIES IN MODERN IRISH

9°. Rather; instead of that. (Removal of wrong impression; but not as strong as 1°).
10°. The *reason* was (is, etc.). Slightly different from 4° and 2°.
11°. Actually (the unexpected). Different from 7° and 2°.
12°. As a result. (But different from 2°, because here the result is given in the other clause, the ᴀṁlᴀɪᴅ clause giving really the *cause*).

Examples :—

1°. Nuaiṗ a tuiɼeaḋ . . . in-ionaᴅ aon laɼaċaṗ ṗláinte beiṫ aṗ Ċaṫal ɼuṗḃ aṁlaiḋ a ḃí neaṗṫ céaᴅ ṗeaṗ ann ṫoṗnuiɼeaᴅaṗ aṗ eaɼla ɼlaċaḋ ṗoimiṗ (C.ᴅ. 11).
After ᴀṁlᴀɪᴅ the direct relative is used superfluously. (See p. 91).

2°. Nuaiṗ a ċuaiḋ na h-uḃla ⁊ na h-eiṫne iṗṫeaċ inɼoile Ċaṫail. iṗ aṁlaiḋ a ḃein ṗiaṗṫaí ḋioḃ iṗṫiɼ na ċoṗṗ (C.ᴅ. 5). *The result was* . . . ni ṗeaᴅaṗ caᴅ na ṫaoḃ ɼuṗ ṫuɼaḋ " Áṗᴅ ṗáoṗaiɼ " uiṗċi muṗaḃ ᴀṁlᴀɪᴅ a ṁeaṗ ᴅuine . . . (ᴍsṗ. 20). *" Perhaps."*

3°. iṗ aṁlaiḋ ḃí an méiᴅ éaᴅaiɼ leaṗṫan a ḃí uiṗċi ṗilṫe ɼo ċṗuaiḋ in aon ċeiṗṫlin aṁáin aṗ láṗ na leaṗṫan (C.ᴅ. 19). He found . . .

4°. Ċeaṗ ṗé, niḋ náṗḃ ionɼna, ɼuṗḃ aṁlaiḋ a ḃí an mac léiɼinn ċun na ṗeola ṫaḃaiṗṫ le n-iṫe ᴅó ó láiṁ (C.ᴅ. 76). As a matter of fact.

5°. An aṁlaiḋ naċ eol ᴅuiṫ an ṫ-olċ uaṫḃáṗaċ ṗo aṫá aṗ an ṗi ? (C.ᴅ. 57). Can it be that . . . ?

6°. Ni haṁlaiḋ a ḃí aon ṫṗúil aċu ɼo leiɼiṗṗi Ċaṫal (C.ᴅ. 51). Not that . . . No, but . .

7°. Ni áiṫeoċaḋ an ṗaoɼal aiṗ ɼuṗḃ aṁlaiḋ a ċeiṫ Aṁlaoiḃ (N. 70). Nothing would convince him that A. had REALLY fled.

8°. Aṗ nóin°ni haṁlaiḋ a ċaḃaṗṗá ḃí ṗéin an ṗuᴅ n-a ṗaiḋ

rí ag faine ort ran a dtabarrá do Brian é (ll. 195).
Surely not.

9º. In' inead ran ir amlaid d'fill Sadb 7 artac na láim (S. 77). Instead.

10º. Ir dóca gurb amlaid a bí féaróg rgáinte uirti (S. 45). The reason was.

11º. Ceapamair go léir gurb amlaid a cuit caor ar do tig 7 go rabair loirgite id' beataid (S. 30). Actually. Notice go rabair (*not* do bir), because this is connected immediately with ceapamair, not with amlaid.

12º. Ir amlaid a táinig a leitéid rin d'uraim acu do'n clearaibe . . gurb ar éigin féadaidír a ruile tógaint in aon cor de. The amlaid clause gives the *result* of what preceded, and the *cause* of what follows.

Exercise XXIX.

Proleptic Amlaid.

1º. He knew not that it was true that an angel was doing it. On the contrary he thought he saw a vision.

2º. If he and his Ultonians are *foolish enough*[1] to come from the North, the result will be—they will come, but they will not return.

3º. Instead of his appetite growing less, they perceived that he was on the contrary becoming *more greedy and voracious*[2] every day.

4º. He found all his clothes rolled up in a hard ball in the middle of the floor.

1. Má tá sé de míc-céille ar . . .   2. Breir airc 7 ampla

5°. We offered him food, but he would not accept it. He actually reviled and insulted us.
6°. When I was at home I used to eat at a single meal, if the truth be told, as much food as would do me nine days and nights.
7°. Can it be that you'd like *to be hanged*[1] to-night?
8°. Is it possible he hasn't come yet?
9°. Not that there is any great love for the truth over there in matters relating to Ireland,—but they have great respect for the cleverness that makes the false *seem true*.[2]
10°. They had no *objection*[3] to it; on the contrary they were very glad to have over them a man who would be able, in case of necessity, to keep them in subjection.

Exercise XXX.

ⱭṁLⱭIⱵ (continued).

1°. He would give no indication that he was in any way jealous. If he did, the result would be that people would laugh at him.
2°. They said that he had, of course, acted on his own initiative, as his friend also, to their thinking, had done before him.
3°. Catiline's frenzy *however*[4] was not lessened. On the contrary he exercised himself all the more vigorously.

---

1. Ⲧu ċⲣoċⲁⲩ.   2. Use ⲓ ⲙoċⲧ nⲁ ꝼíⲣⲓnne.   3. Cuⲣ nⲁ ċoⲓṁniⲃ.
4. Ⱅṁċⲁċ. The student need not fear to use this word. In the form ⱥṁ it occurs at least as early as ⲁn Leⲁⲃⲁⲣ ⲃⲣeⲁc. In S.T. 19 " Ní dia imgabail *ám* tiagmai " " however " suits the context better than " truly."

STUDIES IN MODERN IRISH 83

4°. Is it possible they will be allowed to go and *swell*,¹ the *ranks*² of the enemy?

5° *Surely it is not to be supposed that*³ you would like to be set to swim in the open sea on such a day as this.

6°. The result was that His Majesty and the entire company were *on the point of fainting*⁴ with mirth and laughter.

7°. What is it you purpose in bringing this person to us? Can you possibly wish him to kill us all?

8°. He didn't,— but made the " ᵹꞅuᴀb " ill-use him instead.

9°. Surely you do not possibly mean to say it was I who did it!

10°. Surely he cannot have involved himself in any bond or promise, and that now they should be trying to extort money.

Exercise XXXI.

ᴀṁLᴀıó (continued).

1°. You don't mean to tell me she's not at home?

2°. Instead of that, there is, on the contrary, some misfortune driving us forward and urging us on, *in spite of all our opposition*.⁵

3°. I thought the reason was that he was unwilling to leave her a widow after him when the thirteen years should be up.

4°. Can it be that you don't remember the settlement *made by*⁶ the Saints of Ireland between us, the Kings of Ireland, and you, the poets of Ireland?

5°. If they turned to any other of the kings or nobles of Ireland the result would be, they felt, that they would

---

1. Cuɲ ı méɪᴅ.   2. Sluᴀɡ̇.   3. Ṅí ᴅóċᴀ ɡuɲb ᴀṁLᴀıó.   4. 1 ɲıoċᴛ ᴅul ı Lᴀıɡe.   5. Use ᴀıṁḃeoın intensified.   6. Use active voice.

be putting themselves in the difficulty in which they *had*[1] *been*, when they came to the Leinster King's palace at first.

6°. This hunger of yours is act**u**ally *increased by*[2] food, and this thirst of yours is actually *aggravated by*[2] drink.

7°. When I asked him for the thirteenth apple the result was that it wasn't one, but all the apples, he threw away.

8°. One would have thought that this actually caused him to stay.

9°. Can it be that you don't remember I said I would go away?

10°. Is it possible that the music has put it out of your head?

Exercise XXXII.

Aṁlaiḋ (continued).

1° As soon as *this expression*[3] was heard everyone present was, as a matter of fact, falling on his feet with merriment, laughing at Seán.

2°. Some of them said, if they paid any heed to the basket *or*[4] the two old hags the result would be that the whole district would be laughing at them.

3°. It is not that you have performed a feat; rather you have tricked the whole of us.

4°. Can you possibly mean to say that there is any man here who couldn't do what you have done?

5°. Instead of crushing in some were moving out.

1. Past tense.   2. Use active voice.
3. An focal ꞅan (Irish often uses ꞅin, ꞅan, where English prefers *this*).   4. ná (the clause is virtually negative).

STUDIES IN MODERN IRISH

6°. Some of them were saying that this was not so, but that he had of course taught the animals to perform these remarkable feats.

7°. Finally they were seen coming out, and truth to tell, the man and the woman were wrestling with each other, and the boy behind them *splitting his sides*[1] laughing.

8°. There stood the boy with his face actually *turned behind him*,[2] and the back of his head *in front*.[3]

9°. What would cause another woman fear and trembling has quite a contrary effect on her,—that of hardening her and increasing her energy.

10°. People say that as a matter of fact *he considered it mean*[4] to be in subjection to a woman.

Exercise XXXIII.

Aṁlaiḋ (continued).

1°. I think she actually *considers it a duty*[5] to visit the hosts before she allows her horses *to be unyoked*.[6]

2°. It appears to me the reason was that they thought to earn our gratitude better than the others would have done.

3°. Can you possibly be thinking of *prolonging the interview till*[7] *your*[8] gums freeze with the cold?

4°. It appears to me the reason is that the poor young fellow got ashamed of you.

5°. Instead of that we are in quite the opposite plight.

---

1. Aṅ cup an anma amaċ.   2. 1 leiṫ a ḃroma.   3. 1 leiṫ a ocṫa.
4. ba laṅ leiṗ.
5. Use ní ḟuláiṗ le.   6. Do ṅṅuṗ.   7. Ḃeiṫ aṅ cainnṫ ṅo oṫí ṅo . . .   8. Do not use possessive—(see p. 209).

In a short time it will probably be impossible to find a single man to fight a duel with Cúchulainn.
6°. I venture to say she is in such a state these times that she *hasn't the ghost of an idea what to do with herself*.[1]
7°. On the contrary I was afraid that you might be *gossiping*[2] with someone on the subject.
8°. I was in such a state that I became terrified and imagined I saw the Evil One before me.
9°. Can it be that you think to escape what no mortal ever could avoid?
10°. Think you *that I shall be like*[3] one who promises and never performs?

Exercise XXXIV.

Aṁlaiḋ (continued).

1°. To tell you the truth if I had looked him in the eyes a second time I should have fallen.
2°. Think of this, and instead of being *embittered*,[4] you will on the contrary be rejoiced exceedingly, and consoled with the comfort of patience.
3°. We think sometimes to please others by being with them, whereas we rather disgust them by the evil behaviour which they discover in us.
4°. I have long been in such a state that I would give all I have, or ever had, or ever will have, to have it in my power to marry her.
5° He didn't call her a bold hussy; rather he was sorry that he didn't.
6° Rather each one of the three gave another of them a

---

1. Ná feadair cor léi cad a ḋéanfaiḋ láṁ léi.   2. Caidiṗáil.
3. Suṗ cuma mé nó . . .   4. Use feiṗḃéean.

sword-blow so that the three fell at the door, and the three horses sped off *over*[1] the plain.

7°. He seized the book and when he put it *up to*[1] his eyes to read it he had it, as a matter of fact, upside down.

8°. I suppose your condition is that when you have the book you haven't the power to read it.

9°. What! Could you not watch one hour with me?

10°. We have no more than five loaves and two fishes, unless perhaps we should go and buy food for all this multitude.

11°. *I don't know for the life of me*[2] why he did it unless perhaps he was thinking of something else while he was writing the letter.

We have seen that after ᴀṁʟᴀɪᴅ a direct relative particle is frequently used, where it is logically superfluous. When however the clause following ᴀṁʟᴀɪᴅ is negative, the dependent form of the negative is used :—

Ⱥn ᴀṁʟᴀɪᴅ nᴀċ ᴅʟeᴀġᴛᴀċ ᴅom ᴀn nɪᴅ ɪꝛ ᴛoɪʟ ʟɪom ᴀ ᴅéᴀnᴀṁ ? (Ċ.S. 56).

An early example of the proleptic use of ᴀṁʟᴀɪᴅ is found (Ⱥ.ⱮᴄⱵ. 3) :—

"Amlaid boi in laech sin ; co ngéri chon, co longad chapaill."

"Thus was this warrior—with the edge of a hound ; he ate like a horse."

The direct relative particle which we find used pleonastically with ᴀṁʟᴀɪᴅ is probably due to the direct relative used (for the modal oblique—see p. 90) after *retrospective* ᴀṁʟᴀɪᴅ Thus, because we say—

ᴅeɪꝛɪm ʟeɪꝛ ɡᴀċ nɪᴅ ᴀ ᴅéᴀnᴀṁ ᴀR ᴀ ᴅíċeᴀʟʟ, ⁊ ɪꝛ ᴀṁ-ʟᴀɪᴅ ᴀ ᴅeɪneᴀnn we come to say also with *proleptic* ᴀṁʟᴀɪᴅ—

Iꝛ ᴀṁʟᴀɪᴅ ᴀ ᴅeɪneᴀnn ꝛé ɡᴀċ nɪᴅ ᴀꝛ ᴀ ᴅíċeᴀʟʟ.

1. ꝛé. 2. ní ꝼeᴀᴅᴀꝛ 'on ᴛꝛᴀoġᴀʟ.

CHAPTER III.

Relative Particles.

Section I.

There are many words which serve as relative particles in modern Irish, and the whole matter is somewhat complicated. We shall first enumerate the particles and then consider their uses.

Direct Relative.
- 1°. The particle ᴀ (causing aspiration). This is used normally only for nom. and accusative (Exc., pp. 89-92). It does NOT combine with ꞃo- in the past tense.
- 2°. ᴅo (aspirates). Normally only for nom. and accus. (Exceptions pp. 89-92).
- 3°. ᴀ ᴅ' (before verbs beginning with a vowel, or ꞙ (which is aspirated). Only nom. and accusative (outside cases to be hereafter mentioned—pp. 89-92).
- 4°. ? That is, the relative particle is understood. (Only nom. and accusative. But see pp. 94-95).

Oblique Relative.
- 5°. ᴀ (causing eclipsis). Only oblique (i.e., to express Gen., Dat., Abl. or Instrumental relations; gen. or dat. in Irish). It combines with ꞃo in the past tense, giving ᴀꞃ (aspirates).
- 6°. ɢo (causing eclipsis). Only oblique. Combines with ꞃo- giving ɢuꞃ (aspirates).
- 7°. n-ᴀ (causing eclipsis). Only oblique. Combines with ꞃo- giving n-ᴀꞃ (aspirates).
- 8°. Negative Relative (direct and oblique):—nᴀ́, nᴀċ, nᴀꞃ.

STUDIES IN MODERN IRISH

9°. Compound Rel. ᴀⁿ, ᴀṙ' (direct and oblique).
Examples :—1°. The particle ᴀ'.
(a) Ruᴅ iṛ eᴀᴅ é ᴀ ċuiṛeᴀnn ionġnᴀ mo ċṛoiᴅe oṛm.
(b) ᴀn ḃeᴀn ċoṛ-noċtᴀiċe iṛ í ᴀ ḃí ᴀnn (S. 91).
See also Exx. 2, 4, 5, 6 (p. 22).

This particle did not exist separately in Old Irish, but there are indications of such a particle, either infixed or affixed, in the earliest stages of the language. E.g., 1ᵘ the aspiration in- intí adchí = ᴀn té ᴀ ċíonn. 2° The relative forms of certain prepositions—ara, imme, imma. 3° The suffixed relative in the 1st and 3rd pers. plur. pres. and fut. active of simple verbs,—berme, berte. The development in modern Irish was helped by confusion with the prepositional ᴀ- in ᴀtá, ᴀᴅeiṛ, ᴀᴅuḃᴀiṛt. (Cf. development of ᴅo- from ᴅo ċuᴀiᴅ, etc.). This particle ᴀ' (as also ᴅo and ᴀ ᴅ') is used irregularly for the oblique relative in the following cases :

A.—In temporal clauses :—
1ᵘ. Ḃí ᴀinm Ċᴀiᴅġ in-áiṛᴅe le méiᴅ ᴀ niṛt ón lá úᴅ
ᴀ ġᴀiḃ Sé ᴀṛ ᴀn móiṛḟeiṛeᴀṛ ᴀ leᴀn ó Spáiᴅ ᴀn
Ṁuilinn é (S. 38).
With negatives, however, ná, naċ, náṛ are used. In Middle Irish ná, nach were used when the nuᴀiṛ (uᴀiṛ) clause came first. Otherwise ní was used.
Contrast—*Uair na dernais-siu* sin rega fén for neph- ní.
And—Log doibseo in ní dosgniat *uair nis fetutar* cu mad olc.
2°. ṁá'ṛ eᴀᴅ cá ṛᴀiḃ ᴀn t-ᴀiṛġeᴀᴅ ᴀn ḟᴀiᴅ ᴀ ḃíos
ᴀġ cuᴀṛᴅᴀċ ? (S. 40).
On the other hand we frequently find the oblique forms ; but *not directly* with nuᴀiṛ :—
(S. 62) Ḃí ṛé ᴀġ ᴅéᴀnᴀṁ ᴀmᴀċ ᴀṛ eᴀᴅᴀṛṫṛᴀ um ᴀn
ᴅtᴀċᴀ ġo ṛᴀiḃ ᴀ ṁᴀċtnᴀṁ cṛíoċnuiġte.

(11. 24) Bí ré ar riúbal i ganfior do'n craogal le linn na haimsire n-a raib an beirt buacailli úd ag déanam a bfogluma.

Sometimes both direct and oblique are found in the same sentence :—

(11. 24) Nuair a táinig an t-am n-ar micid do Cadg ua Cealla cuaird a tabairt ó tuaid . . . ní fárócad aon fud é gan Amlaoib do bul ó tuaid in-aonfeact leir.

(eir. 88) Ón lá a tánag annro agur gur taraigead ar an teitin mé.

In double relative clauses, of which the first is ir dóig le . . . and the second a temporal clause, the oblique relative is usual, BUT inversion is the usual practice, the oblique relative going with the "ir dóig" clause (illogically) and the direct with the temporal clause. E.g. (11. 210) . . . ag breitniú na haimrire n-AR dóig leo a bead an t-aro-Ri ag teact a baile. (The two clauses logically implied are—

1°. Na haimrire ba dóic leo (which they thought likely).

2°. Na haimrire n-a mbead an t-aro-Ri . . . . .) (See p. 130).

B.—In modal clauses :—

1°. **Mar a bí** ar dtúir, **mar atá** anoir, ┐ **mar a beid** go brát (Doxology).

Notice the difference in meaning between mar atá (AS there is) ; mar tá (BECAUSE there is) and mar a bfuil (WHERE there is).

2°. Imteocaid do clú ┐ do cáil direac MAR A D'IMTIGEANN uirge an locáin famraid nuair a rataltar air. (5. 18). (a *need not* aspirate the autonomous form).

3°. Do h-innreað cionus ab éiṡin niam do tógaint ar an obair rin (n. 245).

Iñ "How" questions in Connaught the oblique relative is common :—Cia 'caoi (a) bruil tú? In Munster with conur the *direct* is usual, but with cað é an cuma . ? the *oblique* is the normal usage.

C.—A special case of this exception (B) after proleptic a. (classes 2, 3), including dá.

1°. (S. 183) bí iongna a ṡcroiðe orta a feabar DO deineaðar an snó.

See also Exx. 2, (p. 51), 2, (p. 58), 1, 2, 3 (p. 61), 3, 4 (p. 64) 1, (p. 66).

D.—Also after proleptic De (and other prepositional pronouns).

n. 225—b'féiðir ṡur déine-de a déanfar an suiðe an teactaireact do cur timceall uait-re. (a déanfar is really = an cuma n-a ndéanfar).

E.—After proleptic amlaið the direct relative is used where it is logically *superfluous*. See Exx. 1, 2, 3, 4. 6, 7, 8, 10, 11, 12 (pp. 80-81).

F.—With rul, ran (before) the oblique relative is usual in Munster. The direct relative occurs sometimes in Connaught Irish. Keating uses the direct (sometimes understood).

rul do dibreað le Cormac iað (K.H. II, 4865).
rul ruair ré bár (K.H. II, 5041).
rul táinig paðraig (K.H. II, 5372).

G.—In emphatic elliptical sentences :—

1°. ní de a déanfí ri-ollam ać de duine éigin eile.
2°. ní duit-re is cóir é carað liom (Rel. particle understood).
3°. ir liom-ra a baineann an cainnt rin. (Here it

is obvious that *logically* the ᴀ is not direct, being neither nom. nor accus.).

4°. Óip ip dóic leo ꞅup ap méid a ꞅcainnte dóh-eiꞅtpaꞃ leo (Ċ.S. 14).

H.—With the relative clause following comparative or superlative clauses, *when the comparative or superlative clause is not itself relative* :—

1°. Iꞅ ꝼeaꞃꞃ iꞅ eol dóṁ-ꞃa é ná maꞃ iꞅ eol duiꞇ-ꞃe é. Here the meaning of the 1st clause iꞅ eol . . is of course modal, just as the 2nd is.

When the comparative or superlative clause is itself relative then the oblique relative is used in the next clause where the sense allows it :—

2°. Nil éinne iꞅ ꝼeaꞃꞃ ꞅuꞃd eol dó é ná maꞃ iꞅ eol dóṁ-ꞃa é.

3°. n. 180.—Díod an ꝼoꞃmad ann, leiꞅ, ꝼeacainꞇ cia aiꞅꞅe dob' ꝼeaꞃꞃ n-a ṁdead an ꞇ-ollṁúcán déanꞇa.

4°. n. 110.—ní ꞃaid aon nid dáꞃ ꞇuꞅ ꞅé leiꞅ ba ṁó ꞅuꞃ deinead ionꞅna de ná éide aiꞃꞃinn a bí déanꞇa d'éadac ꞃnáꞇóiꞃ.

5°. Im. 85.—Cá in eaꞃnaṁ ꞅóꞃ aiꞃ an nid iꞅ mó n-a bꝼuil ꞅád aiꞅꞅe leiꞅ.

The sense does not allow the oblique relative when the dative relation has already been expressed BEFORE the comparative or superlative clause (outside cia and cad questions : cf. Ex. 3° above with—iꞅ aiꞅꞅe dob' ꝼeaꞃꞃ a bí an ꞇulṁacán déanꞇa). Iꞅ dóṁ-sa iꞅ ꝼeaꞃꞃ iꞅ eol cá luiꞅꞅeann an bꞃóꞅ oꞃm.

I.—In a somewhat rare construction :—

Cad é an ꞃud a bí dꞃuadaꞃ aꞃ aiꞅne a déanaṁ? Cf. also—Sin maꞃ a leanꝼaimid ꞅan conꞇabaiꞃꞇ an bóꞇaꞃ aꞇá ꞇoꞃnuiꞅꞇe aꞅainn aꞃ ꞅabáil.

2°. ᴅo'.
1°. An té ᴅo cuaiᴅ ann.
2°. Ʒuocar ᴅoḃ' ḟeaʀʀ ná é.
3°. Tá ḟior aʒ luċt na h-ionnarḃa caᴅ ᴅ'oiʀeann ᴅóiḃ (TBC. 247).
4°. Taitnḟiᴅ ré leir an uile ᴅuine ᴅo cloisḟiᴅ é.
5°. Ⅎiℓ aʒam aċ an ʒnó ᴅéanaṁ cóṁ h-aiciℓuʒe ┐ ᴅ'ḟeaᴅḟaᴅ é (Ⅎ. 113). Modal dat.—Direct instead of oblique. (Exception B., p. 90).
6°. An cé a ᴅ' iteann mo cuiᴅ ḟeoℓa-ra ┐ ᴅ'óℓann mo cuiᴅ ḟoℓa cóṁnuiʒeann ré ionnam-ra ┐ cóṁnuiʒim re ann.
7°. Suḃáilce ᴅo ḃealuiʒeas ár ʒcroiᴅe ó neitiḃ talṁuiᴅe (Don. 156).
8°. An tan ᴅo naoṁ-coisʀeaʒas ré an t-arán (Don. 222).
9°. An tan ᴅo cuiʀeas neaċ a ᴅóiʒ ... ann a ċumur ḟéin (Don. 314).
10°. Ir ṁire tuʒann ʒráᴅ ᴅo'n croiᴅe ʒℓan ┐ ᴅo ḃronnann ʒaċ naoṁtaċt (Im. 272).
11°. Ir mé ᴅo loiʀʒeann an croiᴅe ʒℓan ┐ ir ann atá áit mo cóṁnuiᴅte.

The above examples afford ample proof of the existence of this ᴅo as a relative particle. It has been developed—(a) from confusion with the prepositional ᴅo of verbs like ᴅo cuaiᴅ, ᴅo ʒeiḃim. These, in absolute construction, are used frequently without the ᴅo, and in relative construction ᴅo tacitly took over the functions of the relative. Furthermore even when ᴅo- is used in absolute construction it causes aspiration in Mod. Irish. The aspiration in O.I. denoted relative use. When this relative force of the aspiration was no longer felt, ᴅo took over the function. This probably conduced to the absolute use of such verbs WITHOUT the preposition. Cf. the influence of ᴀ- in ᴀᴄá, ᴀᴅeıp, etc., on the development of relative ᴀ'.

(b) By confusion, *in the past tense*, with the ᴅo which took the place of the earlier ꝛo-.

(c) Possibly from sentences like 3° above where phonetically the ᴅ- of cᴀᴅ might have been carried on to oıꝛeᴀnn. At any rate, whatever the genesis may have been, the fact is clear. We have undoubtedly in modern Irish the particle ᴅo fulfilling the functions of a relative.

3ᶜ. ᴀ ᴅ'.

This is merely a combination of ᴀ and ᴅo ; or we may look upon the ᴅ' as merely phonetic padding.

1°. Ní puınn pógᴀnᴛᴀcᴛᴀ ᴀ ᴅ'ꝼéᴀᴅꝼᴀᴅ sé ᴀ ᴛᴀᴅᴀıꝛᴄ ó ᴀon ᴛᴀoᴅ ᴀcu (n. 301) (Accus).

2°. ᴀon ꝛuᴅ ın-ᴀon coꝛ ᴀ ᴅ'ıᴀRRꝼᴀᴅ ꝛé (s꞉. 103) (Accus.).

3° Iꝛ mó ᴌeᴀᴛ-ꝛ꞉éᴀᴌ ᴀ ᴅ'ꝼéᴀᴅꝼᴀᴅ sé ᴀ ᴛᴀᴅᴀıꝛᴛ uᴀıᴅ (Accus.).

4° ᴀn ᴛé ᴀ ᴅ'éıRı꞉eᴀnn ꝫo moc bıonn ᴀn ꝛoᴛ ᴀıꝛ (Nom.).

5ᶜ. nuᴀıꝛ ᴀ ᴅ'éıRı꞉ lóꝛeꝛ ᴀꝛ ᴀ cooʟᴀ ᴅo ᴅeın ꝛé mᴀꝛ ᴀ ᴅ'óꝛouı꞉ ᴀın꞉eᴀʟ ᴀn ᴛı꞉eᴀꝛnᴀ ᴅó (Ċ.S. 3).

Cf. the duplication of the preposition ᴅo (ᴀ) before vb. nouns :—ꝛ꞉éᴀʟ ᴀ ᴅ'ınnꝛınᴄ, etc.

4ᵘ. ? (The relative particle is understood. Initial of verb is aspirated).

1ᵘ. Cᴀᴅ é ᴀn ᴛᴀıꝛbe ꝼéᴀᴅꝼᴀᴅ ꝛé ᴀ ᴅéᴀnᴀm ? (Accus.).

2ᵘ Sın é mıʟʟ mé (Nom.).

Like ᴀ, ᴅo, and ᴀ ᴅ' we find the direct relative

understood, instead of the oblique in temporal and modal and the other clauses mentioned on pp. 89-92. Cf. Ex. 2⁰, p. 91.

Exercise XXXV.

(Direct Relatives.)

Irregular use of Direct for Oblique :—

Temporal.—

1° You impressed the fact upon me the last day we were talking about it.

2° You have lost all the time during which the money was out of your possession.

3°. If you arrive at an entire contempt of yourself know that then you will enjoy true peace.

Modal.—

4° Your name and fame shall fade away just as the water of the summer pool disappears when it is trampled upon.

5° We are told clearly how it was she had to be removed from this work.

After proleptic ɑ.—

6°. It is very extraordinary with what difficulty we believe what doesn't please us.

7°. I am much surprised at his exactitude in writing Irish.

8° I will tell them what a heap of money you have gathered together of late.

9° I don't care how soon you give up talking English.

10°. It surprises me that you are staying away from us so long.

With ᴅᴀ ...   11°. Though my eyes are so sleepy I cannot fail to observe what you are at.

12°. Though the food is excellent and fun and merriment abound over it, I cannot keep the thought of that queer marriage out of my head.

13°. The more clearly the truth is unfolded the more boldly it is denied.

14°. The more gently he is taken the more mischief of every kind he makes.

With proleptic ᴅe.—15°. He will do the work all the better if you are looking on.

16°. The troubles that come upon one's friends ought to make one all the more loyal to them.

17°. You will be all the shorter time finishing it if you hurry up now.

18°. You will learn Irish all the more exactly for *confining your*[1] reading to a correct and precise author.

19°. You *will begin to esteem Irish more*[2] *when you have got a deeper*[3] *insight* into its beauties.

20°. You will acquire this insight all the sooner by commencing the serious study of it at once.

---

1. Má ḃeineann tú ɼan aċ ...   2. Iɼ móiᴅe a ċiocɼaiṫ meaɼ aɼat aɼ ...   3. Nuaiɼ a ḃeiṫ eolaɼ níoɼa ḋoiṁne aɼat aɼ ...

Exercise XXXVI.

(Superfluous use of direct relative with ᴀṁʟᴀɪᴅ.)

1°. When my enemies understood that, instead of growing weaker, I had on the contrary the strength of 100 men, they began to get afraid of me.
2°. As a matter of fact he used to come to talk to me every day whenever he got the opportunity.
3°. I came away,—not that I was a bit afraid of him, but, to tell the truth, his boastfulness and self-importance used to get on my nerves.
4°. Is it possible that you can think to impress me with the truth of such a statement?
5°. You may doubt it if you like, but he really did do his best to bring about some settlement of that affair.
6°. He found two-thirds of the people who were there in a state of semi-madness or semi-intoxication.
7°. If I treated you in this way, the reason was that you had just maddened me with your foolish chatter.
8°. When he rushed in thus without invitation or permission the result was that everyone got angry.
9°. I think he was actually afraid that his father might find out what he had done.
10°. Many, seeking to fly temptations, fall on the contrary more grievously into them.

Exercise XXXVII.

(The special meanings of ᴀṁʟᴀɪᴅ are implied, not expressed.)

1°. By doing this a good work is not *lost*,[1] but is changed into a better.

---

1. Cuıp ᴀp neᴀṁ-nıᴅ.

2°. If the day of our death be deferred, let us *believe*¹ *that*² God is merciful to us, because we are not yet well prepared.

3°. Woe be to us if we *are for*³ sitting down and resting ourselves *as if*⁴ we had already met with peace and security.

4°. If you carry your cross unwillingly you will simply be increasing your burden and aggravating your troubles.

5°. Oftentimes when you imagine that you have lost almost everything you have *practically*⁵ won a great deal of merit.

6°. Thou hast not lightened thy burden, but art now bound with a stricter bond *of*⁶ discipline, and art obliged to greater perfection of sanctity.

7°. You would not in that case covet the pleasant things of this life, but would rather be glad to suffer tribulations for God's sake.

8°. Surely you don't mean that you are going to turn the tables on me in that fashion.

9°. It is not that I don't want to go, but to tell the truth I'm afraid I might meet a certain very objectionable person there.

10°. Don't imagine for a moment that I shall ever give up Irish. I wouldn't do such a thing, however generously you might pay me for it.

Section II.

The Oblique Relatives.

5° ᴀⁿ ; ᴀɲ' (with past tense). Examples :—

Genitive — 1°. Sıo é ᴀn ꝼeᴀɲ **ᴀɲ ċoᴅᴀıl mé n-ᴀ ċıȝ ᴀɲéıɲ.**

2°. Sıo í ᴀn ḃeᴀn **ᴀ ḃꝼuᴀıɲ ᴀ ꝼeᴀɲ ḃáɲ ınᴅé.**

1. cuıȝ ın . . ᴀıȝne.   2. Ȝuɲb ᴀıṁlᴀıṫ ᴀcá.   3. Use meᴀɲᴀım.
4. Cóṁ mᴀıċ ᴀȝuɲ ᴅá . . .   5. Ȝeᴀll le.   6. Ċum.

Dative.— 3°. Innpeoċa mé cuiv ve na ȝábanna ır mó a nveaċa mé ṫpíotu (11. nȝ. 3)
4°. Stócaċ acu a vtuȝaimír Seán móp aıp (Ibid,4)
5°. Cé 'p víob mé, nó ce 'mb' ar mé? (Ibid, 6). The a in each case is elided.
6°. Cé 'n ċaoı a bfáȝfainn an aıll ? (Ibid, 8).
7°. Ċuaıṫ mé aȝ an bfeap aR ċeannuıȝ mé na h-uaın uaıv (Ibid, 13).
8° Rinne mé botán beaȝ víobta aR ċuıp mé an plúp ırteaċ ann (Ibid, 16).
9°. An cupaċ a ċup a baıle aȝ an bfeap a mbu leır í (Ibid, 21).
10°. Ċeannuıȝ mé bav bfeaȝ a vtuȝ mé vá ċéav púnt uıptı (Ibid, 38).
In Munster Irish this particle is chiefly used with rul, rap, or when preceded by a preposition (or map = where) :—
11°. Sul a Raıb uaın aȝ an mapcaċ é ċabaıpt ré nveapa vo ȝluaıreavap tpıúp mapcaċ eıle ṫaıpır amaċ (S. 31).
12°. Ir maıpȝ vo'n fear ran TRé a nvéanfap mac an vuıne vo víol (C.S. 75).
13°. Cav é an cómapta a taırbeánann tu vúınn fá a nvemeann tu na neıṫe réo ? (C.S. 228).
14° fan maR a bfuıl aȝat.
Sometimes, as in Exx. 5°, 9° above, a does *not* combine with ro in past tense.
Note.—a, and n-a (oblique relatives) cause eclipsis (when not combined with ro). The following sentences from Canon O Leary's Aıṫpır ar Ċríort and mo Sȝéal féın have an r after the oblique relative. This of course is a printer's error. *In each case the r should be unaspirated :—*
1°. (Im. 48) Cav é an rȝannra ó n-a faorraıp tu féın.

2°. (Im. 120) Pé cuma na focpócad féin an ṡgéal.
3°. (Im. 121) Pé cuma na focapócad mé féin.
4°. (MSf. 135) Pé ball 'n-a polácpócad é.

Exercise XXXVIII.

(Relative aⁿ and aṙ.)

1°. I saw there one of the farmers, whom we used to call Tadhg na n-Ubh.
2°. Why, think you, is the one man called by two different names?
3°. He never told me who he was or whence he came.
4°. I was in a difficulty then to find out a means of leaving the cave.
5°. I went to the woman from whom I had bought the eggs, and asked her to take them back at half-price.
6°. I determined forthwith to send the cows back to the man from whom I had bought them at the fair.
7°. Of these he made a large box into which he put all the money he had.
8°. At the fair of Ballinasloe I bought of him a horse for which I paid £100.
9°. He was awake for some little time before he thought of all that had happened the previous night.
10°. There he was, standing between the two door-posts precisely as he had been the day before.

Exercise XXXIX.

(The Same.)

1°. He must have had a bad attack of fever, for he was three weeks in bed before he was convalescent.

2°. I'm sorry I made those people's acquaintance at all. I had an easy mind before I came across them.
3°. She'd have liked to add something more, but he was gone before she could say another word.
4°. I had to close my eyes lest I should be constrained to watch those eyes moving.
5° When I place before you my reason for having made this request of you I don't think any of you will deny that I had sufficient cause.
6°. Did you notice how he stopped playing just before the cock crew.
7°. It is a good rule not to speak till[1] you are spoken to.
8°. There were, no doubt, some strange customs in this country before the advent[2] of St. Patrick.
9°. You must have the work completed, and render an account of it to me before my father returns.
10°. Think before you speak, and look before you leap.

(Oblique Relatives (continued).

6° ꞅo, ꞅuR.
Dative.— 1°. Ceapaiṁ ꞅup 'mó ouine ꞅo mbíonn an cpeoio úo aiꞅe, ⁊ ꞅo noeineann pi maolú ap buaipc oó (S. 109).
2°. Di pluaip eile ap aꞅaió na pluaipe pin anonn ꞅuRb ainm oí leaba ꞅpáinne (S. 247-8).
3°. O'éipiꞅ liuꞅ piaió ón áic coip cuaió ꞅo paió na capaill aꞅ oéanaṁ aip (S. 33).
Genitive.— 4° Ní oóiꞅ liom ꞅo mbeió an pear eile pin le paꞅáil ip mó ꞅo mbeió a beall 'na cabaip

1. pul.   2, Translate by a *verb*.

7 'na congnaṁ aige ná mar a beiḋ rí agatra nuair a beiḋ Saḋb pórta agat (S. 219).

5° Déarfaḋ ré go raib duine i n-éaġmuir ġormflaiċ ġurb féidir a diabal coiṁdeaċta a ḋ' feircint uaireanta (ll. 265).

Sometimes an apparently irregular use of go, or gur is met with:—

6° Na h-oibreaca ġUR tug m'ataiṙ dom IAḊ le DÉANAṀ tugaid riaḋ riaḋnuire am taob gurb é an t-ataiṙ a ċuir uaiḋ mé (C.S. 237).

7°. Nac é reo an té ġO bfuilid riaḋ aḋ' iarraiḋ é CUR CUN BÁIS (C.S. 245)?

8°. Ir niḋ é ġUR fiú dúinn é TABAIRT FÉ NDEARA 7 é BREITNIÚ ġO MAIT (Sg. 66).

9° Níl a tuille n-a ndiaiḋ ra baile ġUR fiú IAḊ D'ÁIREAṀ (ll. 320).

10°. Dronnaim ruar ort gac rmaoineaṁ róġanta ġO bféadfaḋ aigne crāibteac maċtnaṁ aiṙ, nó é MOTÚ.

The irregularity is only apparent, as the phrases in capitals are merely varieties of expression for phrases with the gen. A. Thus in 6° we might substitute a ndéanaṁ; in 7° a ċur ċun báiṙ; in 8° a tabairt fé ndeara 7 a breitniú go mait; in 9° a n-áireaṁ; in 10° a ṁotú. (In this last instance "go" has already occurred in a dative sense, but is understood after NÓ in a (virtually) gen. sense). We conclude therefore that gur and go in the above examples are VIRTUALLY GENITIVE.

Exercise XL.

(Relatives ġo and ġur.)

Dative.— 1°. This is how he shows the extent of his affection for the person with whom he is in love.

STUDIES IN MODERN IRISH 103

2°. You said, I fancy, that you'd take the man on whom the lot should fall.
3°. These were the horses that were to be given back to those from whom they had been bought, and for which false coin had been given in the king's name.
4°. It isn't *my* death that you need show you are not afraid of, but your own.
5°. If this is the bargain that I was made swear to, I don't think much of it.
6°. His left hand never left the side of his vest inside which the purse rested.
7°. There was one man there whom the priest refused point-blank.
8°. And this is the man, who, people say, has neither faith nor piety.
9°. He that CAN¹ take let him take it.
10°. I have gone through many hard trials of late.
11°. Woe to that man by whom scandal cometh
12°. Anyone who wishes to know Irish thoroughly must be satisfied to study it seriously.

Exercise XLI.

(Relatives ɼo and ɼuṗ.)

Genitive.— 1°. He said there was someone else besides her whose father might be seen in a state of intoxication sometimes.
2°. That is a question the settlement of which is very simple.

1. Cıɼ le.

3°. There are many people who *think*[1] much less of their reputation than their riches.

4°. It's a pity of the man whose relatives live far away and whose neighbours are a hard-hearted lot.

5°. The man whose wealth exceeds his wisdom is generally unwilling to pay for the latter.

6° I'm inclined to think that if he had got a glimpse of the person whose hand was in it *things*[2] would not have gone as smoothly with him as they did.

7°. It is *too much of a good thing altogether*[3] for you to *imagine*[4] that I could fight a duel, for the men of Ireland, with the man whose bones are more to me than all who are alive, I will not say among this great host, but in the whole Gaelic world.

8° What sort of a girl is this with the praise of whose beauty people have us bothered?

9°. When I see the woman whose son fell in battle beside me I will certainly tell her how bravely he fought.

10°. People whose means are better than their manners generally think less of form than fortune.

NOTE 1.—ɼo and ɼuɼ in the two following examples are most easily explained as VIRTUALLY GENITIVE relatives, owing to the ellipsis of n-ᴀ ᴛᴀoɓ :—

1°. ꜰeᴀɼ ʒUR ṁeᴀɼ ᴀn uıʟᴄ ᴅuıne ᴅe ꜰnᴀ

1. Use beᴀnn. 2. ᴀn ɼʒéᴀʟ. 3. 1ɼ obᴀıɼ ɴó-ṁí-ċuıɓɼᴀċ ᴅuıᴛɼe. 4. ᴄeᴀp ıᴛ'ᴀıʒne.

fíníníb (Supply n-a taob) nár maip an peap
ran puam a bí niba ḋilṗe ná é (mS.p 117).
2⁰. Íora éiṡin a puaip bár ┐ ṡo paib pól ṡa
páḋ (supply n-a taob) ṡo bpuil ṗé beo.

NOTE 2.—There has always been a certain clumsiness about
the expression of the genitive relative in Irish. As there was
no inflected relative particle this was inevitable. In early
Irish it was left very much to the reader to infer the sense.
E.g., Intí as énirt iress = He whose faith is weak. Réte ni
réid a mbrith = things whose reference is not easy. A uli
doine is a sailechtu fil is-in coimdid (PH. 222) = All ye men
whose hope is in the Lord. From these Exx. it would appear
that sometimes the relative was expressed, and the genitive
meaning left to inference, while at other times the genitive
of the *personal* pronoun was expressed, the relative nature of
the clause being taken for granted. The modern Irish usage
is at once clear and simple. An oblique relative is used before
the verb, and the *genitive* of the *personal* pronoun is placed
before the word which suits the sense.

Oblique Relatives (continued.)

7°. n-a, n-ar.—
  1°. 'Sé ouḃaipt ṡaċ plait **n-ap maiṫ leip tpiall**.—
    Ṡluaipiḋ ṡo meap, tá an cat ḋá puap,
    Aṡuṗ téiṡmíp ná cómaip (Cat Ċéim in pianḃ).
  2°. An bean n-a bpuil an t-éaḋaċ copcpa uipti (n. 295).

There is an apparently irregular use of these particles (as in
the case of ṡo, ṡup) sometimes, but the same explanation holds
here as in the case of ṡo, ṡup (p. 102).
  3°. An t-aimlear n-a mbeaḋ ḋuine lán-ċeapaiċe ar é
    ḋéanaṁ beaḋ ré cupta ḋe aici pap a mbeaḋ pιor
    aiṡe ṡo paib pí ṡá cup ḋe inaon ċop (n. 95).

4°. Iſ coſmail é le ɼpáinne muſtáiſo n-ɑR ꝺein ꝺuine é tóɼaint ⁊ é cuR na ɼáiſꝺín, ⁊ ꝺ'ꝼáſ ſé 'ɼuſ ꝺein cſann móſ ꝺe (C.S. 185).

Here in 3° for the phrase in capitals we might substitute ɑſ ɑ ꝺéanaṁ, and in 4° ɑ tóɼaint ⁊ ɑ cuſ, so that we may look upon n-ɑ and n-ɑſ as VIRTUALLY genitive.

Exercise XLII.

(Relatives n-ɑ. n-ɑſ.)

(DATIVE.)

1°. The people to whom the questions were put had either to answer them or suffer accordingly.
2°. This is the Holy Spirit of whom Christ promised that the Father would send him to the Apostles.
3°. I pity the enemy on whom she turns at such a time.
4°. The priest's house is naturally the first one that the Bishop turns to on his arrival in a parish.
5°. People say that it was those for whom he used to play his exquisite music that were hardest on him in his poverty.
6°. There was a certain amount of rivalry also, to see which had made the preparations best.
7°. The 1,000 men clad in coats of mail were shown to them, and they were told these were the most formidable foes they had to meet.
8°. The little man called Diarmuid was living in a little hut not far from the house in which his father and mother had died.
9°. John Bull has a great respect for the man he's afraid of.
10°. He asked me what district I was from.

Exercise XLIII.

(Relatives ⁊-ᴀ, ⁊-ᴀʀ.)

(Genitive.)

1°. Isn't it a wonderful thought that you are one of those for whose sake Christ died?
2°. Assuredly these are the men whose names will be on people's lips throughout the country as long as God is in heaven and man on earth.
3°. The Saviour who had been promised from the beginning, and for whose coming the human race had been waiting, came at the appointed time and did His appointed work.
4°. I wonder who is the man in whose house I slept last night.
5°. The man whose wife is always quarrelling with him is sure to envy the celibate.
6°. A people whose language, for melodiousness and precision, is superior to most others, should surely have never given it up.
7° People who live in glass houses shouldn't throw stones (Emphasis on *glass*).
8° It is only fitting that a man whose father was a very lowly person should himself be always humble.
9° No one can have any respect for people whose God is their belly.
10°. If it is a thing which ought to be talked about, why don't you give us your opinion about it at once?

REMARK 1.—Sometimes n-ᴀ and ɡo occur in the same sentence :—

Ùpoptú ċun na h-áice il-á mbeið ᴀoiḃneᴀp píopuiðe ᴀɡᴀinn, ⁊ ɡo ḃpᴀnpᴀið pé ᴀɡᴀinn (Im. 2).

REMARK 2.—The second ɡo in the following sentence is probably influenced by the first :—Ip ᴀoiḃinn ðo'n cé ɡo ðcᴀḃᴀppᴀip-pe ceᴀɡᴀpɡ ðó, ⁊ ɡo múinpip ᴀp ðo ḃliɡe é.

Unless we take it as the conjunction ɡo with ellipsis of " ᴀ ṁáð " after ᴀɡup. Such use of the particle ɡo to denote (in conjunction with an accusative pronoun) the accusative relative is allowed, when it is necessary to avoid ambiguity.

REMARK 3.—Note the construction of the following :—

Sið é ᴀn cé ɡuR Leis é.

Cé'Rð ᴀs tú ? Sin é ᴀn áic ᴀRð ᴀs é.

Cé 'R ðíoḃ tu ?

Cᴀð é ᴀn ceᴀnntᴀp n-ᴀRð ᴀs é (Acts xxiii. 34).

In these sentences observe that the preposition cannot be put *before* the relative. Why ? Because the preposition is required, in the prepositional-pronoun form, to act as the predicate (in conjunction with the relative particle) to the verb ip. Another proof that *the subject* can never appear immediately after the copula—(see p. 36).

Development of ɡo, ɡup.

Several influences have been at work in the development of " ɡo " as a relative particle. Cf. the *relative* " that " in English in reference to the *demonstrative* " that " and the Latin conjunctions *quod* and *quia* (a neuter plural) in reference to the relative QUI.

1° It has developed from ᴀɡ ᴀ (preposition + oblique relative ᴀ).

In Middle Irish oc a frequently became ca ; so ᴀɡ ᴀ

became go through the stage ga (being unstressed).
(a) Bíd follus anossa in fírinde oc in tií ca mbia (P.H. 92).
(b) An ní ó bfuil gaedeal gtar.
    Is teare ga bfuil a feancar (K.H. II, 18).
(c) An ceirt-breiteam ag a raibe an lod Morainn aige¹ (B.K. 18).
Observe the double ag. When the prepositional pronoun occurred at the end the attention was diverted from the preposition before the relative, and this of course facilitated the passage from ag a to ga, go.
(d) Uactarán ag a mbíod an crioc uile fá n-a rmact (BK. 51).
Here we have a dative relative followed at the end by a genitive personal pronoun. The latter helps to convert the dat. relative ag a into the gen. relative ga, go.
(e) Rí ag a Raibe mórán d'uairlib Éireann ag cor n-a agaid (BK. 86).
See previous remark, and note that the long stressed vowel in rí facilitates the transit from ag a to ga.
(f) Gac mnaoi díob ag ar maip a fear ag teact in Éirinn dóib (K.H. II, 94).
Notice that in the modern language there is a difference in meaning between ag ar maip a fear (= with whom her husband lived) and gur maip a fear (= whose husband lived). The passage quoted from Keating has the meaning of the modern gur.
(g) . . . do mnáib na dtaoireac ag ar marbad a bfir (K.H. II, 114) = whose husbands were slain. See

---

1. That this double use of the preposition came in early is seen from such passages as PH 148—duine, FOR-a ta omun báis FAIR.

preceding remark, and note (p. 105) on the difficulty of expressing the genitive relative.

(*h*) Aon mac ouine uaṗail aʒa ṗaiḃe oiʒṗeact móṗ n-a cómaiṗ.

Here the meanings of the preposition and of the genitive were at first felt distinctly (T.B. 11).

2°. The conjunction "ʒo" has had some influence also. The conjunctional meaning passes very easily into the relative, so much so that it is difficult sometimes to determine which was in the writer's mind.

The following Exx. will be found instructive :—

(*a*) Ḃí ṗé na ṗuiḃe aṗ catoiṗ móṗ áṗo ʒUR ḋóic leac ʒo ṗaiḃ an uile ḃLúiṗe ḃí ḃéanca ḃ'óṗ caṗca (S. 97).

(*b*) Caḃ é maṗ ḃuine é ṗeo ʒO ṗmaccuiʒeann ṗé ʒact ⁊ ṗaiṗṗʒe ⁊ ʒO noeinio ṗiaḃ ṗuḃ aiṗ (Luke viii. 25). The first "ʒo" is clearly conjunctional; the second very easily passes over to the relative sense.

(*c*) Cá ḃṗuil an ṗeompa ḃíḃ ʒO n-iceaḃ an Cáiṗʒ i ḃṗocaiṗ mo ḃeiṗʒiobul? (Luke xxii. 11).

Here, if we add **ann,** the transition to the relative sense is easy.

(*d*) ṗéacainc an ḃṗaʒaḃ ṗé aon ṗuḃ ʒo ḃṗéaḃṗaḃ ṗé ʒṗeim a ḃṗeic aiṗ (eiṗ. 40).

Here there is practically no difference in meaning whether we take "ʒo" conjunctionally or relatively :—

"that he might take hold of it" (conj.).
"that he might take hold of" (rel.).

The two senses meet in the following Exx. from Connaught Irish :—

11. nʒ. 8.--Ní ṗaiḃ an t-eiḃean ṗéin aʒ ṗáṗ ann le ʒo ḃṗéaḃṗaḃ ṗuḃ aṗ ḃic ḃeo imceact aṗ ac an t-éan.

Ibid, 40.—ní ṗaiḃ ḋionnóiḋ ġaoiṫe ann le ġo ḃfeaḋfaḋ ṡinn imṫeaċṫ.

3°. The natural contrast between ná and go as *conjunctions* facilitates the use of go as an affirmative *relative* corresponding to the negative RELATIVE ná. This we may express by the proportion—
As Conj. ná : conj. go : : Rel. ná :——Rel. go.

Examples :—

11. 168.—Ḃí a lán neiṫe ḃeaga ag ṫeaċṫ ċun cuiṁne ṫairṁg,—neiṫe ḃeaga naR cuir sé ḃlúiṗe ṗuime ionnṫa nuair a ċonnaic ṡé ar ḋṫúir iaḋ, aċ gur cuir sé móṗán ṗuime anoir ionnṫa.

sg. 88.—An arm ná fuil eoluṗ aige air agur go ḃfuil eoluṗ ag an naṁaiḋ air.

Cf. also—Iṡ mairg an ṫé ná fuil airgeaḋ aige (7 a ḃaḋ)
go gcóṁnuigeann a ġaolṫa a ḃfaḋ uaiḋ 7
gur ḋream ḋúṗ-ċṗoiḋeaċ a ċóṁaṗṗain.

Development of n-a, n-aṗ.

1° From the combination of certain prepositions with the oblique relative a we get the form n-a. Thus—i n-a, ó n-a, go n-a (with), ṫṗé n-a le n-a, and (earlier) ṗia n-a (before).

2° Possibly from accidental occurrences like—
an ḃean n-a ḃfuil an ṫ-éaḋaċ coṗcṗa uiṗṫi,
where the final n of ḃean might have attached itself to a, or been reduplicated.

3°. Possibly also from the Middle Irish reduplicated form of the compound relative a^n (in an-, an a n-). Mine dena-su in a n-apraim-si (D. I. 228).

Examples:—
(a) Ӡać τρεαbċαρ ὸαοιne **le n-αρ** mian (for earlier **léρ'**) ιαὸ ϝéιn α beιτ oρ cιοnn na n-αιnṁιὸτε ειLε ní ϝυLáιρ ὸóιb ὸíċεαLL α ὸéαnaṁ αρ ӡan α ρаοӡαL ὸο ċαιτεαṁ ι n'ὸíτ úρLαbρа (Cατ. I).

(b) Ọí ρé ρа ὸριιć n-α ὸρεαcа ρé αρ ὸτúιρ é (S. 20).

(c) San áιτ 'n-αρ bαιn an óρὸóӡ Lειρ (αn ὸταLαṁ) (S. 23).

(d) Iρ ρεαρρ ειρӡε αρ maρ οὸαιρ 7 ρаοċαρ éιӡιn ειLε ὸéαnaṁ n-α mbειὸ τаιρbε αnn 7 n-α mbειὸ ροċαρ ann.

When **ann** followed, the prepositional force of the n- before α was no longer felt, and n-α became merely an oblique relative.

(e) Ọυbαιρτ ρé Le ӡаć heαn ὸíοb ρεαρаṁ αmυιċ αρ αӡαιὸ na ϝυιnneοιӡε n-α ραιb α ϝεαρ ϝéιn **LαιSτιӡ ὸε.**

Further Remarks:—

I.—In addition to the particles enumerated so far, relativity was expressed in other ways in Middle Irish:—

10°. The old indefinite pronoun nech (later noċ) was sometimes employed. The relative meaning was unconsciously attached to it.

Uan Dé nech tocbus pectha = Uan Dé a τóӡann ρεαċτа.

11°. An infixed pronoun was sometimes used:—

in tu ro-t-bris na dee? = Αn τυ ὸο bριρ na ὸéιτε?

P.H. 130 is é in fegad-sin ro-t-cuir Petar dochum aithrigi díchra.

The following peculiar usages will be of interest:—

P.H. 129. "Nach do muintir in fhir Galilee ATATHAR DO CROCHAD duit si?"

With this cf. the Ulster Irish—

Ӡοιὸé τά cυ α ὸεαnаὸ?

STUDIES IN MODERN IRISH 113

Munster Irish prefers to turn thus—
Cao cá agac á (= o'á) véanam?
P.H. 128.—Cia fors-a taid d' iarraid? Whom are ye seeking?
P.H. 120.—Is e so in t-Ísu oc a ra-ba Hiruath d'iarraid.
P.H. 127.—A ní dia tanacais do dénum.

II.   **The Relative in Scotch Gaelic.**

There is a close resemblance to the modern Irish forms
1°. a' (or understood) :—
   PB. 7.—'n uair THig Samhuinn.
   PB. 10.—'S droch-dhìol air a' ghunna
       'BHEIR builli 'n ad thaobh.
   DS. 14.—Nuair cHunnaic e slatag òir agus slatag
       airgid a' cur nan car diubh air an réidhlean.
   DS. 14.—Nuair A cHunnaic e coileach òir agus cearc
       airgid a' ruith roimhe air a' bhlàr.
2°. Oblique :—AM before labials ; otherwise AN.
   AM :—C. na nG.—1.   tríd am bheil = cré n-a bruil.
   DS.—9. àireach ghabhar d'am b'ainm Gorla-nan treud.
   With g' = Irish o'á :—
   DS. 13. agus a dh'aon ni g'am faic thu na toir
       sùil air = agur aon nío oá breiceann tú ná
       cabair rúil air.
   AN.—C. na nG.—2.—air an d'éirich Grian = ar ar éiris.
   DS. 10.—nach dean mi fois no tàmh a latha no dh'oidhche
       GUS AN lorgaich mi mach i (conjunctional use with gu).

114   STUDIES IN MODERN IRISH

DS. 9.—Ag an robh triùir mhac agus aon nighean.
DS. 14.—ràinig e 'n t-àite 's an robh na tri mairt mhaola.
DS. 19.—gun ghluasad as an àite 's an d'rinn e 'm fàgail.
DS. 21.—Anns an cuirte seachad i = 'na ₅cuıʀcí ċaʀc í.
DS. 22.—ge b'e àit 'an tèid thu
DS. 22.—tar an d'iarr e air dà thrian d'a sgìos.
= maʀ aʀ ıaʀʀ ʀé aıʀ . . .
With g' = Irish d'á :—
DS. 13.—a dh'aon ni g'an cluinn thu, na toir sùil air.
3°. Neg.-nać. DS. 20.—fonn theud air nach robh e eòlach.
DS. 22.—air nach laigheadh an codal, agus air nach éireadh a' ghrian.
4°. Compound Relative na (Mid. I. ina, ana, inna).
DS. 22.—ghabh thu gu cridheil sùnndach na thairg mi.
DS. 22.—gus am biodh aige na dh' fhòghnadh dha féin agus dha-san a thigeadh 's a dh' fhalbhadh.
DS. 23.—thoir leat na dh' fhòghnas air do thurus.

Section III.

Double Relative Construction.

The double relative construction is a very remarkable phenomenon of Modern Irish, but as far as I know, no one has yet called attention to it. If we compare the sentence—ıʀ ᴅóıġ lıom ġuʀ ʀġʀíoḃ ʀé leıcıʀ ınᴅé,
with—   Cıa ıʀ ᴅóıġ leac ᴅo ʀġʀíoḃ an leıcıʀ ?
we are at once struck by the peculiarity. In the first sentence

the clause— ꞅuꞃ . . . ꞅnꞈé is subject to the verb ıꞃ. In the second one the ꞅuꞃ clause disappears, and instead we have two relative sentences combined in one :—

Cıa (ṁé an ċé) ıꞃ ꞈóıṡ leaċ? and
Cıa (,,   ,,   ,,) ꞈo ꞃṡꞃíoḃ an leıċıꞃ?

But observe that the meaning of the second question is influenced by the meaning of the first. There is *dependence in thought*, although that dependence is not clearly expressed. Similarly compare—

(a) meaꞃann ꞃé ṡo ḃꝬuıl a lán aıꞃṡıꞈ aıṡe.

Here meaꞃann ꞃé is *not* relative, and is followed by the usual ṡo- clause. But observe the change when meaꞃann ꞃé becomes relative :—

(b) Cóṡꞃaꞃ uaıꞈ ṡaċ a **meaꞃann ꞃé** a ċá aıṡe

The ṡo clause disappears and we have a double-relative construction again. There is even a further change introduced, because the two relative sentences taken separately would be :—

1° Cóṡꞃaꞃ uaıꞈ ṡaċ a meaꞃann ꞃé, and
2°.   ,,   ,,   ,,   ,, ḃꝬuıl aıṡe.

But as ṡaċ a has already taken effect on meaꞃann ꞃé, we have the simple relative form aċá, when the two parts are combined in one.

Again we should say—

(a) ꞈo ṁeaꞅaꞃ ṡo nꞈéanꝬı an ꞃṡıaċ níoꞃ Ꝭeaꞃꞃ ṡo móꞃ ná maꞃ ꞈo ꞈeıneaꞈ.

But when ꞈo ṁeaꞅaꞃ becomes relative—

(b) Cá an ꞃṡıaċ ꞈín a ḃéanaṁ ṡo maıċ ; níoꞃ Ꝭeaꞃꞃ ṡo móꞃ ná maꞃ a ṁeaꞅaꞃ a ꞈéanꝬı é (TBC. 245).

Here we have the two relative clauses combined :—

1° ná maꞃ a ṁeaꞅaꞃ
2°. ná maꞃ a ꞈéanꝬı é.

with of course the usual dependence in thought.

Once more—

(*a*) Déarfainn go bfuil faid cúig flat ionnta.

But when déarfainn becomes relative the go clause becomes relative also :—

(*b*) Ní cuimin liom anois cad é an faid a déarfainn atá ionnta (msf. 123).

Here again we have TWO relative clauses joined in one, with, however, dependence in thought :—

    1°. Cad é an faid a déarfainn

    2°. ,, ,, ,, ,, a tá ionnta.

Again—

(*a*) Is dóic liob gur mé an Slánuigteoir.

But when is dóic liob becomes relative the gur disappears :—

(*b*) Ní mise an té is dóic liob is mé (Acts xiii. 25).

This is a good example of the dependence in thought involved in the double sentence, as distinct from the separate relative clauses. In this case one of the relative clauses is patently false :—

    1°. Ní mise an té is dóic liob

    2°. Ní mise an té is mé (contradictory).

The falsity and self-contradictoriness of the second element is taken away by the dependence in thought upon the first. In the following exercises in order to bring home the phenomenon clearly to the student, two sentences are given opposite each number, the second one only involving a double relative.

Exercise XLIV.

(Double Relative.)

1. *a.* Don't you think that something should be done?
   b. What do you think should be done?

2. a. Do you think I could give you any assistance?
   b. What assistance do you think I would be able to give you?
3. a. People say that this man is stronger even than Murchadh.
   b. This is the man who, people say, is[1] stronger even than Murchadh.
4. a. She thought the subscription would be greater than it was.
   b. I suppose it was greater than she thought it would be.
5. a. I thought the fever would get a greater hold upon me than it did.
   b. I think it got a greater hold upon me than I thought it would.
6. a. She said she met some bad companion.
   b. Who is the bad companion that she said she met?
7. a. She thought the amount she gave him would be good for him.
   b. She would give him only the amount she thought would be good for him.
8. a. I never thought I should see such a thing in my life.
   b. I observed there one thing that I never thought I should see in my life.
9. a. Would you like people to do to you as you would do to them?
   b. Do unto others as you would like others should do unto you.
10. a. I should like the child to be called by an Irish name.
    b. What name would you like the child to be called?

1. Aoeipteap atá . . .

Exercise XLV.
(The Same.)

1. *a.* You see that I have flesh and bones,—which a spirit has not.
    b. A spirit has not flesh and bones as you see that I have.
2. *a.* You say your son was born blind.
    b. Is this your son, who, you say, was born blind?
3. *a.* You thought it was promised to you more fully than you can get it now.
    b. You can get it now more fully than you thought it was promised to you.
4. *a.* I didn't think that such a thing would be done to us so soon.
    b. That is a thing which I never thought would be done to us so soon.
5. *a.* I should think that Brian was a better man than Murchadh.
    b. He asked me which I thought was the better man, B. or M.
6. *a.* Anyone ought to know that he might expect some such trickery from you.
    b. All this trickery was only what anyone ought to know he might expect from you.
7. *a.* We thought that the man towards whom Brian turned was their leader.
    b. Brian turned towards the man we thought was their leader.
8. *a.* I thought it would be done much better than it was.
    b. It was done much worse than I thought it would be.
9. *a.* I felt that the work ought to be undertaken after this fashion.
    b. This is how I felt the work ought to be undertaken.

10. *a.* He thought the business wanted of me here was the one he mentioned in the letter.
   b. I suppose he mentioned in the letter what business he thought was wanted of me here.

Exercise XLVI.

(The Same.)

1. *a.* It was thought that he would have made greater haste than he was able to.
   b. He was unable to make as much haste as it was thought he would.
2. *a.* She would have liked people to go to her own country house.
   b. She told me it was to her own country house she'd have liked people to go.
3. *a.* I thought that the night which had arrived was suitable enough.
   b. There came a night which I thought was suitable enough.
4. *a.* I thought I should reach Belfast sooner than I did.
   b. I didn't reach it as soon as I thought I should.
5. *a.* I thought by the time I had arrived in the centre of the city that the sun would have been much farther west than it was.
   b. By the time I reached the centre of the city the sun was not at all as far west as I thought it would be.
6. *a.* I know you would wish me to do at once the business which brought me here.
   b. It occurs to me that the business which brought me

here, and the one which you would wish me to do, are identical.

7. *c.* They thought you were going to ask them to do something that they would have done quite willingly.
   b. They were very glad to have it to say that they would do quite willingly the thing they thought you were about to ask them to do.
8. *a.* I don't think a person who speaks Irish would need to spend any great length of time learning to read and write it.
   b. How long do you think a person who speaks Irish would need to spend learning to read and write it ?
9. *a.* You'd imagine that, when a thing was cast aside once and for all, it would not come back again with redoubled force.
   b. It is just when you'd imagine a thing had been cast aside once and for all that it would come back with redoubled force.
10. *a.* I don't consider there's much difference between denying one's Faith and siding with the enemies of the Faith.
    b. What difference do you think there is between denying one's Faith and siding with the enemies of the Faith ?

Exercise XLVII.

(The Same.)

1. *a.* If a person is fully determined to deny me all rights I don't think he has any claim to receive any right from me.
   b. If a person . . rights, what claim do you think he has to receive any right from me ?

2. *a.* They thought they had a right to be treated as well as the King of Leinster had treated them.
   b. They were in the habit of satirizing any king who didn't treat them as well as they thought they had a right to be treated.
3. *a.* He thought there was I don't know what there.
   b. I don't know what he saw or what he thought was there.
4. *a.* The nurse thought she was needed longer than she really was.
   b. She remained longer than she thought she was needed.
5. *a.* Her mind was so much unhinged with love of you that I never thought she could do such a thing, whatever happened her.
   b. Her mind . . . of you, that she did a thing I never thought she could have done whatever happened her.
6. *a.* He thought it would be useful for him to send the messages round like this.
   b. He sent the messengers round like this just as he thought would be useful for him.
7. *a.* Saevius' letter, which the Senator in question read before the Senate after a few days, had come to him, he said, from Faesulae.
   b. After a few days he read before the Senate Saevius' letter which, he said, had come to him from Faesulae.
8. *a.* He considered that every one of those, either on account of his evil deeds, or of the loss of his property, was a fit subject for the revolution.
   b. At the same time Lentulus was in Rome, and in accordance with orders received from Catiline, was engaged, either personally, or through his emissaries, in coaxing into the conspiracy everyone whom he

considered, either on account of his evil deeds, or the loss of his property a fit subject for the revolution.
9. *a.* You think I am one that I am not.
   b. I am not the person that you think I am.
10. *a.* It was thought that the school into which the lad was put was suited to him.
    b. The lad was put into the school which it was thought was suited to him.

Exercise XLVIII.

(The Same.)

1. *a.* If the people who have come here are sent home without giving them any satisfaction whatever, I think the people who sent them will do something desperate.
   b. If these people are sent home without giving them any satisfaction what do you think the people who sent them here will do?
2. *a.* Everyone knew that the war was coming, and everyone was asking himself how many men he should have to muster for it.
   b. Every day some prince arrived, with a query as to the quota he should be required to muster for the war which everyone understood was coming.
3. *a.* He feared that his friend had acted treacherously towards him, and this fact was worrying him exceedingly.
   b. The treachery of which he feared his friend had been guilty was worrying him exceedingly.
4. *a.* He hoped everything would turn out exactly as it did.
   b. Everything turned out exactly as he hoped it would.
5. *a.* The others did not think they would see him as soon as they did.

b. They saw him coming towards them long before they thought they would.
6. a. He said the enemy were thinking of doing something terrible.
   b. What did he say the enemy were thinking of doing?
7. a. If I thought that anyone would make any attempt to stop the work I should do my best to keep it from everyone.
   b. I did my best to keep it from everyone that I thought would make any attempt to stop the work.
8. a. They said there ought to have been more of them there than there were.
   b. There were not as many of them there as they said there should have been
9. a. I tell you I have undertaken a certain obligation in regard to Irish, but it has nothing to do with this matter.
   b. This matter has nothing whatever to do with the obligation which I tell you I have undertaken.
10. a. They hoped that Irish would die when people began to teach it, but when they found it wasn't dying they issued a rule designed to stop the teaching, fearing that this teaching might do harm, other things being neglected on account of it.
    b. When they found that Irish wasn't dying when people began to teach it, the rule which I said above had been issued was put in full force.

Exercise XLIX.

(The Same.)

1. a. I maintain that this sort of Irish should not be put in books for the people, and I think too that the other

kind would be too hard for them yet, and that it therefore should be excluded also.

    b. I should put into it the sort of Irish which I consider ought to be put in books for the people, and I should exclude from it the sort I think would be too hard for them yet.

2. *a.* You would like people to be kind to you as you are to them.
    b. Be kind to people as you would wish them to be to you.
3. *a.* I shouldn't wish people to do to me what I ought never to do myself.
    b. What I shouldn't like people to do to me I ought never to do myself.
4. *a.* I tell you meditation on the pains of hell is calculated to cure one of a sinful inclination.
    b. If meditation is so painful now what think you will hell-fire be hereafter?
5. *a.* I am certain I ought to have everything done well against the coming of death.
    b. When I have everything done as I think I ought to, I see clearly that I have nothing done.
6. *a.* Thou wouldst have a pleasing ointment poured upon Thy Sacred Feet.
    b. Heartfelt contrition is the pleasing ointment which Thou wouldst have poured upon Thy Feet.
7. *a.* I desire all glory and all honour to be rendered to God.
    b. If a man is guided by grace it is to God he would have all honour and glory rendered.
8. *a.* He says that Cormac arrived soonest.
    b. Who does he say arrived soonest?
9. *a.* I tell you I should rather learn Irish than any other language.
    b. Which language do you say you would rather learn?

10. *a* Don't tell me this is the man who did such an ugly deed.
   b. Is this the man who, you say, did such an ugly deed?

Section IV.

(Treble, Quadruple and Quintuple Relative Clauses.)

1⁰. Ir minic nuair ir ria ir dóic leac a bím-re uaic gurb ead ir giorra bim duic (Im. 160).

Here we have 3 relative clauses combined :—

(a) an uair (nuair) ir ria ⎫ It is clear that the
(b) ,, ,,   ir dóic leac ⎬ meaning of the first
(c) ,, ,,   a bím-re uaic ⎰ and last is influenced
                              ⎭ by that of the second.

But this dependence in thought is not clearly expressed.

If we begin the above with the words—Cad é an uair adubairc ir ria, etc., we have a *quadruple* relative construction. If we wish to say in Irish—" What think you did he say he thought would suit the school best ? " we shall have *quintuple* relative construction, five relative clauses being ranged side by side in one sentence :—

(a) Cad é an fud ir dóic leac ?
(b) ,, ,, ,, ,, a dubairc ré ?
(c) ,, ,, ,, ,, do mear ré ?
(d) ,, ,, ,, ,, ab 'fearr ?
(e) ,, ,, ,, ,, a d'oirfead do'n rcoil ?

It will run as follows in the actual sentence :—

2⁰. Cad é an fud ir dóic leac adubairc ré do mear ré ab 'fearr a d'oirfead do'n rcoil ?

Here the meaning of the last question involved is influenced by the other four.

3°. Má bíodar ollaṁ roimir rin ar ɼac aon nіṫ a ḋéanaṁ ar an ɼcuma ba ḋóic leo dob' ḟearr a caicnreaḋ léi, bíodar niba cuɼca na ḋiaiḋ rin cuiɼe (N. 95).

Here we have the three relative clauses :—
(a) ar an ɼcuma ba ḋóic leo.
(b) ,, ,, ,, do b' ḟearr.
(c) ,, ,, ,, a caicnreaḋ léi.

4°. Bi ḋúil aɼ na rearaiḋ ɼo léir ɼac ɼnó a ḋéanaṁ ar an ɼcuma ba ḋóic leo do b' ḟearr a caicnreaḋ léi.

5° If we want to say in Irish—" In what way do you think he said they thought things would best work out at a profit for them?" we shall have a series of FIVE relative clauses :—
(a) Caḋ é an cuma ir ḋóiɼ leac? (*lit*. What way
(b) ,, ,, ,, ,, aḋubairc ré? do you think
(c) ,, ,, ,, ,, do ṁearaḋar? likely?)
(d) ,, ,, ,, ,, ab' ḟearr?
(e) ,, ,, ,, ,, n-a raɼaḋ an rɼéal i dcairbe ḋóiḃ?

In the completed sentence it is to be noticed that the oblique relative of the LAST question involved, is transferred to the FIRST question, thus :—
Caḋ é an cuma n-aR ḋóic leac aḋubairc ré do ṁearaḋar ab' ḟearr a raɼaḋ an rɼéal i dcairbe ḋóiḃ? (Cf. p. 90 and Ex. 7°, p. 130).

6° Cf. C.D. 41.—" Ní baoɼal ná ɼo raɼaḋ an cóir ra creo baill ba lúɼa 'nar ḋóic leo a ciocraí ruar leo."
Here there are three relative clauses :—
1°. ra creo baill ba lúɼa (Rel. understood).
2°. ,, ,, ,, ba ḋóic leo (which they thought likely).

3°. ɼá ᴄɼeo ḃáɩll n-á ᴅᴄɩoᴄɼáí ɼuáɼ leo.

(Observe that the oblique relative is necessary here if the clause stood by itself. In multiple relative construction, however, the oblique rel. is shifted to the "ᴅóɩċ" clause, and the direct relative which belongs naturally to that clause is transferred to the ᴄɩoᴄɼáí clause.

Exercise L.

(Treble, Quadruple and Quintuple Relative Clauses.)

1°. When does he say she thinks you are farthest away from them?
2°. I tell you that this is the way he said he thought would best please all concerned.
3°. We are all anxious of course to study Irish in the way which we believe will bring us to a knowledge of it soonest and best.
4°. Who, think you, did he say they thought would be the best to do the deed?
5°. What did he say you would wish me to do for you?
6°. Which of the two did they say they would wish him to release?
7°. This is the greatest oath which he swore to our father he could give us.
8°. These are the greatest things we heard you did in that place.
9°. This is the person to whom I think he pardoned most.
10° Who do the people say he thinks I am?
11°. He asked me which of these three I thought he would say was neighbour to him that fell among the robbers

Section V.

Double Relative.

Apparent Exceptions and Abnormal Usages.

We sometimes meet sentences in which we find a go, ṡup, naċ, or nár clause unexpectedly, in view of what has been said about double relative construction. It is necessary to discuss the various cases which may turn up :—

1°. An té aoeiṗ ríḃ-ṗe ġuṅḃ a ḃuṗ nōia é (John viii. 54). Here the ġuṗ clause may be explained and defended on two grounds :—(a) to avoid the somewhat unusual iṗ ṗuṗ n'Oia (with omission of pronoun—see p. 45); (b) aoeiṗ ríḃ-ṗe has the force of "of whom you say." Though formally the relative is accusative it has the force of a genitive, and in this case we shall find that the double relative construction is not permissible. When the 1st clause has a genitive relative a conjunctional clause is required afterwards either as the object of the transitive verb of the 1st clause, or as the subject of the 1st verb (if it was "iṗ"). E.g., "Siḃ é an té n-ap ḃóiġ leaṫ-ṗa n-a ṫaoḃ ġup ṗuġaḃ na ḃall é." "This is the person OF WHOM you think, etc.

2°. Canaḃ iṗ ṫoil leaṫ go n-ollṁóċaimiṗ é? (Luke xxii. 9). This is only an apparent exception. The "go" is relative, not conjunctional. The two clauses taken separately would be :—

(a) Ca ionaḃ (i.e., canaḃ) iṗ ṫoil leaṫ?

(b) Ca ionaḃ go n-ollṁóċaimiṗ é. (For "go" here one could of course say either a (unusual in Munster, however) or n-a.

3°. Níl éinne is feapp ṠUR̃ḃ eol ṫó ran ná map ṫob eol ṫuicse é (TBC. 1).

Only an apparent exception : ṡup is the relative, *not* the conjunction. The two clauses are :—

(a) Níl éinne is feapp. ⎫ Meaning of the
(b) ,, ,, ṡupḃ eol ṫó ran. ⎬ second of course
⎭ is influenced by
  the first.

4°. Tá buaipc móp tpom tagaiṫe opm,—buaipc náp mearap piam ṡupḃ' féidip a leiṫéid do ṫeaċc ap ṁnaoi (TBC. 133).

Various explanations of ṡup are possible :—

(a) ṡup may be taken as gen. relative ; buaipc ṡup d'féidip a leiṫéid do ṫeaċc ap ṁnaoi—is quite a normal relative construction.

(b) náp may be the negative conjunction (buaipc (ċom tpom ran) náp . . not the negative relative. In this case there is no room for double relative construction ; ṡup = conjunction.

(c) náp may be the negative GENITIVE relative (with easy ellipsis of n-a taoḃ) and in this case also double relative construction is neot permissible—(see case 1°) ; ṡup would then be th conjunction.

5°. Do fuapad bainne na mbpoc, fud ba dóiċ le haoinne R̃ÁRḂ féidip a d' faġáil, pé cuapdaċ a deanfí dó (ṡ. 63).

Only an apparent exception, náp is the negative *relative* (genitive), not the negative conjunction. Observe, however, if one said fud ṠUR dóiċ . . the following náp would then be the conjunction, because ṡUR would be genitive relative (with ellipsis of na taoḃ). (See 4°c., 9° and remarks under case 1°).

F

6°. D'féroip go bréaḋfá-ṛa a innṛint ḋúinn ... caḋ é an tṛeo baill n-a mbeaḋ aon ḋeallṛaṁ go ḋtiocṛaimír ruaṛ leiṛ an ṛgéal (5. 202).

Here we may take "go" as the conjunction; as the relative in the first clause is DATIVE and the sense of the clause incomplete, the conjunctional clause is required to complete the sense. *This case differs from the next one and from example* 5° *on p.* 126, *in both of which there is* TRANSPOSITION *of direct and indirect relatives.*

7°. Ḃí gaċ aoinne ag breiċniú na h-aimṛiṛe n-aṛ ḋóiċ leo a ḃeaḋ an t-Áṛḋ-Rí ⁊ a ċuallaċt ag teaċt a ḃaile (n. 210).

The two relative clauses here are:—

(*a*) .. na h-aimṛiṛe ba ḋóiċ leo (*lit.*, the time they thought likely).

(*b*) na h-aimṛiṛe n-a mbeaḋ.

We have double relative construction, but what is peculiar is that we have inversion of the direct and oblique forms. Cf. next case.

8°. Caḋ é a ṁinicíġe ḋo ṛuaṛaṛ é ṛan áit náṛ ṁeaṛaṛ a ġeoḃainn é (Im. 187).

This looks abnormal, because the second clause could not stand by itself—ṛan áit a ġeoḃainn é, would not be correct. Cf. Ex. 6, p. 126. It is more abnormal even than the second clause in No. 7°, because there one could conceive the direct relative being used even if the clause stood by itself, inasmuch as it is a *temporal* clause—(see p. 89). The explanation is that here again we have *inversion*. It would be quite normal to say ṛan áit ḋo ṁeaṛaṛ ná ṛuiġinn é. When the negative relative is shifted to the first clause, the direct relative of that clause (which is

9°. Cad é an brig a bí ag ámlaoib leir an rult a bein ré ... de'n pud sur dóic le haoinne go n-éircreað ré a béal na taob? (11. 299).

The go may be explained in two ways :—(a) sur is gen. relative (influenced by na taob at the end) and so go is the conjunction—(see case 1°). (b) sur may be the *conjunction* (de'n pud [a bí cóm náireac ran] sur . . .) and so of course there is no room for relative construction at all. Observe that one might have said—'De'n pud ba bóic . . . in which case go would be genitive relative. Cf. case 5° and remarks.

10°. Tá an obair déanta agam go dtí ro ar cuma nár mear aoinne i dturac barra gurb féidir í déanam (Sg. 113).

Three possible explanations :—(a) nár = genitive negative relative with na taob understood, and so sur is conjunction (case 1°). (b) If nár is accusative then sur can be taken as virtually gen. relative, inas much as í déanam is equivalent to a (gen.) déanam —(see p. 85). (c) nár is the negative *conjunction,* and so there would be no relative construction at all.

11°. Ir minic a bein duine intaob pórta an pud a ceap ré ná déanpað ré coidce (Sg. 110). This is quite regular. ná is the negative *relative* (not conjunction). If the negative were put with ceap (as it might be) the sentence would run—nár ceap ré a déanpað ré.

12°. Cun gac tíre n-ar dóic léi go bragað rí a beag nó a mór d' aon pud i bruirim nirt (n. 251). Here the

two relative clauses, taken separately, would be normally—
(a) cun ᵹać tiṗe ba ḋóić léi,
(b) ,, ,, ,, ᵹo bṗaᵹaḋ ṗí . . . (or n-a).
When the second clause is oblique temporal, or oblique local, there is a tendency to transfer the oblique relative to the iṗ ḋóić . . . clause, and use the direct form with the temporal or local clause (cf. cases 7° and 8°). Here, while the first clause *has* the oblique relative, the second one retains it also. Or the 1st clause being incomplete in sense ᵹo may be conjunction. Cf. case 6°, p. 130.

When the first is a comparative or SUPERLATIVE clause it is usual to leave the direct relative in it. Cf. Examples H 2°—5°, p. 92).

13°. An ṗuḋ ᵹuṗ ṁeaṗaiṗ ᵹuṗ ṗuḋ ṗóᵹanta é (Im. 120).
Whether we understand the first ᵹuṗ as conjunction, or (with ellipsis of na taob) as gen. relative, the second ᵹuṗ *must* be the conjunction; there is no room for relative construction at all. An alternative construction of course would be—an ṗuḋ ḋo ṁeaṗaiṗ ba ṗuḋ ṗóᵹanta (Double Relative).

14°. Aᵹuṗ ᵹo ḋeiṁin iṗ aᵹ caineaḋ a ćéile a bíḋ ṗiaḋ nuaiṗ iṗ ḋóić leo ᵹo mbíḋ ṗiaḋ aᵹ molaḋ a ćéile (Im. 206).
Here apparently the **nuaiṗ** clause is not FELT as a relative clause, although *de facto* it is one. The stress is not upon *the point of time*, but upon *what they think* at that time. If we wished, not so much to contrast what they are ACTUALLY doing with what they THINK they are doing, but rather to point out that it is JUST WHEN they think they're praising one another, they are actually indulging in blame, we should use the double relative construction :—nuaiṗ

ir vóic leo a bío riav as molav a céile ir as cáineav a céile a bív. *This is a very good example of the beautiful subtlety of Canon O'Leary's Irish.* Cf. also Im. 40:—bímív so minic as sáiří nuair ba ceart sur as sol a beimir. Here the stress is on the contrast between laughing and crying—"we often *laugh* when in all reason we ought to *weep*." But if the stress is upon our laughing JUST WHEN we ought to cry, the Irish will run—bímív so minic as sáirí an uair ba ceart a béimís as sol.

REMARK I.

Double Relative Construction occurs after such expressions as the following, when THEY are relative :—

1°. vo ceapav (any tense of course).
2°. ir voiš le ,,
3°. vo ṁearar, etc. ,,
4° avéarrainn ,,
5°, a cuišim ,,
6°. ba toil le ,,
7° ba ṁait le ,,
8°. ir feann ,,
9°. mar a cionn rib ,,

REMARK II.

The following combinations may occur :—

1°. Direct Relative (Nom. or Accusative) in both clauses.
2°. Direct in first (compar. or superl. clause); indirect in 2nd.
3°. Direct in both **for indirect.** (See exception H., p. 92, and remarks).
4° Direct in first ; direct for indirect temporal in second (See ex. under 14°, above).

5°. Direct in first ; indirect in 2nd. (Interrogative Sentences. See p. 139).
6°. Indirect in first,; direct in 2nd. (By an INVERSION for direct in 1st + temporal oblique in 2nd. See Ex. 7°, p. 130).
7°. Indirect in first ; direct in 2nd. (By an inversion for direct in 1st + indirect *local* in 2nd. (See Ex. 8, p. 130).
8°. Indirect in both. Abnormal. (See Ex. 12, p. 131).

Section VI.
Negative Relatives.

The negative particles ná, nac, nár, besides their *conjunctional*, have also a *relative* value. The following exx., arranged according to case, will make the matter clear :—
I. Nom. (or Gen.) :—

(*a*) Ar ball do teartócad rud eigin uaca nárb 'feroir a d' ragáil (5. 3).

Here according to the way a d'ragáil is understood nár will include either the Nom. or Gen. Relative ; if a d' is merely the preposition do (duplicated in each of its two forms) then the Rel. is of course Nom. If it be the gen. pron. a (with d' as phonetic padding) then the relative is gen.

(*b*) Sometimes of course there is no such ambiguity :—
Sin rud ná raib ann lem' linn-re (Nom.).

(*c*) Mearaim gur mian é nac feroir a d'ragáil (5. 52). Nom. or Gen. See remarks under (*a*). It is only with the NEGATIVE relative that this ambiguity can exist. Also there would be no ambiguity if the preposition do were used simply in that form. When the sentence is affirmative the form used determines the sense both of the relative and the particle ᴀ (or ᴀ ᴅ'); mian ir eaᴅ é ʒup puipirᴄe ᴀ ᴅ'pᴀʒáil—can only have *one* meaning (Gen. Rel.). Similarly mian ir eaᴅ é ᴅo ᴅ'puipirᴄe ᴀ' ᴅ'pᴀʒáil—can only have one meaning (Rel. nom.).

(*d*) Sin ceirᴄ naċ puipirᴄe ᴀ péroᴄeaċ (Sʒ. 53). Ambiguous construction. Rel. may be nom. or gen. according to the meaning attached to ᴀ.

II. Genitive.

See examples under I. Of course as in the case of the Nom. we sometimes have a quite unambiguous genitive :—

Ruᴅ ᴀb eaᴅ é NáR ʒáᴅ laḃairᴄ na ᴄaoḃ.

III. Dative.

(*a*) Ḃa ᴄeaċᴄaipeaċᴄ é NáRḂ pulᴀip ᴅiúlᴄaᴅ ᴅó (TBC. 5).

(*b*) Ḋeineaᴅap painnᴄ cainnᴄe, cainnᴄ Ná paiḃ puin⁻ ruime aʒ aoinne acu innᴄi (S. 129).

IV. Accusative (or Gen.).

(*a*) Sap ap ᴅeineaᴅ an ᴄeiċe pin ḃí cpuaḃᴄan ⁊ ḃpúᴄ ⁊ peiᴅm ap Ulᴄaiḃ Ná péaᴅpairóir ᴀ peapaṁ puinn eile aimpipe (TBC. 246). If ᴀ = the prep. ᴅo then the rel. is accus. governed by péaᴅpairóir (and peapaṁ dat. governed by ᴀ). But as cpuaḃᴄan ⁊ ḃpúᴄ ⁊ peiᴅm may be taken closely together ᴀ might be the gen. ᴀ and then the rel. would be genitive (and peapaṁ would be accusative governed by péaᴅpairóir).

(*b*) Oḃaip aḃ eaᴅ í Ná péaᴅpainn ᴀ ċup uaim (mSp. 160). There is the same ambiguity of construction here. If ᴀ = ᴅo then the rel. is accusative and cup is dative ; if ᴀ is the gen. pron. then the rel. is genitive and cup is accusative.

(*c*) Ċuʒap pé nᴅeapa ʒo minic polṁap éiʒin Ná péaᴅainn ᴀ ᴄuipʒinᴄ inp na ʒnóᴄaiḃ cpeiᴅim ᴀ ḃíoḃ ap piúḃal aiʒe (N. 169).

(*d*) ᴅo meapaᴅ pinn ᴀ ᴄaḃairᴄ ap an plóʒaᴅ po le ḃpéiʒ, le ʒeallaṁainᴄ Ná meapaᴅ ᴀ ċómlionaᴅ.

If ᴀ = the prep. ᴅo, and meapaᴅ is understood autono

mously, then the rel. is accusative, governed by meapaó, (Nom. if meapaó is understood as a passive) and cómlionaó is dat. If ᴀ = the gen. pronoun (the gender of ḃṗéiṡ and ṡeaʟʟaṁainc is no obstacle to its being so considered—see p. 217) then the rel. is gen. and cómlionaó is accus. governed by meapaó, if the latter is understood autonomously; if it is understood passively, of course, cómlionaó will be Nom. The virtual gens. ṡo, ṡuṗ (p. 102) n-á, n-aṗ (p. 106) are paralleled in the neg. rel. in the following sentence :—ṅíʟ baca pa ciṡ pin ṅáR ḃ'éiṡean peippeac oo ṡaḃáiʟ cun é caḃaiRc aḃaiʟe ón ṡcoiʟʟ (Cl. 7). Here cun é caḃaipc is equivalent to c un a caḃapca, and so we may look upon ṅáR as gen. neg. relative : "for the bringing OF WHICH it was NOT..."

Section VII.
Comparative and Superlative Adjectives.

Formally there is no such thing in Modern Irish as a comparative or superlative adverb. In O.I. the comparative and superlative of adjectives were changed into adverbs by prefixing the dat. sg. of the article, e.g., int serbu = more bitterly, ind lugu = less, in máam = mostly. This construction has become obsolete, and all comparative and superlative forms are now *formally* adjectives, though *virtually* they may be adverbs. They can never be *parsed* as adverbs. Hence we frequently have to use *the double relative construction* to express the English comparative and superlative *adverb*. E.g., "No one knows better than you how to do that" is in Irish—"ṅíʟ éinne is peaRR ṡuRḃ eoʟ oó cionnuṗ é píúo a óéanaṁ ná maṗ iṗ eoʟ ouicṗe é," where peaṗṗ is of course an adjective (formally). Similarly "the work he knows best" is in Irish "an oḃaiṗ is peaRR acá αn eolus αιʒe" (S. 34), where again ꝼeαꞃꞃ must be *parsed* as an adjective.

Even in such a sentence as—τά ꞃé níoꞃ ꝼeαꞃꞃ αnoıꞃ ná mαꞃ τo ϸí, " ꝼeαꞃꞃ " is an adjective. (Níoꞃ of course is not a part of the adjective at all).

Exercise LI.

Comparative and Superlative ADJECTIVES.

(Double Relative.)

1°. He told me he would come whenever it suited my convenience best.
2°. The best tradesmen came to *him* because he fed and paid them best.
3° Where is the man who has to fight harder than he who's trying to keep himself in subjection?
4° Nothing he brought with him caused more surprise than a set of cloth of gold vestments which you'd have thought was made of pure gold it was so beautiful.
5°. If there's one thing which more than another surprises me in the matter of the Irish language it is the extraordinary good sense displayed by the people who are directing the work.
6° He is still without the one thing which he needs most.
7°. Those who advance furthest in the spiritual life oftentimes meet with the heaviest crosses, because through their great love for God they feel separation from Him most keenly.
8°. Nothing satisfies a man more than to realise that his will is in accord with God.

138   STUDIES IN MODERN IRISH

9°. The Gael ought to know his own language best.

10°. If the life of a language is in speech he who is ignorant of Irish phonetics should never speak it because he speaks it worst of all.

Section VIII.

Interrogative and Relative.

(Single Relative Clauses.)

Sentences like—1°. Caḋ na taoḃ ná raḃair annro inḋé?
    2°. Cia ḋó ꞅo ḃruiliꞅ ꞅá taꞅairt rin?
    3°. Cia leir an peann?
present a difficulty to learners of Irish. It must be understood that all such sentences are elliptical. E.g.,

1°. is equivalent to—Caḋ [é an ruḋ] ná raḃair annro inḋé na taoḃ where ná includes the gen. relative. I.e., What is the thing *on account of which* you were not here yesterday? The subject is an ruḋ .   na taoḃ, the predicate of course is Caḋ, and é (in the expanded form of the question) is the temporary subject. It is usual, however, to find the prepositional pronoun or the prepositional phrase *immediately after the interrogative* in the short elliptical form of the sentence, which is the usual form in actual speech. Sentence 2° (above)
= Cia (hé an té) ꞅo ḃruiliꞅ ꞅá taꞅairt rin ḋó?
       | _____/
    P. s   S
Similarly sentence 3° = Cia (hé an té ꞅur) leir an peann?
                          | _____/
                          P   s ·   S

It will be noticed that the *oblique* relative is used in such sentences, and this form is required by the sense. The Déisi forms are corruptions of the true idiom, and are highly undesirable. They allow such questions as—Ciá teir atá ré ag cainnt? Cia cuige cuireann tu na leabra ran? Cad air atá ré ag trácc? W. Munster, Connaught and Ulster are against these forms. And even if they were not we should strongly object to them on the ground that they would frequently destroy the distinction between single and double relative clauses, and make it impossible to differentiate pairs of sentences with quite distinct meanings. E.g., the sentence :

(a) Cad cuige adubairt rí ná raib aon mait innti? has quite a different meaning from—

(b) Cad cuige go ndubairt rí ná raib aon mait innti? (a) is a DOUBLE relative question including the two relative clauses :—

1° Cad é an rud a dubairt rí?
2°. ,, ,, ,, ,, ná raib aon mait innti cuige?
and means—**What did she say she was no good at ?**

(b) On the other hand is a *single* relative question the full form of which would be—

Cad é an rud go ndubairt rí ná raib aon mait innti cuige? and means simply—
Why did she say she was no good ?

To allow the direct form of relative where the meaning of (b) is intended is destructive of the language and should not be tolerated.

Similarly the two sentences—
(a) Catoin adubairt ré a bead ré ann ?
(b) ,, ,, go mbead ré ann?
are quite different in construction and meaning ; (a) is a double relative sentence, involving the two questions :—

1°. Catoin adubairt ré? (i.e., ca tan adubairt ré = What time did he speak of ?)

2°. Cátoin a beáḋ ṗé ann?

and means—When did he say he would be there? (referring to the time of his **being there,** not to the time of **his making the statement.**)

Whereas (*b*) is a single relative sentence, meaning—

On what occasion **did he make the statement** about his being there (**at some time or another not referred to in the question at all.**)

Again (*a*) Caḋ n-a ċaob áḋeiR riḃ ɢo mḃíonn buaiṗeaṁ oraiḃ? is a **double** question involving the two relative sentences

1° Caḋ (é an ṗuḋ) aḋeiṗ riḃ?

2° ,, ,, ,, ,, ɢo mḃíonn buaiṗeaṁ oraiḃ na ċaoḃ?

and means—

About what do you say you are troubled?

whereas (*b*) Caḋ na ċaoḃ ɢo nḋeiR riḃ ɢo mḃíonn buaiṗeaṁ oraiḃ? is a single question, meaning simply—

Why do you make the statement that you are troubled? A most important idiom is here at stake. We must allow no tinkering with it.

Exercise LII.

Interrogative and Relative.

(Single Relative Clauses.)

1°. You know very well for whose sake I have lost both my riches and my reputation.

2°. How surprised they would have been had they known whom he was expecting.

3°. I cannot make out why you said it at all, or to whom you are referring.

4°. Who *is* this man whom so many people seem to know so well?

5°. She didn't tell me at all who it is she knows so well in the city.
6°. He didn't care who it was he took the goblet from as long as he got the drink.
7°. When I heard this I couldn't help wondering who it was that she was so fond of.
8°. He told me *point blank*[1] that he *was at a loss*[2] to understand my motive in giving him so much money *in advance*.[3]
9°. Though she watched very carefully she was unable to discover any *specific*[4] fact that would have enlightened her as to who the person was against whom all the mischief was brewing.
10°. If I were in your case I should confess at once for whose sake I had done such an unseemly action.

---

1. Ṡan ḟiacal oo ċup ann.   2. Ṡo ṗaiḃ ceipṫe aiṙ.   3. Roiṁ ṙé.   4. Áiriṫe.

CHAPTER IV.

The Verbal Noun.[1]

Section I.

The verbal noun is a fruitful source of blundering to the learner, and of worry to the teacher. A great deal both of the worry and the blundering could be avoided if teacher and learner would remember that these forms are NOUNS, and should always be treated as such. Even teachers seem to forget this sometimes. In a book printed and published for the purpose of teaching Composition I have found the following extraordinary information (in the vocabularies) :—

do tabairt ar iasacht=to lend.
do leanamaint=to follow, succeed.
do bogad=to steep (as flax).
do beit ag teastbáil ó=to be wanted.
do beit toilteanac cuige=to agree to it.
do tuitim amac=to take place.
do cur ar ionad=to dislocate.
do cotugad=to hand-feed.
do teact suas le
do breit ar } = to overtake.

ag imteact=leaving, going.
ag fagáil=getting.
ag formad le céile=grudging.
ag sabáil air=beating him.
ag brat air=depending on him.
ag baint=cutting.
ag inbear=grazing.
ag cur a tuairisci=inquiring for him.
do teact ar=to obtain.
do caiteam=to wear.

Now one might as well give the following information, which would be equally correct,—*and equally misleading* :—

ag leabar=a book ; do Seán=John ; ag Liam=William ag tobar=a well ; ar sliab=a mountain ; D'uair a' cluig=an hour.

There is no sense or reason in putting these nouns *in the dative case* in a vocabulary. There is just as little sense in putting the *verbal* nouns quoted above in the dative case,—as if they were never used in other cases, Nom. Gen. Accus., or

---

1. For formation of verbal noun see pp. 248-

STUDIES IN MODERN IRISH 143

in the dative with any other preposition than the one given in the vocabulary. It is infinitely more harmful indeed with *verbal* nouns, because this is just the tendency of the learner, which it is the teacher's business to correct, not to foster. It is all the worse when we find verbal nouns given in the dative,—the use of which in the dative (at least with the preposition given) is comparatively rare, e.g., (I quote from the same book) :—

Do cur isteac air = to interfere with.

Do cromad ar obair = to set to work.

Do luige ar obair = to set to work.

Do tornugad ar obair = to set to work.

Sometimes we find the correct form (nom.) given side by side with the incorrect (dat.) :—

géillead (do) = to submit
Do cur ar reilb = to evict
éirge ar = to cease, to give up.

} cuir 'n-a luige air
  ag áiteam air } = persuading

ag dul i nolcar = getting worse.

The best way to realise the construction of the verbal noun is to remember that it *is* a NOUN, and may be found in the Nom. Gen. Dat. or Accus.

1°. Nom.—

(a) Ba dóbair airir **cailleamaint** ar a mirneac (S. 260). How could one expect a student to write such a sentence correctly if we told him in the vocabulary—Do cailleamaint = to lose ; Do cailleamaint air = to fail ?

(b) So—ba mait liom,

Dul ann ; fanamaint annro ; imteact ; druidim riar ; a innsint duit ; a cur n-a luige ort . . . etc., etc.

In many places the particle a has become petrified

in the phrases a ḋul and a ḃeiṫ in the Nom. and Accus. (The particle was originally the gen. pronoun).

2°. Genitive.—

(a) Cailín ḋeag CRúiṪe na mḃó.
(b) fear innsṫe sgéil.
(c) Ceard ḋéanṫa crocán sgriaḋ (K.).
(d) Ṫáim ċun a ḋéanṫa anoir.
(e) Ḃí ré ḋireaċ ċun imṫigṫe.
(f) Ḃíoḋar ollaṁ ċun gluaisṫe.
(g) Cuaiḋ ré ċun cóṁnuiḋṫe i gCaraṙnaum (Cs. 8).

Exceptions :—The Genitive form is not used :—

1°. In phrase nouns :—In-aġaiḋ gaċ caraḋ 1 aṫrú ḋá ḋtéigeaḋ ar an sceol ṫéiḋeaḋ a ċoṁṫrom ḋ'aṫrú ar gluaireaċṫ na nḋaoine (S. 239). So,— ṫugṫaċṫ ċun géilleaḋ ḋ' uaċtarán (Im. 47). Tréir gaḃáil ḋe ċoraiḃ ann, etc., etc.

2°. With proleptic a (contrast example ḋ above) :— g. 42—Ṫánas annro ċun a iarraiḋ ar Ḋia mé ṫósainṫ ar an raoġal nó mé ḋ'fuarsailṫ ar an gcruaḋtan ro n-a ḃfuilim.
TBC. 188—Caḋ na ṫaoḃ ḋuiṫ ranaṁainṫ riar ṫréir a ráḋ go ḋṫiocfá?
So—Ḃí ré aḋ'iarraiḋ aḋéanaṁ amaċ cé ḃí ann. Ḃí ré aḋ'iarraiḋ a ċur na luiġe orm gur aige féin a ḃí an ceart.

3°. Certain nouns resist inflexion,—e.g., ċun maireaċṫainṫ, buaċṫainṫ, aireaċṫainṫ. Im. 257 :— ċun ḋóláir ná ċun croiḋe-ḃrúġaḋ. Aoinniḋ 1 ḃfuirm ṫaḃairṫ suas (msf. 33).

3°. Dative :—

(a) Do h-órḋuiġeaḋ gan aoinne ḋe'n ṁuinnṫir n-a mḃeaḋ a gcaraill raġálṫa acu ḋ'imṫeaċṫ ón bráigre go ocí go mbeað an capall ðéanac cabμca amac, ⁊ an ꝼeaμ ðéanac μáμca (S. 211).

(b) Deinið móμán ðaoine móμán cainnce, ⁊ ðá bμí͝s μin ní ceaμc a cuμ 'n-a scainnc ac beagán μuime (Im. 173).

(c) Do cogaμ iað ó cuμać gan iað μéin ðo ðéanaṁ aon μuða cun an coga μan ðo cuilleaṁ (Im. 228).

(d) So—leaðaμ ðo léigeaṁ, an ðoμaμ ð'oμgailc μgéal ðo cuiμginc, etc.

4° Accusative :—

(a) Ní ꝼéaðμainn a cuiμginc cað é an bμí͝s acá leiμ (S. 42).

(b) So—Duðaiμc μé liom—

Dul a baile ; ꝼanaṁainc annμo ; imceacc : oμuiðim μiaμ ; a cuμ na cóṁaiμle . . . ; a innμinc ðóið . . a cuμ n-a luige oμća . . . etc., etc.

In phrases like "to understand the story," story of course is accusative governed by understand. But in the Irish "an μgéal ðo cuiμginc" the case of μgéal cannot possibly be settled by cuiμginc.

A great scholar has observed :—" An infinitive may be said to be completely formed when the nom. is no longer regarded as a case-form belonging to the nominal system, and the construction no longer follows the analogy of its original use as a noun-form : e.g., dounai, domenai : dare." (Brugman II, 470). Again—" The infinitives which least deserve the name are the Irish because . . . they retained the construction of nouns " (Ibid, 471). We may go further and say that the Irish verbal noun SHOULD NOT BE CALLED AN INFINITIVE AT ALL.

Cuiμginc is a NOUN and cannot govern μgéal ; the only instances in modern Irish in which nouns govern *preceding* words are the genitives of the personal pronouns—mo capall,

a leabar, etc., and the *governed* word is in the genitive.*
The case of "rgéal" in the phrase in question is determined
by its relation to the rest of the sentence. If I say—

ba maic liom an rgéal do cuirginc

rgéal is of course Nom. (the subject to ba,—at least the
fundamental noun of the Subject). This is evident if we say
merely—

ba maic liom an rgéal.

But the addition of do cuirginc, do léigead, do rgriobad,
etc., does not affect the construction. These phrases merely
tell the *purpose* in respect of which "the story would be
GOOD in my estimation." If on the other hand the sentence
is—

níor féadar an rgéal do cuirginc,

rgéal is of course accus. governed *by* féadar.

Yet some of our most popular text-books on Composition
tell us that even in the first case rgéal is accusative. It is
bad enough to have people **Anglicizing** our language; but
when the Anglicizers are reinforced by the "Latinizers," it
is time to extend a helping hand to the student victim. The
above phrases have been compared to the Latin accusative
and infinitive. Sometimes of course there is no accusative!
and there is *never* an infinitive. The true construction is
shown by such sentences as—PH. 232 "túcad damsa comus
cech *neich* (bus maith liumm) do denum a nim ⁊ hi talmain."
neich is genitive of the neuter ní. The insertion of the relative
clause doesn't affect the matter in hand; if we do not connect
immediately cech neich do denum, we must connect "bus
maith liumm do denum" and the relative "a" understood
is *subject* to bur, NOT accusative governed by dénum (!) or
anything else.

* A word like déiric (originall =love of God) is only a survival.

Cf. also Ml. 42a4.—Ni guid *digail* du thabairt foraib (*digail* is *accusative* governed by *guid*). He prays not that punishment should be inflicted on them.

Ml. 103c15.—Iarsindí dob-roíga sa i m-mess fíra do brith for cách. (After I had chosen you to pass righteous judgment upon all ; mess (accusative)).

Wb. 10d6.—Arisbés leosom *indaim* dothuarcuin indarbe = for it is a custom among them for the oxen to tread out the corn (in daim Nom.). In this example, however, there could be no question, even in the minds of some of our grammarians, of making ɪnoaɪm governed by do thuarcain. It is the subject of the action in question, the object being ind arbe—see pp. 150 sqq.

So,—GM. (ZCP. II, 10) deis (o'éɪr) meɪc oé do chur do cum báis. (Meic is gen., governed by deis, *not* accusative gov. by chur !)

If the sentence is " níl aon bpeic agam aɲ on ɲséal oo cuɪɲsɪnc " ɲséal is *dative* governed by aɲ. Even where the preposition in such cases does not inflect the noun (say of 2nd declension) it cannot be maintained that the noun is accusative governed by the verbal noun (!) or governed by any other word. If I were to say (as I might) níl aon bpeic agam aɲ (mo bróg do ɲgaoɪleao) we should have here simply a Nom. absolute, by reason of the phrase noun. In W. Munster it is more usual to say—aɲ mo bróɪg oo ɲgaoɪleao.

Section II.

Subject and Object of ACTION expressed in Verbal Noun Phrase.

One can sometimes avoid cumbrousness and turn the expression neatly by using a phrase containing the verbal noun, preceded by the *subject* of the action in question, and followed by the *object*, which will of course be in the GENITIVE case. The *subject* may be a relative particle expressed or understood. Its case of course is not determined by the verbal noun. E.g.,

(a) ní tu* ba maiṫ liom d'ḟaġáil báiṡ aṗ an ṡcuma ṡan.
Other examples of the construction :—
(b) is aic an ṡġéal é tuṡa do ḋéanaṁ an tiġe ṡeo ḋúinn ṡo léiṗ ⁊ a ṗáḋ ná leoṡṡi ṫú ṡéin iṡteaċ 'o' tiġ ṡéin! (Dṗ. 16).
(c) pé 'cu tá nó ná ṡuil, is í buime na Cléiṡe *ba maiṫ liomṡa d'ḟaġáil báiṡ aṗ dtúiṗ ṡaṗ a ḃṡaṡṡá-ṡa báṡ (Ṡ. 36).
(d) Tuṡa do ċoṡġ do ċṗann-taḃaill ó ṡeaṗaiḋ Éiṗeann (TBC. 87).

Exercise LIII.

Verbal Noun.

1°. It is easier for a camel to go through the eye of a needle than for a rich man to enter the Kingdom of Heaven.
2°. Her courage almost failed her again.
3°. He said if they fought bravely they wouldn't allow a man of them to escape to tell the tale.
4°. For every change and turn that came upon the music a corresponding change took place in the movements of the people.
5°. I have come here to ask God to take me out of life or else to rescue me from the hard plight in which I find myself.
6°. If anyone hath ears to hear let him hear.

(* Rel. particle understood.)

7°. Orders were given that none of those who had received their money should leave the house until the last farthing had been paid and the last claimant was satisfied.
8°. I can't understand the meaning of it.
9° I have chosen them from the beginning without their having done anything to merit that choice.
10°. I should like to go home for a year or two when the war is over.

Exercise LIV.
(The Same.)

1°. I should much prefer to stay here for the night, than to start for home in all this rain.
2°. If you tell me to go I will of course comply at once.
3° I shouldn't like such a thing to happen you in my house.
4°. If you really don't wish me to go tell your man to unyoke the horses and stable them again.
5°. I can easily start early in the morning if the rain has stopped.
6°. When I reach home safely—if I ever do—I will register a vow never to come here again.
7°. It may be that you intend to give me an invitation on some other occasion, but I tell you here and now that I will not accept it.
8° Furthermore, when I have a party at my house you needn't expect to get an invitation from me.
9°. The long and the short of it is that I am persuaded that you are much too proud to treat your friends as you would have them treat you.
10°. I will say just one word more, that if I have inconvenienced you on the present occasion, I am determined that it shall be the last.

Exercise LV.

(Subject and Object Expressed.)

1°. Neither they nor their wives would have been satisfied that anyone but you should have settled matters between them.

2°. *What I have asked must be done*[1] : that I should take off your head to-night, and you take off mine to-morrow night,—if you are able.

3°. Should your father have had no inclination to die, at the time they wanted him to die, *you think*[2] that Gormfhlaith would have helped him to die?

4°. I am surprised that he chooses these weapons.

5°. I see that some of you have a plan in your minds; and that *this plan is*[3] that the Kings of Munster should turn their *backs*[4] on this great host, and that we should all go home by mutual agreement.

6° And the ruler of the synagogue, being angry *that*[5] Jesus had healed on the Sabbath, answering, said to the multitude . . .

7° In this is my Father glorified that you bring forth much fruit and that you become my disciples.

8° It is impossible for us to go and make such a request of him, *after having promised*[6] that we would bring him the money, and having failed to do so.

9°. They asked them *whether they would prefer*[7] to go to celebrate the feast in Gleann an Sgáil or that Guaire should bring them the feast to their own house.

---

1. Use type 4 Identification.   2. ɩp é ꝺo ṁeaṟ.   3. Type 2 (ná).
4. Ꝺṗuɩm láṁa.   5. Coɩrs.   6. Cṗéɩṗ ṗɩnn ġá ġeallaṁaɩnc.
7. Cɩa' cu ba ṗoġa leo.

10°. Was not *this*[1] the bargain—that I should give you as much money as would buy you leather for 13 years, and that you should come with me *at the expiration of*[2] that period?

When the object of the action is a pronoun then both subject and object precede the verbal noun :—Ɒ'ꜱoṁuiʒ ꝛé nápƀ 'péiɒiꝛ a maiċ ɒo loċ coiꝛʒ **mé ʒá** ċaƀaiꝛċ uaim aꝛ ꝛon an ċSlánuiʒċeoꝛa (S. 62).

Of course mé is here formally in connection with ƀeiċ (ɒo ƀeiċ understood). If the genitive pronoun is proleptic, then of course the REAL object comes AFTER the verbal noun :—

ƀí peaꝛʒ aiꝛ coiꝛʒ mé ʒá ċuꝛ na luiʒe aiꝛ ʒuꝛ aʒam péin a ƀí an ceaꝛċ.

When the verb to which the noun belongs is intransitive the subject of the action will come BEFORE the verbal noun, when they are combined in a phrase :—

Aꝛ ṁiꝛɒe leaċ miꝛe ɒo ƀul leaċ aꝛ cuaiꝛɒ ? (eiꝛ. 23).

Exx. from Keating of Subject and Object expressed :—

1°. KH. II 360.—Miꝛe ɒo ṁaꝛƀaɒ na ʒColla.

2°. ,, ,, 362.—Ʒo ɒċiocpaɒ ɒe ꝛin plaiċeaꝛ Éiꝛeann ɒo ꝛoċċain a ʒcloinne.

3°. ,, ,, 362.—Cia an ċíꝛ n-aꝛ ṁaiċ leaċꝛa ꝛinn ɒo ƀéanaṁ peaꝛainn cloiɒiṁ ?

Another way of expressing subject and object of the action is—

KH. Ʒo ꝛoċċain Ceaṁꝛaċ ɒóiƀ
Aꝛ ċaƀaiꝛċ an aiꝛʒiɒ ɒí ɒó.

Section III.
Verbal Noun in a Passive Sense.

The verbal noun, being the *name* of the action, it is natural inasmuch as the action can be considered from the point of

---

1. é will do. 2. nuaiꝛ

152   STUDIES IN MODERN IRISH

view of the object as well as of the agent, that the verbal noun should occasionally be used in a passive sense. It is so used in three ways :—

1°. with Le : ηιι ϫοιnnιϋ ιe ϋéαnαṁ ⱭnnƤo ȺʒⱭιnn Ⱥnoιρ ; ƇⱭ ιeιƇιρ ⱭʒⱭm ιe ƤʒƤíoϋⱭϋ ċun mo ṁⱭƇⱭρ, etc.

2°. with ⱭR : ƇⱭ Ƥé Ⱥρ ƤⱭʒⱭιι ⱭʒⱭƇ. Not as common as 1° or 3°. ƇⱭ Ƥé Ⱥρ ƤoʒⱭιι = He is outlawed.

3°. with ϋO : ĊeⱭρ Ƥé nⱭ ρⱭιϋ Ⱥon Ƈριιʒeϋ'ƤeⱭρρ n-Ⱥ ρⱭċⱭϋ Ƥé ó Ⱥιnm Ⱥn ϋιƇeⱭṁnⱭιʒ ϋo ƇⱭϋⱭιρƇ Ⱥιρ, nⱭ é Ƥéιn ϋo ƇⱭϋⱭιρƇ Ⱥιnme Ⱥn ϋιƇeⱭṁnⱭιʒ Ⱥρ ϋυιne éιʒιn eιιe (S. 166).

PH. 92. " Apair-siu tor mor do chrannaib DO DÉNUM co ndech-sa ind."

Exercise LVI.

(Verbal Noun in Passive Sense.)

1° If thou be the Son of God command that these stones be made bread.

2°. It is expedient for thee that one of thy members should perish rather than thy whole body be cast into hell.

3°. Take heed *that ye do not*[1] *your justice*[2] before men to be seen by them ; otherwise you shall not have a reward of your Father who is in Heaven.

4°. Gather up first *the cockle*[3] and bind it into bundles to burn, but the wheat *gather ye*[4] into my barn.

5°. *For*[5] them that sat with him at table he commanded it to be given to her.

6°. From that time Jesus began to shew to His disciples,

1. Ⱥʒυρ nⱭ . . .   2. ϋυρ ϋρíoρⱭonƇⱭċċ-ρⱭ.   3. Ⱥn coʒⱭι.
4. Use ϋeιnιϋ . .   5. Ⱥρ ρon . . .

that HE[1] must go to Jerusalem, and suffer many things from the ancients and scribes and chief priests, and be put to death, and the third day rise again.

7°. It is better for thee to go into life *maimed*[2] or *lame*[3] than having two hands or two feet to be cast into everlasting fire.

8°. His lord commanded that he should be sold, and his wife and children, and all that he had, and payment to be made.

9°. He commanded that something should be given her to eat.

10°. It were better for him that *a mill-stone*[4] were hanged about his neck and he were cast into the sea.

11°. When he understood from the centurion that Jesus had died he ordered the body to be given to Joseph.

12°. If the householder knew at what hour the thief would come he would surely watch and not suffer his house to be broken open.

---

1. é péin.   2. ar leat-láiṁ.   3. ar leat coir.   4. bró ṁuilinn.

CHAPTER V.

(Partitive de.)

The partitive uses of the preposition de are important. They occur chiefly:—

1º. After adjectives or nouns of magnitude, multitude, intensity, description, etc.

(a) Ní beag de feo an rgeon do cuireadair ra leanb ro (S. 26).

(b) Ir {fial / umal} rciall de leatar duine eile (Proverb).

(c) Ní beag liom de fult beit gá cup i bfeirg, ⁊ annran gá maolú (TBC. 5).

(d) Gan a faid rin de luigeacán na bliadna orc! (S. 97).

(e) Ar úféidir go mbead ré de mí-fortiún air go rruiocrad an t-áirreoir é, ⁊ go ndéanfad ré a leitéid de gníom? (N. 199). Cf. a malairc rin de rgéal.

(f) Toirg go mbead a dóitin de cúram do gac soinne n-a cár féin (Im. 50).

(g) Ir fearr leir rúd órlac dá toil féin aige ná bannláṁ d'á lear (Proverb).

(h) MSF.—60.—Tá ré cóṁ bunadrac cóṁ creideaṁnac d'fear ⁊ atá le fagáil ra bapúntact.

2º. After proleptic a, ré, ro; and after ran proleptic (or otherwise)—

(a) Da ṁait an rgéal a beit de tubairte uirti é gá pórad (S. 112).

(b) Ní raib ré d'uain aige a tuille do rád (S. 88).

(c) Beid ran de marla ⁊ de guit ar a gclú ⁊ ar a

STUDIES IN MODERN IRISH 155

gcáil an vá lá ir an faio a beiò grian ar rréir
7 vaoine ar talam (N. 320).
(d) Tá SO ve veirrigeact eatorta . . .

3° After a negative (or gan) with ac (= English " any "
with negative, or " the only ")—
(a) ní feicim féin o'uairleact in a lán acu ac
mórcúir 7 votigear 7 tarcuirne (S. 60).
(b) ir truag gan an rgéal mar reo agat . . . 7
gan ve toil agat ac mo toil-re (Im. 166).
(c) ní tarrann ré ve luact raotair ná ve tuar-
aroal ar a veag-oibreaca ac Dia féin (5. 215).

4°. *Before* the compound relative. (These cases can generally be brought under one of the other headings):
(a) an té ir breagta v'á breacaiò rúil vuine
ruam ar an raogal ro (S. 61).
(b) an fear ir fearr v'á raib ann.

5°. *After* the compound relative :— (Cf. 1°)
(a) veir Diarmuid nac beag ve feo a bruil v'ór
7 v'airgeav 7 ve faiòòrear aige (S. 130).
(b) tréir ar cugamair ve gráò 7 ve cion 7
v'annract vá céile (TBC. 165).

6°. After comparatives. (Can generally be brought under
one of other headings):—
(a) an Donn Cuailgne ir ainm vó, 7 ir fearr ve
tarb é ná an finnbeannac (TBC. 8).
(b) veir ré . . gurb fearr ve rígnear ran ná
aon rígnear a curri orta le mion-coimeargan
ó veag-buiòniò (TBC. 123).
c) ba meara ve vuine mé ag teact uata vom
(Im. 36).

7°. By a sort of inversion the noun of description comes *after* ᴅe :—
TBC. 94.—Ná cuptap teaccaipe cúgam-ra le **coṁa** ᴅe'n tragar ran aipir.
Notice that if ragar comes first the genitive is more usual after it than partitive ᴅe. But we say a leitéiᴅ rin ᴅe cóṁa, *not* cóṁa ᴅá leitéiᴅ rin.

Exercise LVII.

Partitive ᴅe.

1°. There one hour of suffering will be more sharp than a hundred years here *spent in*[1] the most rigid penance.
2°. Give it not over until thou receivest some *crumb*[2] or drop of divine grace.
3°. He was looking at me so fixedly with his two eyes that *a certain*[3] inexpressible terror came upon me.
4° People say that the barony of Cooley is *wonderfully*[4] prosperous.
5°. He saw a houseful of dark little folk around him.
6°. Our *natural reason*[5] understands the difference between good and evil, but is not strong enough *to fulfil*[6] all it approves.
7°. Who am I that I should *dare*[7] to speak to thee?
8°. He is so wanting in intelligence that he has not come yet to speak to you—or to me—about the marriage.
9°. Before he had time to write the letter his friend arrived.
10°. He was the only person who had sufficient courage to come towards them and speak to them.

1. Use ᴅe.   2. míp beag.   3. 1appact ᴅe . . .   4. Use a partitive ᴅe phrase.   5. Ciall ᴅaonna.   6. beapt a ᴅéanaṁ ᴅo péiṅ . . .   7. Use ᴅánact.

Exercise LVIII.
(The Same.)

1°. Let us not suffer our glory to be tarnished by flying from *the standard*[1] of the cross.
2°. Never have any other aim but this—that thou please Me alone.
3°. It is good for nothing anymore but to be cast out and trodden on by men.
4°. A sign shall not be given them but the sign of Jonas the prophet.
5°. Everytime I have gone amongst men I have been a worse man on my return.
6°. Not on bread alone doth man live, but on every word that cometh from the mouth of God.
7°. For every idle word that men shall speak they shall render an account for it in the day of judgment.
8°. Then shall contempt of riches weigh more than all the treasures of *wordlings*.[2]
9°. And Jesus went into the Temple of God and cast out all them that sold and bought in the Temple.
10°. The humble knowledge of thyself is a surer way to God than the deepest search after science.

Exercise LIX.
(The Same.)

1°. Wouldn't it have been a much greater pity to marry them *considering*[3] the *circumstances*.[4]
2°. It is a greater *struggle*[5] to resist *vice*[6] and *passions*[7] than to *toil at bodily*[8] labours.

---

1. Omit. 2. Lucht ṗaoġaltaċta. 3. Aġur. 4. An rġéal . . .
5. Ġníoṁ. 6. Droċ-ṁian. 7. Dubáilcí. 8. Allur a cur díoc . . .

3°. It were more *just*[1] that thou shouldst *accuse*[2] thyself and *excuse*[3] thy brother.
4°. Is not this a greater *loss*[4] than if thou wert to lose the whole world?
5°. I consider Irish a much more precise and more melodious language than English.
6°. There is no other way to God than that of earnest prayer and patient suffering.
7°. The *tale bearer*[5] is a worse sort of person than the liar.
8°. I was so situated that my only *way of egress*[6] from the cave was to fall into the sea.
9°. I thought that more wonderful than all the wonderful tales I ever heard.
10°. This business, for badness, has beaten all previous records.

CHAPTER VI.

Noun Phrases.

When two nouns (one of which may or may not be verbal), a pronoun and a noun, or some other combination, are closely united in meaning in a phrase, the first element (or the second, if it be an adjective ; see Ex. 14°, p. 159) sometimes resists inflection (gen. voc. or dat.) when a governing word precedes. This may be called—

A.—The Bracketed Construction.

On the other hand, the phrase does not always preserve its unity in this way, but the first element submits to government. This we may call—

B.—The Un-bracketed Construction.

---

1. Ceapc. 2. Daopaḋ. 3. Saopaḋ. 4. Donap 5. Ciúrsalóip.
6. Seipc ap úul amaċ.

STUDIES IN MODERN IRISH 159

A thir1 kind of noun-phrase consists of—
   C.—Nouns used adverbially without prepositions.
A.—The Bracketed Construction :—
1°. D'aipigeaṗ ḋuine ġá páḋ . ꜱo paiḃ a ḋó 7 ḋá
   ċuiṗciún aꜱ (bean an táḃaiṗne) aiṗ (S. 16).
2°. Fuaiṗ ṗé an ṗṗápán 7 ceaḋ (capanꜱ aṗ) (S. 20).
3°. Coiṗꜱ (an paiḋḃpeaṗ ꜱo léiṗ a ḃeiċ aiꜱe) (ꜱ. 4).
4°. Ó, a íoṗa, a (ṗoluṗ na ꜱlóiṗe ṗíopuiḋe), a (ṗóláṗ anma
   an ḋeopaiḋe) ní ṗéaḋann mo ḃéal laḃaiṗc leac
   (Im. 141).
5°. Ó, a Ḋia, a (ṗuaipceaṗ ꜱan ceopa) (Im. 153).
6°. A Ċiꜱeaṗna íoṗa, a (ṗoluṗ an cpoluiṗ ṗíopuiḋe) (Im.
   153).
7°. A (páláṗ aoiḃinn na caċaṗaċ ċuaṗ) ! (Im. 195).
8°. 1 ꜱcaiċeaṁ (oipeaḋ aꜱuṗ aon lá aṁáin) (Im. 118).
9°. ꜱeallaim ḋuic ná ṗuil aon lopꜱ aꜱam aṗ (i ṗeiṗcinc)
   aiṗíṗ (S. 204). Here where the first element is a
   pronoun (not gen.) preceded by a prep. governing
   the dative, the unbracketed construction is impossible.
10°. Ḃí an cpiúp píoꜱan aṁuiċ annpan 7 a caoꜱaḋ ban
   coiṁḋeaċca 1 ḃṗoċaiṗ (ꜱaċ píoꜱan ḋíoḃ).
11°. Ḋuḃaiṗc ṗé le (ꜱaċ bean ḋíoḃ) peaṗaṁ aṁuiċ aṗ aꜱaiḋ
   na ṗuinneoiꜱe n-a paiḃ a ṗeaṗ ṗéin laiṗciꜱ ḋe (Ḋṗ.
   21).
12°. Cun (an c-aoinne aṁáin pin ḋo ċup ċun cinn) (MSF. 68).
13°. Cun (cuṗaċ a ċaḃaiṗc ḋóiḃ) aṗ an ḃṗuaṗꜱailc (Ser. 171).
14°. Amḃaṗa cá, coṗaċ aꜱac opċa ꜱo léiṗ aċ aṗ (Ṡile ḃeaꜱ)
   (S. 18).
15°. Ċuaiḋ ṗé amaċ aiṗíṗ cimpal (an cṗímaḋ h-uaiṗ) (ĊS. 55).
16° Ċun (aon ullaṁuꜱaḋ ḋéanaṁ) (Ser. 2).
17°. Cá pí aꜱ ṗeiċeaṁ le (clann an uilc) (Ser. 87).

B.—The Un-bracketed Construction :—
1°. Tréir ʋiablaiʋeaċċa éiȝin a ʋéanaṁ orca ċuȝ ré ċúiċi irceaċ iaʋ (S. 16).
2°. Nuair a ċáiniȝ rí ar a ȝlúiniʋ ċun na braiʋreaċa ʋo ráʋ (S. 68).
3°. le linn na cainnce rin ʋo ráʋ ʋó ʋ'ṗéaċ ré ar ṁicil (S. 74).

Sometimes we find A. and B. combined in the same sentence :
1°. n. 7.—ʋioʋar créir na manaċ ʋo ʋíbirc aȝur (iaʋ réin a ʋainȝniú ann).
2° Ȝ. 2.—aʋ'iarraiʋ na n-aoir ʋo ṗeaċainc 7 aʋ' iarraiʋ (an molaʋ ʋo ċuilleaṁ).

C.—Nouns used adverbially without a preposition :—
1°. ar ċáiniȝ ȝaċ rí an líon a ȝeallaʋ? (TBC. 37).
2° nil rí acu nár ċáiniȝ breis 7 líon a ċríoċa céaʋ.
This could be explained as a *genitive relative* clause : " there's not a king more than the complement OF WHOSE CANTRED has not come." But more probably " breir 7 líon " are used adverbially, and the sentence means : " Not a king of them but has come WITH more than the complement of his cantred."
3° cá an leaċ-rȝéal ran ró-ċaol iarraċċ (TBC. 188).
4° cá an cráċnóna buille beaȝ ȝlar ann réin.
5° cá ré pas beaȝ ruar.
6° Cearaim naċ roláir nó bíor ar ma ṁeaʋair ruʋ éiȝin (S. 105).

Exercise LX.
(Phrase Nouns) A.—Bracketed Construction.
1°. After a little while he stopped coming.
2°. He gathered from her substantial knowledge of the whole business from beginning to end.

3°. It's an extraordinary thing that one couldn't leave home for a short space of time but you must go and get sick.
4°. But Jesus did not trust Himself unto them for that He knew all men.
5°. This shield was depriving Aodh Fionn of his night's sleep.
6°. He told *each of the women*[1] to stand outside opposite the window inside which her husband was.
7°. There's not the slightest possibility of my doing it as quickly as you think it can be done.
8°. I have heard people saying that he owes the lady of the hotel *about*[2] £200.
9°. The doctor told him to eat as much as he could, and gave him permission to get fat as fast as he liked.
10°. Because he has all that money he imagines he can do as he pleases.

Exercise LXI.
(B.—The Unbracketed Construction.)

1°. While saying these words he began to tremble hand and foot.
2°. I must not be depending on one of these little apples to relieve my thirst.
3°. His mother told him what Séadna had said while giving her the money.
4°. However this business *turns out*[3] there's an *end to*[4] Sadhbh's talk as to her having a claim on Séadna.
5°. It was no human being that took the mantle from you but a briar caught it *just as*[5] the hound dragged you after her.

1. Ṡaċ bean ḋíoḃ.   2. Suap le.   3. Ḋeipe . . . ap.
4. Ḋeipe le . . .   5. Ḋípeaċ le linn . . .

6°. This I consider is the best way to do that work.
7°. He attempted in every possible way to condemn this man to death.
8°. She likes to know with what complement each royal leader has come.
9°. The cold had gripped me—just a little bit—and I was afraid of the fever.
10°. They had just expelled the enemy out of the country and settled themselves and their partisans on the lands vacated by them.

CHAPTER VII.
Prepositional Phrases.—Section I.

These may be either—
- A.—Substantival.
- B.—Adverbial.
- C.—Adjectival.

A.—Substantival. A substantival prepositional phrase may be either Nom., Gen., Dat or Accus.

1°. NOM.—S. 19.—Níorb fiú ouic gan fanṁaint liom. Here the prepositional phrase is subject to the verb bá.

Madh áil let *gan beith a péin* (Poem ascribed to Colum Cille, Ed. Kuno Meyer, Ériu IV. 17).

2°. GEN.—Ar feaḋ a bfaḋ; tréir a bfaḋ; 50 ceann a bfaḋ; toirg (gan iaḋ a beiṫ ann) (C.S. 5). Cun (gan é ḋéanaṁ) MSF. 137.

3°. DAT.—S. 130.—Deir Diarmuiḋ ... gur aníor ó (in aice an baile móir in áit éigin) é. C.S. 251.—Táimre ann ó (roiṁ Ábraham a beiṫ ann). MSF. 159.—Bí cúir eile agam le (gan an rcoil ḋo caiṫeaṁ ċuige).

4°. ACCUS.—Dubairt ré liom (gan fanṁaint a ċuille leir). D'órouig ré ḋom (gan ḋul a baile).

B.—Adverbial. Dubairt ré liom, gan fanṁaint le freagra uaim, nár ṁirḋe ḋom imṫeaċt láiṫreaċ (Contrast A. 4°).
Le neart buile ḋo ḋein ré é.
Bí ré ar meirge; rin é a bí inḋán ḋuit, etc.

C.—Adjectival.
> Ⅎeaṗ gan ṁaiṫ iʁ eaḋ é.
> Duine le Dia iʁ eaḋ é.
> Ⅎeaʁ ʁé leiṫ ᴘiaṁ é.
> Duine aᴘ leaṫ-ʁúil.
> Maċ do Ċaḋg iʁ eaḋ é.
> Leaḃaʁ liompa é.
> A ċlú do leiṫ eolasa is eagna
> (KH. II. 14).

But care must be taken here. One mustn't say, e.g., do ċuiʁ an ċainnt sa leitiʁ feaʁg oʁm, but "an·ċainnt a ḃí ʁa leiciʁ (making the phrase *adverbial*). So, *not*—do ʁgʁíoḃaʁ ċun fiʁ ionaid an Rí imḃ'láṫ Cuiaṫ, ga ʁáḋ leiʁ ciall a ḃeiṫ aige, *but*—aċá imḃ'láṫ Cuiaṫ. The *adverbial* sense clings more naturally. Sometimes apparently adjectival uses border on the adverbial :—

> S. 28. Sídí annʁo aʁ an dcaoḃ ṫiaʁ ḃíompa í.
>
> Sg. 118. An é ʁin an ʁagaʁṫ úd a noċt an t-éiṫead i ndiaiḋ an doċtúʁa?

When the *noun* which the prepositional phrase qualifies is *verbal* the adjectival use fades into the adverbial :—

> CS 3.—An ṫeiṫe ċun na h-éigiʁṫe.
>
> g. 77.—Ní ʁaiḃ iḃʁad ṫʁéiʁ na cainnṫe ʁin idiʁ an ṁáṫaiʁ ⁊ an ingean go dtí guʁ ḃaineaḋ geiṫ . . . aʁ a ʁaiḃ idṫig na Ṫʁom-ḋáiṁe.

Sometimes, outside the stock phrases mentioned above, the use is clearly adjectival :—

> S. 73.—Ċeap Miċil ná feacaiḋ ʁé eigʁe ʁiaṁ aċ é aʁ ċeann na caillige ʁa ʁgéal fiannaiḋeaċta.
>
> n. 120.—Aʁ gaċ áiʁd i gcian iʁ igċóṁgaʁ.

Exercise LXIII.

(Prepositional Phrases.)

1°. It is great wisdom not to be *rash*[1] in our doings, nor to *maintain*[2] too obstinately our own opinion.
2°. A *pure spirit*[3] tries to be free from all *self-seeking*[4] in the works which he does.
3°. T. Manlius Torquatus ordered his son to be put to death, because he had fought with the enemy contrary to orders received.
4°. I wrote to my friend in Cork asking him to visit me *the day after*[5] the fair.
5°. I don't very much like the stories in this book.
6°. The people in these districts don't seem to take very much interest in Irish.
7°. I promised to write to Diarmuid in Dublin giving him an account of those queer things in the letter from my friend in Belfast.
8°. The language in the letter disturbed me not a little.
9°. In the king's place I should certainly have ordered them *off the premises*[6] at once.
10°. The account of the murder in the papers was *not exactly*[7] misleading, still on reading it one would have been inclined to say it was no murder at all.

Prepositions.
Section II.

The meanings of the Irish prepositions must be studied very carefully. To aid the student we give here some of the

---

1. Ró-obann.   2. Seapam.   3. An té go mbíonn an aigne glan aige.   4. Use cperoeamaint.   5. Lá 'p na bápac tpéip . .
6. Cup cun piúbail . . .   7. Ní hamlaro . . .

more important usages—
- I. *Before* Nouns.
- II. *After* Nouns and Adjectives.
- III. After *Verbs*.

I. Prepositions *before* Nouns.

(a) The preposition ar :—

1°. Frequently modal,—to denote state or condition : ar reacrán, ar meirge, ar buile, ar crocad, ar rilead, ar deiġilt (separated).
ar boġad (loose), ar mire, ar díbirt, ar tarang (drawn), ar ionntaoib,
ar eaglă, ar ránaideact aigne (in a state of distraction), ar rtaid na ngrárt, ar rodar.

2° Of time :—ar ball, ar dtúir, ar uairib, ar an neomat, ar a ré a clog, ar teact a baile dó.

3°. Of place :—ar torac, ar deire, ar aġaid (opposite), ar an raoġal ro, ar lár, ar muir, ar tír.

4° Of the part affected (cf. 3°) :—ar cluair, ar rġórnaiġ, ar láim, ar coir, do rug ré ar cluair orm.

5°. To denote the *passive*, with verbal nouns :—ar labairt, ar raġáil.

6°. †In respect of, causal.—ar áilneact, ar feabar, ar a olcar liom, ar aoibnear. Do cinn r' ar mnáib a cóm-aimrire **ar áilneact ┐ ar breaġtact**.

7°. Of measurement :—ar faid, ar leitead, ar doimne, ar aoirde.

† But le is preferred when ar follows in another sense :—do buaid ré le h-olcar AR an sceol ba meara dár airiġear ruam (Cl. 5).

STUDIES IN MODERN IRISH 167

8°. Dependent upon :—ᴀɼ ƀeᴀᵹᴀ́ɴ ꝼᴀᵹᴀ́ʟᴛᴀɪɼ, ᴀɼ ʟeᴀᴛ-ʟᴀ́ɪᵯ, ᴀɼ ʟeᴀᴛ-ꝼúɪʟ, ᴀɼ ɼoɴ Ɗé.

9° Of price :—ᴀɼ ċéᴀᴅ púɴᴛ, ᴀɼ ɼᵹɪʟʟɪɴᵹ.
Ɗo ƀɪúʟᴛᴜɪᵹ ɼé mé ᴀɼ ᴘɪɴᵹɪɴɴ.

10°. Miscellaneous :—Nᴀ́ ᴄᴜɪɼ ᴄᴀoɪ ᴀɼ ᴄᴀ́ɪɼᴅe ; ᴅo ċᴜɪɼeᴀɼ ᴀɼ ċᴜmᴀɪɴċe ɴᴀ Mᴀɪᵹᴅɪɴe Mᴜɪɼe é ; ɴíʟ ᴀɼ ċᴜmᴜɼ ᴅom é ᴅéᴀɴᴀᵯ.

11°. Of feelings, burdens, etc. (cf. 3°) :—Ꞇᴀ́ ᴀ́ᴛᴀɼ, eᴀᵹʟᴀ, ƀɼóɴ oɼm. Ċᴀᴅ ᴛᴀ́ oɼᴛ? Ƀí ɼé ᴅe ċɼᴀɴɴ oɼm ..

(b) The preposition ᴀɼ :—

1°. Modal :—Ⱥɼ eᴀᵹᴀɼ (disorderly), ᴀɼ ɪoɴᴀᴅ (dislocated), ᴀɼ ᴀ ċéɪʟe (asunder), ᴀɼ ɼeɪʟƀ (evicted).

2°. Temporal :—Ⱥɼ ᴀ ɴ-ᴀɪᴛʟe, ᴀɼ ɼo ᴀmᴀċ, ᴀɼ ɼᴀɴ ᴀmᴀċ.

3°. Local :—Ⱥɼ ɼo ᵹo Ċoɴᴄᴀɪᵹ ; ᴀɼ ᴀɴ mƀoɼᴄᴀ.

4°. Various :—Ⱥɼ ᴀ ᴀɪɴm (by an abusive name).

5°. Cause or origin :—Ⱥ ꝼeɪɼᵹ ᴀ ƀeɪɴ ɼé é. Nᴀ́ ƀí ᴀᵹ mᴀoɪᴅeᴀᵯ ᴀɼ ᴅo ᵯᴀɪᴛeᴀɼ.

(c) The preposition ċᴜm :—

1°. The end or purpose, the result ; (generally after verbs of motion, *metaphorical* or otherwise) :—
Ċᴜm ᴄɪɴɴ, ċᴜm ᴛoɼᴀɪᵹ, ċᴜm ᴅeɪɼe, ċᴜm ɼᴜɪme, ċᴜm ᴛᴀɪɼƀe, ċᴜm ᴄɼíċe (Rᴀᵹᴀɪᴅ ɼé ċᴜm ᴄɼíċe ᴅᴜɪᴛ = it will turn out to your advantage), ċᴜm ᵹʟóɪɼe Ɗé, ċᴜm oɴóɼᴀ ɴᴀ ɴÉɪɼeᴀɴɴ. So with conjunction before verbs.

2°. Local :—Ċᴜm ᴀɴ ᴛoƀᴀɪɼ, ċᴜm ɴᴀ ɴ-Éɪᵹɪɼᴛe.

3°. Temporal :—Ċᴜm ɴᴀ ƀeᴀʟᴛᴀɪɴe ; ċᴜm ᵹo ᴅᴛɪoᴄꝼᴀᴅ ɼé.

4°. The use with abl. of accompaniment in ᵹo ɴ-ɪomᴀᴅ ɼéᴀᴅ is confined to poetry.

(d) The preposition Do :—
  1º. Of purpose (generally after verbs of motion) :—
      Dúr (< do ḟıuṟṟ) = for the purpose of finding
      out ; ḋ'ḟeaċaınṫ = to see. (In W. Munster
      the preposition in this phrase is now dispensed
      with, ḟeaċaınṫ being used absolutely). Also
      in vb. n. phrases :—ṟgeal do ṫuıṟgınṫ, obaıṟ
      do ḋeanaṁ, etc.
  2º. Causal (frequently with confusion of de and do).
      De (do) ḋeoın ; doṫ' aıṁḋeoın ; dom' ḋóıg ;
      do péıṟ. (Cf. L. Secundum).
  3º. Temporal :—Do gnáṫ, de (do) ṟıoṟ. (The ac-
      companying word generally refers to time).
  4º. Motion towards ; (cf. 1º) :—Do'n ṫobaṟ. (Almost
      obsolete in Munster, go, go ḋṫí, ċum and
      various prepositional phrases now taking its
      place).
  5º. To denote the agent, with verbal nouns :—Aṟ
      ṫeaċṫ a ḃaıle ḋom. (Cf. L. pugnandum est
      nobis) ag ṫaḃaıṟṫ an aıṟgıd dı Ḋó.
  6º. Possessive :—Cad ıṟ aınm ḋuıṫ ?

(e) The preposition de :—
  1º. Origin or cause :—(Cf. proleptic de with com-
      paratives). D'eagla [with eagla, de empha-
      sises the CAUSE ; te the accompanying circum-
      stances, aṟ the state of the agent]. De ṁéıḋ
      (out of), de ḃaṟṟ (as a result of), de ḋṟuım.
      De ḋeaṟgaıḃ (mostly of evil), de ḃṟíg ; céṟ'
      ḃıoḋ ṫu ?
  2º. Temporal :—De ló ıṟ d'oıḋċe.
  3º. Of the material (as distinct from instrument) :
      lán d'uıṟge ; do líon ṟé an coṟċán d'uıṟge

STUDIES IN MODERN IRISH   169

do líon ré an copcán le cupán. Do deineaḋ
ragarc de; do dein licíní pinne de.
4°. Local :—Do léim ré anuar de'n capall.
5°. Partitive :—Cuid díoḃ, dpaon d'uirge na laoi
    etc.

(f) The preposition in :—
    1°. Modal (of state or condition) :—i gcóir; i gceart;
        (also ra ceart, and n-a ceart, = alright).
        I n dán do; in-aċrann in (entangled with);
        in-aimrir (in service—cf. caitin aimrire);
        in-eagar; 'n-a cuir a táinig ré (MSF. 179).
    2°. Local :—Imearg; i leit; i gcoinne; iḃpocair;
        iḃpiadnaire; in-agaiḋ; ingar; iḃpogur; iḃpad
    3°. Temporal :—i gcionn; ra deire; in-aon uair a
        cluig amáin;
    4°. Purpose, result :—i rocar, i lear, rocairḃe,
        i roilear. Ragaiḋ ré rocairḃe duic luac nó
        mall.
    5°. Comparative with ḋul, etc. :—ḋul inaoir;
        i ḃpeaḃar, i ḃpuaire, roceo, i dcanaiḋeacc,
        i gcocuigceacc, i ndánaiḋeacc, etc. Strictly
        speaking tá ré ag ḋul i ḃpuaire = it is getting
        COLDER; tá ré ag éirge fuar = it is getting
        COLD. Cf. 4°.

(g) The preposition le :—
    1°. Local :—le hair, le coir, leir an ḃralla (on the
        wall, of things HANGING), leir an aill (over
        the cliff, of anything FALLING, or HANGING).
    2°. Temporal :—le fada, le gairid, le déiḋeannaige,
        le mí, le linn.
    3°. Cause, or accompanying circumstances :—led'

STUDIES IN MODERN IRISH

toil, le toil a céile, le neapc peipse; tasann mait le cáipve; le h-easla.

4°. Instrumental :—le rcin, le peann, le cloideam, le lám-láidir.

5°. Object, result :—le puact 7 le pán; le pilidcact, le h-asaid.

6°. To denote the *passive* with transitive verbal :—
le pasáil, le déanam.

7°. To denote purpose or futurity with noun of intransitive verb :—le teact, le dul a baile, etc.

8°. With adjectives denoting likeness (and analogically) unlikeness, instead of O.I. ppi :—Copmail le, etc.

9°. With nouns and verbs of addressing, listening (for older ppi) :—Labaip le, éipteact le.

10°. Ownership : subjectivity :—Ip liompa é. Ip dóig liom ná tiocpaid ré.

In reference to (2°) above notice the difference in meaning between—

Táim annro le reactmain ; díor ann le reactmain nuaip a táinis reir an

D'panar ann ap pead reactmaine

Panpad ann 50 ceann reactmaine eile.

I pit na reactmaine dead as iarsac.

Rasad a baile i scionn na reactmaine pin.

Asur tiocpad tar n-ar tréip reactmain a caiteam ra baile.

In le reactmain we are looking back upon the period *just* spent.

In ap pead reactmaine we are looking back upon or forward to a period, but not in connection with the present moment =

for the space of a week. There is frequently the same relation between ar feaó and 50 ceann as there is between tréir and 1ycionn.

50 ceann reaccṁaine = "*for* a week," looked at from the beginning.

1 ycionn reaccṁaine = "*after* a week," looked at from the beginning.

Tréir reaccṁaine = "*after* a week," looked at from the end.

Iric, or 1 ycaiceaṁ na reaccṁaine means in the course of the week, during the week.

The earlier use of "te" to denote the agent with passive verbs is to be discountenanced in modern Irish. In W. Munster it is never used by good writers and speakers; "te" is best reserved to express the "*instrument*."

(*h*) The prep. ó :—
    1°. Local separation :—Ó Corcaiġ 50 b'lát Cliat.
    2°. Temporal separation :—Ó roin ; rao ó ; ó aimrir Páoraiy 1 leit.
    3°. Agent (with passive) :—Do hoironiġeaó ó Óia é (developed from 1°).
    4°. In general, the origin, cause ; motive of an action : (developed from 1°).

Tuġann ré uaió a lán airġio ġac bliaóain.
Ón iomao óúil in airġeao ir eaó táġann an t-aiṁlear 50 minic.

(*i*) The preposition mar :—
    Chiefly in such phrases as—mar ġeall ar ; mar báfr ar ġac noonar.

(*l*) The preposition ór (mostly pronounced ar, except in ór áro, ór freal) :—

In ór cómair, ór áru, ór íreal, ór cionn, etc.

(m) The preposition ré :—

1°. Of motion :—rén ocuaic; ré'n scnoc ruar. Cf. L. sub, Sansk. úpa.

2°. Of time :—ré maroin (before morning); ré látair (at present).

3°. Of place :—Amuis rén rpéir; ré luise na sréine.

4°. Modal :—ré féan, ré fonar, ré brón, ré brácas an donair, ré slar (cf. 3°).

5°. Special :—Cá'n sorc ré prácaí; cuirim ré suide an pobuil (pray publicly for). Fosa do tabairc ré (to attack). Cuireab ré sráb rasairc mé (MSF 106).

6°. Partitive :—San a cúis ficib rén scéab locáirte b'rasáil uairb (MSF. 167).

7°. Multiplicative :—Ré dó, ré trí, etc.

8°. Causal :—Cad rár crutais Dia rinn?

(n) The preposition ran (formed from ar reab na, ar reab an) :—

1°. Of time :—Ran na naimrire.

2°. Of place :—Ran an ralla, ran an úrláir, ran bótair. Sometimes with accus. of pronoun :—lab as sluairreáct ran é (MSF. 88).

(o) The preposition um :—

1°. Of time :—Um Nodlais, um trátnóna.

2°. Causal :—Uime rin.

3° Local :—Cuir ré uime a cuid éadais.

STUDIES IN MODERN IRISH 173

II. Prepositions after Nouns and Adjectives :—

1°. **Aiṗeaċ** aṗ—Im. 36. Níoṗ ḟág ṗan iad gan ḃeiṫ . . . .
   go h-ana-aiṗeaċ oṗṫa ṗéin.
   Also **aiṗeaċ do**. Aiṗe do : Ṫaḃaiṗ aiṗe dod' gnó ṗéin.
   Aiṫne ag . . . aṗ : tá aiṫne maiṫ agam aiṗ.

2°. **Ḃṗíġ, ciall, míniú** ṫe ; ḃṗíġ ṫeiṗ, the *meaning*, force of it.
   Ciall ṫeiṗ —the *sense* of it ; míniú ṫeiṗ, the interpretation of it.
   Ḃeag ṫe . . . do (with the usual distinction between the subjective (ṫe) and the objective (do) : Ní ḃeag liom dóiḃ é.
   Ní ḃeag liom de. Ní ḃeag duiṫ ṗan.
   Ḃṗeiṫ aṗ : Níoṗ ṗéadaṗ ḃṗeiṫ aiṗ (overtake).
         Níl aon ḃṗeiṫ agam aiṗ (it is quite impossible for me).
   Ḃáiġ ag . . . . ṫe : tá ana-ḃáiġ agam ṫeaṫ (love, sympathy).
   Ḃaiḋeaṁail aṗ, ṫe : Iṗ ḃaiḋeaṁail aṗ a ċéile ṫuċt aon-ċeiṗde.
   Ḃuiḋeaċ de = thankful to ; ḃuiḋeaċaṗ ṫe Dia = Deo gratias.
   Mo ḃuiḋeaċaṗ do ġaḃáil ṫe = to express my thanks to . . . a ḃuiḋe ṫe . . . thanks to . . . that . . . .
   Ḃeann ag . . . aṗ : Níl aon ḃeann agam oṗt.
   Ḃuiḋe (from which ḃuiḋeaċ is derived) means originally good-will. (Cf. Gk. πυ-ν-θάνομαι; π because of θ (Grassman's Law). Cf. tá gaċ aoinne ḃuiḋeaċ dem he's very popular.

3°. **Caoi** ag . . . aṗ : . . . ċum : Ní ṗaiḃ an ċaoi aga:

cuige (I hadn't the opportunity). Ní ṗaiḃ aon ċaoi agam aṙ é ḋéanaṁ.

"Aṙ" is of course preferred when cum is required to introduce a purpose afterwards :—Caoi ḋ'ḟaġáil AR é ḋéanaṁ, CUM ḋo a ċuṙ ó ċéile.

Cóiṙ cum . . ; cion ag . . . aṙ : tá ana-ċion agam oṙt.—ceanaṁail aṙ . . .

Coinne ag . . . le : ní ṗaiḃ aon ċoinne agam leiṙ.

1gcomóṙtaṙ le : compared with. (So 1gcompaṙáiḋ le).

4°. **Dóiċ** le . . . aṙ : níoṙ ḋóiċ leat aiṙ go ḃḟuil aon tṙaiḋḃṙeaṙ in aon ċoṙ aige.

Dúil ag . . . in : níl aon ḋúil agam ann. Dúilṁaṙ i ṗuḋ.

Deiṙe le, aṙ : pé ḋeiṙe ḃeiḋ AR an ngnó ṙo, tá ḋeiṙe le cainnt Saḋḃ. Whatever the *upshot* of this business may be, *there's an end to* Sadhbh's talk.

5°. **Éaḋ** aṙ . . . cun.—Ní ceaṙt ḋuit éaḋ a ḃeit oṙt cuige.

Eagla ag, aṙ . . . ṙoiṁ.—Níl aon eagla oṙm ṙoimiṙ anoiṙ, aċ táinig iaṙṙaċtin ḋ'eagla agam ṙoimiṙ an uaiṙ úḋ.

In such cases ag, as distinct from aṙ, generally implies that the feeling is more or less voluntary.

Eolaṙ ag . . . aṙ : níl aon eolaṙ agam aṙ an ngaeḋilg.

6°. **Foṙmaḋ** le :—ná bí ag foṙmaḋ leiṙ.

Fuaċ ag . . . ḋó :—táinig fuaċ agam ḋó.

Faġáil aṙ :—níl aon faġáil agat aṙ é ḋéanaṁ.

Feaṙg ag, aṙ . . . cun :—bí feaṙg oṙm cuige ; táinig feaṙg agam cuige. Also—bíoṙ iḃfeiṙg cuige.

STUDIES IN MODERN IRISH 175

Fonn, ꜰʟᴏʀꜱ ᴀʀ . . . ċum :—ḃí ꜰonn ⁊ ꜰʟᴏʀꜱ oʀm ċum ᴀn ḃíᴅ.

Follᴀṁ ó :—ᴛá ᴀn áɪᴛ ꜰoʟʟᴀṁ ó ᴅᴀoɪnɪḃ ʟe ꜰᴀᴅᴀ.

Fᴀɪʟʟɪġe ᴀ ᴛᴀḃᴀɪʀᴛ ɪ . . . ᴛuꜱ ʀé ꜰᴀɪʟʟɪġe ᴀnn : ḃí ʀé ꜰᴀɪʟʟɪġᴛeᴀċ ᴀnn.

7° Gráḋ ᴀꜱ . . ᴅo :—ḃíoḋ ꜱʀáḋ ᴀꜱᴀᴛ ᴅo Ḋɪᴀ nᴀ ꜱʟóɪʀe ; ᴛɪocꜰᴀɪḋ ꜱʀáḋ ᴀꜱᴀᴛ ᴅó (Im. 38). But ḃí ʀé ɪ nꜱʀáḋ ʟéɪ.

Gráɪn ᴀꜱ . . ᴀʀ :—ᴛá ꜱʀáɪn ᴀꜱᴀm ᴀɪʀ.

Gáḋ ᴀꜱ . . . ʟe :—níʟ ᴀon ġáḋ ᴀꜱᴀm ʟeɪʀ. But with ɪʀ—ní ꜱáḋ ḃuɪᴛ é. ᴛá ʀé nᴀ ġáḋᴛᴀʀ ꜱo móʀ = He is in great need of it.

Gᴀɪʀɪᴅ ʟe ᴅuʟ :—ɪʀ ꜱᴀɪʀɪᴅ ʟe ᴅuʟ ᴀn méɪᴅ ʀɪn, ʀeᴀċᴀʀ ᴀn ċuɪᴅ eɪʟe ᴅe.

Gʀeɪm ᴀꜱ . . . ᴀʀ :—ᴛá ᴀnᴀ ġʀeɪm ᴀɪꜱe ᴀɪʀ : ꜱʀeɪm ᴅo ḃʀeɪᴛ ᴀʀ ꜰuᴅ.

Gʀeᴀmuɪġᴛe ᴀʀ :—ᴛá ʀé cóṁ ꜱʀeᴀmuɪġᴛe ʀɪn ᴀʀ Ḋɪᴀ nᴀ ꜱʟóɪʀe ná cuɪʀeᴀnn ʀé ᴀon ᴛʀuɪm ɪ neɪᴛɪḃ ꜰᴀoġᴀʟᴛᴀ.

8°. Iᴀʀʀᴀċᴛ ᴀʀ :—ᴅo ḃeɪneᴀʀ ɪᴀʀʀᴀċᴛ ᴀʀ é ꜰᴀġáɪʟ. But— ḃí ʀé ᴀᴅ' ɪᴀʀʀᴀɪḋ é ḋéᴀnᴀṁ.

Iᴀʀʀᴀċᴛ ᴅe :—ᴛáɪnɪꜱ ɪᴀʀʀᴀċᴛ ᴅe'n ᴛʀᴀɪnnᴛ ᴀnn. ᴛá ɪᴀʀʀᴀċᴛín ᴅe'n ꜰuᴀċᴛ ᴀnn ꜰóʀ.

Ionnᴛᴀoɪḃ ᴀʀ :—níʟ ᴀon ɪonnᴛᴀoɪḃ ᴀꜱᴀm ᴀʀ. But—ní ḣᴀon ɪonnᴛᴀoɪḃ é = he's not to be trusted ; one can't rely on him.

9°. Láɪṁ ʟe :—ʟáɪṁ ʟe ᴛíʀ ⁊ ʟáɪṁ ʟe muɪʀ—on the land side and on the sea side. Sometimes ʟáṁ ʟe . . .

10°. Meᴀʀ ᴀꜱ . . . ᴀʀ :—ᴛá ᴀnᴀṁeᴀʀ ᴀꜱᴀm ᴀɪʀ.

Muɪnɪġɪn ᴀꜱ . . . ᴀʀ :—ᴛá mo ṁuɪnɪġɪn ᴀ Ḋɪᴀ nᴀ ꜱʟóɪʀe.

Muinigin in :—Mire atá cun lucc mainigne ionam a d'fuargailt (Im. 159).

11°. Neamruim ag .. in :—ir iongantac an neamruim a bí agam ann.

Neamruimeamail in :—ir dítcéillide an fud beit neamruimeamail ingnótaíb creidim.

Neamruim a cup i rud :—neamruim a déanam de.

Neart ag ... ar :—níl neart agam aip.

Neart do ... (generally without ar) :—⁊ neart duit tarraing ar ar do dícеall.—ar neart a beit dom i pórad. San neart a beit dó an cior d'arougad (MSF. 25).

12°. Ollam ar, cum :—táim lán-ollam ar é déanam anoir. (See caoi ar, cum). Nílim ollam cun a déanta fór.

Oireamnac do (person) :—níl ré oireamneac duit indaon cor.

Oireamnac cun, ar (of an action) :—ní fó-oireamnac an duine é cum a leitéid a déanam ; tá ré oireamnac go mait aip.

Orvonuigte ó :—bí ré orvonuigte ó Dia go dtiocfad an dílinn.

13°. Páirt do gabáil le duine i rud ; páirteac ann.

14°. Riactanac do (person) ... cum (action).

15°. Súil le (hope, expectation of a thing) : ní raib aon trúil agam leir, go dtiocfad ré.
Dá mbead 'fior acu cia leir go raib an trúil.
Cf. tá súil le Dia agam.

… STUDIES IN MODERN IRISH 177

Staḋ ḋe :—Duḃairt ré liom rtaḋ ḋe teact. But the *verb* is also transitive.

Do rtaḋ ré an capall. Cf. also níor rtaḋ ré aċ as cainnt.

Socair ar :—Táim rocair ar imteact láitreaċ. But also—tá ré rocair am' aisne asam so n-imteoċaḋ láitreaċ.

Spéir in :—Ná cuir rpéir i mbiaḋ ná i méir.

Suim in :—There are 3 constructions :
ruim a ċur i ruḋ.
ruim a ḋéanaṁ ḋe.
ruḋ ḋo ċur i ruim. Don. 146 :—sur luṡ cuirteár i ruim iaḋ ná loċta eile.

Searaṁ ar :—ar an aor ós atá ár rearaṁ.
Mo fearaṁ inḋiu oraiḋ!

Searaṁ in :—Díoḋ ḋo fearaṁ ionam-ra (Im. 175).

Sárta le : satisfied with.

16°. **Toilteanaċ** ar, ċun :—(cf. caoi ar, ċun).
Toraḋ ar :—Sin a ḃfuaraḋ ḋe toraḋ ar.
Toraḋ ar :—Tá toraḋ ar ḋo faotar = you labour with fruit.
Tusta ḋo :—Ná bí pó-tusta ḋo ḋ'toil féin (Im. 40) (of *things*).
Tusta ċun :—Ná bí pó-tusta ċun ḋul inḋiaiḋ neiṫe raosalta (of *action*).
Tustaċt ḋo :—Tustaċt ḋo'n peaca (Im. 45) = proneness to vice (of things).
Tustaċt ċun :—Tustaċt ċun séilleaḋ ḋ'uaċtarán (Im. 47) = a ready obedience (of action).
Taitiġe ar :—Níl puinn taitiġe asam ar an scainnt.

Caitiġe a ḋéanaṁ ḋe puḋ :—Ḋul i ḋtaiciġe ḋe ; ḋul n-a caitiġe.

Cruaġ aġ . . ḋo :—Cáiniġ cruaġ aġam ḋí.

Tarcuirneaċ le :—Ḃeiṫ tarcuirneaċ leir an té ná fuair puinn.

17°. Uain ar, cun. (See caoi ar, cun). Ní raiḃ uain aġam AR é ḋéanaṁ. By a mixture of this construction, and that with proleptic ré (ní raiḃ ré ḋ'uain aġam é ḋéanaṁ) we get the third construction :—ní raiḃ uain aġam é ḋéanaṁ (without ar).

III. Prepositions after Verbs.

1°. Áitiġim ar : convince, argue down one's throat.
2°. Ḃac ḋo : ná ḃac ḊÓ ; also ná ḃac leis, and ná ḃac é. Cf. níl ḃac ORT ann.

Ḃain le :—" Caḋ é rin'ḋon té rin ná ḃaineann ran leo" ?
„ ḋe :—Ḃain ḋíot ḋo ḣata. Ḋo ḃaineaḋ an tearpaċ ġlan ḋe.
„ ar :—Ḃainfar ceol ar.
„ ó :—Ḋo ḃaineaḋ a lán airġiḋ uaiḋ (ó is the correlative of aġ ; ḋe of ar. Hence tá an brón (buairt, eaġla, imfníoṁ, etc.) imtiġte ḊÍOM But tá mo ċuiḋ airġiḋ (mo ċáiṗḋe, an rrarán, etc.) imtiġte Uaim.)
„ ḋo :—Caḋ ḋo ḃain ḋuit ?
Without preposition—ḋo ḃain ré amaċ an ḃóṫar árḋ ; na rráṫaí ḋo ḃaint.

Ḃeir ar :—Seize, overtake. Níl aon ḃreit aġat ar é ḋéanaṁ.

Beiɼ ċun :—bring to (a person)
Beiɼ ó :—bring from.
Beiɼ ᵹo :—bring to (a place)

" Beiɼ beannaċt óm ċroiḋe ᵹo tíɼ na hÉiɼeann ċum a maiɼeann ꝺe ḟíolɼaḋ Íɼ ir Éiḃiɼ." (Ꝺonnċ Ruaḋ).

Beiɼ le :—bring with :—beiɼ leat luaċ ċúiᵹ púnt.

3°. Coɼᵹ aɼ. Ná coiɼᵹ é aɼ imṫeaċt. But coɼᵹ a ċuɼ le . . . .
Caḋruiᵹ, cuiꝺiᵹ le :—ᵹo ᵹcuiꝺiᵹiḋ Dia leat.
Cuiɼ ruar le = put up with.
Cuiɼ ríor aɼ = talk about ; describe.
Cuiɼ ruar ꝺe = give up ; éiɼiᵹ aɼ.
Cuiɼ ríor le = assign for (cúiɼ a ċuɼ ríor le . . .).
Cuiɼ ruar ċun = instigate to . . .
Cuiɼ ċuiᵹe :—to attempt it ; ir uiriɼte é ḋéanaṁ, aċ cuɼ ċuiᵹe.
Cuiɼ le :—send with ; add to :—ᵹan cuɼ leir ná baint uaiḋ ; cuiɼ le céiɼꝺ = apprentice to trade.
Cuiɼ ríor aɼ :—send FOR. Cuiɼ ríor aɼ an raᵹaɼt.
Cuiɼ ré :—to settle down, reside ; cuiɼfiḋ mé fúm ran áit reo.
Cuiɼ ꝺe :—to get over :—tá ré cuɼta ḋíom aᵹam anoir.
Cuiɼ ꝺíot = be off. Ḃí ré aᵹ cuɼ ꝺe = he was *talking* away. Cuiɼ ré alluɼ ꝺe.
Cuiɼ aɼ a ḟúil ꝺo ḋuine = make a thing apparent to a person.
Cuiɼ taɼ :—to *put past* a person ; not to suspect him ; ní cuiɼfinn taiɼir é.
Caillim le :—spend (lose) ON a person :—ꝺo ċailleaḋ a lán aiɼᵹiꝺ leat.

Caillim ap :—(the dat. of disadvantage) :—do cailleaḋ a lán airgid ort = you lost a lot of money.

Caiṫim le :—1°. throw at :—do cait ré cloċ liom.
2°. spend at :—ná cait a ṫuille aimrire leir.

Car le :—1°. (autonomous) = to meet. Cia hé a ḋubairt rí do carad léi?
2°. to cast up to :—ní ḋuit-re ir cóir é carad liom.
3°. to try :—bí ré ag carad le h-éirge.

Caill ap :—fail (either absolutely, or with personal object). Do ċaill ar a mirneaċ. Ná caill orm.

Cinn ap :—1°. determine :—do cinneaḋ ar ċómairle. Cf. cinnte ; cinneaṁaint.
2°. fail (impersonal) like do teip. do ċinn orm é ḋéanaṁ.

Cait ar : spend :—an oiḋċe do caiteaṁ ar. So—do ṫugadar ar an oiḋċe rin.

Claoiḋe le = to keep at ; cumil de (rub TO) ; ceangal de (tie TO) ; ceangal le (fasten WITH).

Cuiṁnigim ap = think of, remember.

4°. Deinim paid ap :—obey, accede to request. Bí ré ag déanaṁ amaċ ap eadarṫa (It was NEAR . . .)
Deinim taiṫige de :—practise. Deinim anonn ar . . . go over to (Cl. 24).
Deinim de :—change into : do deineaḋ ragart de. The active forms are used with this preposition in the sense of the *passive*. Do ḋein airgead der na licíniḋ rinne.—Dogéna ben dí = she will become a woman (GM. ZCP. II. 22).
Dein do : do or make for :—bí cataoir ṗúgáin aige do ḋein ré féin dó féin S.6).)

STUDIES IN MODERN IRISH 181

Ðein le : do with :—caÐ Ðo Ðein ré leir?
Ðul ar :—1° getting reduced. 2°. escape.
Ðul i bfuaire, roteo, etc. :—getting colder, hotter, etc.
Ðul le :—1°. resembling :—tá ré ag Ðul le n-'ataip.
    2°. engaged at, taking to :—tá ré ag Ðul le
    filiÐeáct ; Ðo cuaiÐ ré le rcoluigeáct.
Ðul Ðo :—due to : Cia méiÐ aipgiÐ atá ag Ðul Ðuit?
  Also suits, becomes : téiÐeann an hata ran Ðuit
  go háluinn.
Ðul Ðe :—1°. bí ré ag Ðul Ðíom an áit a baint amac.
    2°. Ðo cuaiÐ Ðá gcuiÐ fíona (Their wine
    failed).
Ðíol ar : pay for :—Ðíolfaid cú ar, luac nó mall.
  Also Ðíol ar—an mó a Ðíolair ar an gcapall.
Ðíol le :—to sell to :—Cia leir gur Ðíolair an capall?
  Cia Ðó ... would mean—*For* whom did you sell?
Ðiúltuig Ðo :—refuse :—Ðo Ðiúltuig ré Ð'é Ðéanaṁ.
  But also transitive followed by ar (of the price) :—Ðo
  Ðiúltuig ré mé ar rgilling.

5°. Éirig ar : give up. Comáin leat, nó éirig ar.
  Éirig Ðo : happen to. CaÐ Ð'éirig ÐoÐ' coir?
  Éirig le : succeed. Cionnur Ð'éirig leat?
  Éirig a (Ðo) : go to : éirig a coulaÐ ; éirig a baile.
  (Here there is confusion between éirig = rise, and the
  old imperative of the verb téigim, viz. eirgg (cf. Gk.
  ἔρχ-ομαι)).
  Éirt le : listen to :—Éirt le fuaim na h-abann ⁊
  geobaiÐ tu breac (Proverb).
  (Also feit le fuaim na h-abann ⁊ geobaiÐ tu breac.
  Cf. feiteam).
  Éirt is also used without a preposition, 1°. in the sense

of "keep quiet," 2° in the sense of "hearing" (confessions), 3° hearing Mass.

6° ꝼóıꞃ ᴀꞃ :—help :—ꞃo ᴠꝼóıꞃıᴅ ᴅıᴀ oꞃᴀınn. Cf. Lat. *sub*venio, SUCCURRO.

ꝼéᴀċ ᴀꞃ :—look at : ꝼéᴀċ ᴀıꞃ ꞃın ᴀnoıꞃ !

ꝼéᴀċ ᴌе :—try : ꝼéᴀċ ᴌеıꞃ.

ꝼéᴀċ é :—examine it.

ꝼéᴀċ ċun :—look to : ᴎıoꞃ ṁıꞃᴅe ᴌıom ꝼéᴀċᴀınᴄ ċúꞃᴀm ꝼéın.

ꝼᴀn ᴌе : wait for : ᴎıoꞃᴅ ꝼıú ᴅuıᴄ ꞃᴀn ꝼᴀıṁᴀınᴄ ᴌıom.

Also (like ᴀꞃ) intensive :—ꝼᴀn ᴌеᴀᴄ (oꞃᴄ) ꞃo ꝼóıᴌ. (Cf. ᴅ'ımᴄıꞃ ꞃé ᴌеıꞱ, ᴅ'ımᴄıꞃ ꞃé ᴀıꞀ).

ꝼᴀꞃ ᴀꞃ, ꝼé :—leave to : ꝼᴀꞃ ꝼúm-ꞃe é. ᴅ'ꝼᴀꞃ ꞃé ᴀn ꞃᴌeᴀnn 'ꞃᴀ ꞃᴀıᴅ ᴀnn ᴀꞃᴀmꞃᴀ.

ꝼıᴀꝼꞃuıꞃ ᴅe :—enquire of, from.

7°. ꞃᴀıᴅ ᴅo :—be *at* a thing, or a person :—ᴄáım ᴀꞃ ꞃᴀᴠáıᴌ ᴅo'n ꞃᴀeᴅıᴌꞃ ᴌе ꝼᴀᴅᴀ.

ꞃᴀıᴅ ᴀꞃ :—to beat, attack :—ᴠí ꞃé ᴀꞃ ꞃᴀᴠáıᴌ oꞃm.

ꞃᴀıᴅ ᴅe :—(of the instrument of attack) : ᴠí ꞃé ᴀꞃ ꞃᴀᴠáıᴌ oꞃm ᴅ'ꝼuıꞃ.

ꞃᴀıᴅ ᴌе :—to be engaged in, to take up :—ᴅo ꞃᴀıᴅ ꞃé ᴌе ꝼıᴌıᴅeᴀċᴄ. Also with ᴠuıᴅeᴀċᴀꞃ and ᴌеᴀᴄ-ꞃꞃéᴀᴌ, to denote the person thanked or the recipient of an apology :—mo ᴌеᴀᴄ-ꞃꞃéᴀᴌ ᴅo ꞃᴀᴠáıᴌ ᴌеᴀᴄ. ⎫
„ ᴠuıᴅeᴀċᴀꞃ „ „ „ ⎭

ꞃᴌᴀn ᴀꞃ :—clear out : ꞃᴌᴀn ᴀꞃ mo ꞃᴀᴅᴀꞃċ.

But—ᴅo ꞃᴌᴀn ꞃé ᴀn ċᴌᴀıᴅe (cleared the fence).

8°. ımᴄıꞃ ᴌе :—go off with ; or the preposition is merely intensive : ımᴄıꞃ ᴌеᴀᴄ.

STUDIES IN MODERN IRISH 183

Like éiriġ le, it is sometimes used in the sense of *succeed*.

Cionnur o'imċiġ le Séaona ? (lit. *fare* with).

Imċiġ ar : intensive : imċiġ orc ; o'imċiġ ré air.

„ oe : depart from (of things that are said to be " on " a person).

„ ó : depart from (of th n s that are said to be " at " a person).

„ ċun : of the end or destination. D'imċiġ ré ċun oeirio.

Iarr ar, ask of, request.

9°. Lean oe :—cling, cleave to ; continue :—Leanraṙ oe reo ; oo Leanaoaṙ a ġcora oe'n lic-oirupe.

Lean oo :—continue : ná lean ooo' ċuio clear a ṫuille.

Lean ar :—chiefly intensive :—lean orc.

Lean le :—chiefly intensive :—lean leac.

Lean rian ar :—probe thoroughly :—cá orm leanṁainc rian ar an rġéal.

Líon le :—fill with (of the instrument).

Líon oe :—fill with (of the material).

Labair le :—speak to.

Labair ar :—speak of.

Labair oo :—speak of (sometimes). An tír sin dar' labramur = This country of which we have spoken (GM.—ZCP. II, 276).

Leiġ oo :—allow :—ní leiġreao uó a ċuio clear a o'imirc orm rearoa.

Leiġ le :—allow to *take* or give :—ní leoġraṙ oo ċuio oroċ-ċainnte in airġe leac.

Leiġ ó :—allow to be taken from :—ní leoġraio riao uaċ a é.

184 STUDIES IN MODERN IRISH

Leig ar :—pretend :—ná bí gá leogaint ort gur amaḋán tu, mar ní heaḋ.
Leig de :—give up, leave off :—leig deḋ' clearaiḋeact fearḋa.

10°. Maitim do :—I forgive :—mait ḋuinn ár gcionta.
Méaḋuig ar :—increase (impersonal). Do méaḋuig ar an mbuairt aige.
Maoiḋim ar :—boast of :—ní maoiḋte ḋuit ar do maitear.

11°. Sgar le :—separate from :—níor mait liom rgarmaint leat.
Sgar ó :—separate from (transitive) :—níor féadar iad a rcaramaint ó céile.
Sgar de :—separate from (sometimes, chiefly in Ulster).
Scaoil le :—yield to, let alone :—dá mb'áil liom rcaoileaḋ leir an uair úd (give him ' carte blanche ').
Scaoil tar :—not to notice, interfere with :—do rcaoil ré tairis mé.
Scaoil ó :—let away without hindrance :—do rcaoil ré uaiḋ mé.
Scaoil cun :—give promptly, let a person have a thing at once :—rcaoil cúgainn an rgéal (S. 12). It seems likely that Nora's "cait uait an rtóca ran, a ṗeig, 7 SCAOIL cúgainn an rgéal" is suggested by Peig's occupation; rcaoil means to loosen, unravel, let out.

Scaoil le ⎫   ⎧ liom.
„ ar ⎬ of a weapon :—do rcaoil ré urcar ⎨ orm.
„ ré ⎭   ⎩ rum.

Smaoinim ar, meditate, cogitate upon.

11° Searaim do :—support :—Searócaḋ-ra ḋuit. Or of the

person interested in a thing. Seapócaiv ré vom go
ceann camaill eile. It will *last me*, etc.

Seapaim ap :—am dependent upon. Cá mo peapam
inviu opaib-re !

Seapaim in :—am dependent upon. bíov vo peapam
ionam (Im.).

12°. Ceapcuig ó :—want :—Cav a ceapcuig uaic ?
Cabaip le :—bring with : Or—vpuim láma vo cabaipc
le = to turn one's *back* upon.
Coil a cabaipc vo vpúir.
Coiligim cum = consent to. (Cf. the adjective coilte-
anac).
Cabaip vá céile = reconcile.
Cabaip vo :—give to.
Cabaip cun :—bring to.
Cabaip ó :—give *away* :—cug ré uaiv a lán aipgiv.
Cabaip ap :— call, name :—Cav é an ainm ba mait leac
a cabappí aip ?

Cabaip pé :—1°. attempt.
    2°. attack.
Cá . . . ag :—have.
Cá . . . ó :—want.
Cá . . . ap :—of the feelings :—brón, átar, buaipc,
eagla, etc.
Cá . . . pé :—intend :—cá púm vul go Copcaig imbái-
reac.
Cá . . . cun :—1°. am about to :—cáim cum é véanam
láitreac.
    2°. attack. Cátar cúgac !

With the verb ir, cun denotes the reference of a remark

or an action :—"a ṗeana-cṗoċ ṗúiġ iṗ cúġac-ṗa ṗan!"

Tá ... le :—1°. am with, on the side of :—an té ná ṗuil liom tá ṗé am' ċoinniḃ.

2°. advise, counsel, discuss with :—ní ḣaon ṁait ḃeiṫ leaṫ!

Tá ... ṗoiṁ :—is before; in store for; is intended.

Tóġ ... aṗ :—blame a person : ná tóġ oṗm é.

Tóġ ... ó :—take away from : "tóġ uaim é iṗ ġan uaim aċ é!"

Téiġim ḋe (impersonal) :—fail, find impossible :—ḋo ċuaiḋ ḋíom é ḋéanaṁ.

Also of things—fail (absolute) : ḋo ċuaiḋ ḋe'n ṗíon.

Téiġim ḋo :—1°. Suits—tá an oḃaiṗ ṗin aġ ḋul ḋuit ġo mait. Ní ṗó-olc a ṗaġaḋ ġṗeaṗ cooluta ḋom anoiṗ.

2°. is due to :—Caḋ é an tuaṗaṗḋal atá aġ ḋul ḋuit anoiṗ?

Téiġim in ... ḋo :—Raġaiḋ ṗan l'Ótaiṗḃe Ḋuit, etc.

Téiġim aṗ :—1°. Become reduced :—Ḋo ċuaḋaiṗ aṗ ġo móṗ! Cf. ḋo ċuaiḋ ann = it shrank.

2°. Ḋo ċuaiḋ ṗé a ṗaḋaṗc an tiġe.

Téiġim le :—Resemble :—Téiġeann ṗé le n-a átaiṗ.

Téiġim aṗ :—1°. In various phrases like aṗ ceal, aṗ ṗeaċṗán, aṗ ṗán, aṗ loṗġ, aṗ an aonaċ.

2°. Go against :—Ḋo ċuaiḋ an cluiċe oṗm = I tosl the game.

Téiġim aġ :—Of the victor in a contest, aṗ denoting the vanquished :—Ḋo ċuaiḋ aġ na tṗí Colla oṗta— The three "Collas" defeated them

Téiġim ó ... ġo :—of movement (real or metaphorical).

STUDIES IN MODERN IRISH 187

Téigim tré, tríd :—1°. go through (lit.) do ṗaṡaḋ ré ríoḋ tré ṗoll ċaraċair aṡ loṅṡ aiṗṡiḋ.
2°. suffer, endure :—is mó céim cruaiḋ n-ar ṡaḃar(=ḃeaṡar) tríd le tamall.

Téiġim tar :—1°. lit.—do cuaiḋ na ba tar teorainn.
2°. metaphorically—ní raṡainn tairir rin. I am quite *content with* that.

Tiṡim, taṡaim ar :—1°. of feelings, calamities, etc. :—
táiniṡ brón, fearṡ, cruaḋtan, orm.
2°. of persons, and things other than feelings, etc. Táiniṡ ré a ṡanḟior orm ; tánṡaḋar aniar aḋtuaiḋ (unexpectedly) orainn.

Tiṡim irteaċ ar = become accustomed to, proficient in.

Tiṡim irteaċ le = agree with, am consonant with, fit in with. An tuirṡe in Éirinn n-a ḋtiocfaiḋ ré irteaċ leḋ' ċaotaṁlaċt féin.

Tiṡim lairtiṡ ḋe ḋuine = I circumvent a person, get the better of.

Tiṡim ḋe :—result :—Sé tiṡ ḋe rin ná ná tiocfaiḋ ré a ṫuille.

Tiṡim do :—purpose :—Táiniṡ ré d'á féaċaint.

Tiṡim ó . . . ṡo :—local. Teaċt tar = tráċt ar.

Tiṡim ó (origin) :—ó ḃuiḋin a tiṡ ḃruiṡean.

Tiṡim le :—1° possibility :—ní tiṡ liom é ḋéanaṁ.
2°. come with, in the sense of offering no resistance (like boṡ le) :—Ruṡ ré ar an ṡcataoir 7 táiniṡ rí leir ṡo héarṡaiḋ.
3° Agrees :—tiṡ leir rin an méiḋ aḋeir plató.

Exercise LXIV.

(Prepositions.)

1º. This is the Christian's chief comfort so long as he *sojourns*[1] afar from Thee in this mortal body.
2º. Some are preserved from great temptations, and are often overcome in *daily*[2] little ones.
3º. It is wonderful *that*[3] any man can *heartily*[4] rejoice in this life knowing as he does that he is in *a state of banishment*.[5]
4º. The desires of your heart ought to be examined and kept in moderation.
5º. You ought to be sorry that you are still *so inconsiderate*[6] in speech, *so little able to hold your peace*,[7] so disorderly in your manners.
6º. It's a pity one should be so easily distracted when one begins to pray.
7º. When it was evening, after sunset, they brought to him all that were *ill*[8] and that were *possessed*[9] of devils.
8º. *In*[10] *judging*[11] and in *looking into*[12] oneself one always labours with fruit.
9º He does well who *regards rather*[13] *the common good*[14] than his own will.
10º. A deed is not done in charity if it *is accompanied by*[15] *hope of retribution*[16] and *desire of our own interest*.[17]

1. ᴀɼ ᴅeıɼıʟᴄ.   2. 1 n-ᴀɡᴀıᴏ́ ᴀn ʟᴀc.   3. Insert ᴀ ɼᴀ́ᴏ before "that."   4. ıomʟᴀ́n.   5. Emphatic.   6. Cóṁ beᴀɡ ḃɼeıᴄnıú ɼᴀɼ . .   7. Cóṁ beᴀɡ ɼᴘeım·ᴀɼ ᴅo cᴀınnᴄ nuᴀıɼ . . .   8. Áɼ ᴀ ɼ́ʟᴀınᴄe.   9. Use simply "in."   10. nuᴀıɼ.   11. Mᴀcᴄnᴀṁ.   12. ḃɼeıᴄnıú.   13. Iɼ mó ᴀɡ   .   14. Cᴀıɼḃe ᴀn ɼoḃᴀıʟ.   15. Ḃıonn ᴀnn.   16. Súıʟ ʟe ᴄuᴀɼᴀɼᴅᴀʟ.   17. Súıʟ ʟe ᴄᴀıɼḃe ᴅó ɼéın.

Exercise LXV.

(The Same.)

1°. *It doesn't follow from that*[1] that they ought not to be very humble and very *careful of*[2] themselves.
2°. Be not too *free*,[3] but restrain all thy senses under discipline.
3°. *How great is*[4] human *frailty*[5] *which*[6] is always *prone to vice* ![7]
4°. *It will give a man great confidence*[8] of dying happily if he has a ready obedience.
5°. Perfect men do not easily give credit to every report, because they know man's weakness which is prone to evil, and very subject to *fail*[9] in words.
6°. *Endeavour*[10] *rather to do*[11] the will of another than your own.
7°. In all things look to thy *end*,[12] and how thou wilt be able to stand before *a severe*[13] judge to whom nothing is hidden.
8° No one can serve two masters.
9°. The patient man is *easier*[14] *moved to*[15] compassion than to anger.
10°. A true *internal man*[16] that is *free from*[17] *inordinate*[18] affections can freely turn himself to God.

1. Ní fágann san ná . 2. Aireac ar. 3. Ró-ċugta dod' ċoil féin. 4. Cad é mar ná fuil rá' aċ. 5. Earba nirt. 6. Not relative. 7. Tugtact do'n ṗeaca. 8. An té go mbíonn . . . aige . . . ní mirde dó fuil a ḃeiṫ aige le . . . 9. Díoġḃáil a ḋéanaṁ. 10. Foġluim. 11. Use níor tugta ċun. 12. Deire ar . . . 13. Say "the," and form new sentence with "severe." 14. Túirge. 15. Use ag. 16. A ḋ'ḟéacann lairtiġ. 17. Follaṁ ó. 18. Ainṁearardá.

STUDIES IN MODERN IRISH

Exercise LXVI.
(The Same.)

1°. *They*[1] that are *grounded and established in*[2] God can by no means be proud.
2°. Learning is not to be blamed nor the mere knowledge of anything that is *good*[3] in itself and ordained *by*[4] God.
3°. Stand purely and with a full confidence in God, and thou shalt possess Him.
4°. I am quite ready to leave everything *to*[5] you. What money I have is *of little use*.[6]
5°. It is vanity to *follow*[7] the *lusts of the flesh*.[8]
6°. It is vanity to mind only this present life, and not to look forward to those things which are to come.
7°. *Study*[9] to withdraw your heart from the love of visible things.
8°. Leave vain things *to*[10] vain people ; but *mind thou*[11] the things which God hath commanded thee.
9°. I am wearied *with*[12] often reading and hearing many things.
10°. The holy fathers in the desert long ago *renounced*[13] all riches, *dignities*,[14] honours, friends and kindred.

Exercise LXVII.
(The Same.)

1°. If the salt *lose its savour*[15] wherewith shall it be salted?
2°. If the master *is long in coming*[16] the servant will grow careless.

1. An té. 2. Sreamuiġte go daingean ar . 3. Tairbeaċ.
4. Ó. 5. Fé. 6. Gairid le dul. 7. Toil a ċabairt do . . .
8. Drúir. 9. Ḃreicniġ ar conur . 10. Aġ. 11. Féaċ féin
ċun. 12. Ó. 13. Druim láṁa do ċabairt le . 14. Teidiol.
15. Dul i leaṁar. 16. Riġneas a ḃéanaṁ de ċeaċt.

3°. He went up to them into the ship and the wind ceased, and they *were far more*[1] astonished within *themselves.*[2]
4°. The wine failing, the Mother of Jesus said to Him—They have no wine.
5°. They add and take away according to their own inclination, and not according as it is pleasing to the Eternal Truth.
6°. They are filled with so great a love of the Deity, *and such overflowing*[3] joy, that there is nothing wanting to their glory.
7° God speaks in many ways to us without respect of persons.
8°. If we would but use a little *violence*[4] on ourselves in the beginning we might afterwards do all things with ease and joy.
9°. If you *were sensible*[5] how much peace you would *secure for yourself*[6] by good behaviour, *I should say*[7] you would be more solicitous for your spiritual progress.
10°. A man should *establish himself*[8] in such a manner in God as to have no need of seeking many comforts from men.

Exercise LXVIII.

(The Same.)

1°. The longer a man is *negligent*[9] in resisting the weaker does he daily become in himself, and the stronger the enemy becomes against him.

1. Do méaduiġ ap . . .   2. Use aiġne.   3. Cóm cuilte de.
4. Use dian.   5. Cuiġ it' aiġne.   6. Cuip i n-áipite do . .
7. Ní meapaim ná . . .   8. Speamuiġte ap . . .   9. Dein paillíġe de.

2°. Turn your eyes back upon yourself and *see you judge not*[1] the doings of others.

3°. If you consent to see him I shall not refuse to send him to you.

4°. The charity of Christ is never *diminished*,[2] and the greatness of His propitiation is never *exhausted*.[3]

5°. If you *have not*[4] this grace, but rather find yourself *dry*,[5] continue in prayer, *sigh and knock*[6] and *give* it not *over*[7] till you receive some crumb or drop of divine grace.

6°. No man is *worthy of*[8] heavenly comfort who has not diligently *exercised himself*[9] in holy compunction.

7°. What happened you that you did not give up that unpleasant work?

8°. Do this for me, and I shall obey you in that other matter, and make you a priest.

9°. I had not time and no opportunity to write you a letter sooner.

10°. You have grown quite thin since I saw you.

---

1. ná bac do . . . ap . . .   2. Dul i luigead.   3. Foiú a déanam
4. Use i n-éagmais.   5. Cup, tirim.   6. Use bí ag . . .
7. Stad.   8. Oireamnac do . . .   9. Caitige a déanam de . . .

CHAPTER VIII.

On Ellipsis, and Change of Construction.

If we compare the English sentence—"I did not delay anywhere, but went home immediately" with the Irish—"Níor ḟanaṛ i n-aon ḃall aċ ḋul a ḃaile láiṫreaċ" (S. 42), we are struck by the change of construction in the latter language. This apparent change of construction is due to ellipsis. E.g., in the sentence given we may supply, after aċ, the words iṛ é ḋeineaṛ. The starting-point of this very common feature of Irish construction may very well be found in such sentences as P.H. 221.—Ar ní derna aithrige acht dul in derchainiud, where we may consider both dul and aithrige as governed by derna ; cf. also MSF. 71—Ní hé rin a ḋeineaṛ aċ aġaiḋ a ṫaḃairṫ aṛ an ġcnuc. The construction spread early, however. E.g., P.H. 258.—Dia n-oscailter in chomlasa ⁊ diabul do ligad is-tech ann.

This change of construction (due to ellipsis) is found chiefly (*a*) in adversative clauses introduced by aċ or non-adversative clauses introduced by aġus, following negative clauses ; (*b*) in clauses following other clauses introduced by má, ḋá, nuaiṛ.

Examples :—(*a*).

1°. Níor leiġ ré aoinniḋ aiṛ aċ an biaḋ do ċaiṫeaṁ cóṁ maiṫ ⁊ ḋ'ḟéaḋ ré é (S. 68). Here, after aċ, we may supply is aṁlaiḋ a ḋein sé . .

With this sentence compare—Níor leiġ ré aoinniḋ aiṛ aċ é beiṫ iġcruaḋ-ċáṛ : "He merely pretended that he was in difficulties,"—where there is no ellipsis or change of construction.

2°. Cad na taob ná preabann tú láitreac agur i do leanamaint? (S. 164). Here, after agur, we may supply "ná deineann tú."

3°. Cad na taob nár tánair-re ⁊ do beart féin do críocnú gan oul ar dtúir ⁊ é innrint do méid? (TBC. 188). Here, after the first agur we may supply "nár deinis."

4°. Muna brágrair an áit rin ⁊ glanad ar mo rabairc go diaiṗ cuirread cómarta ort a leanraid díot an faid a beid cor cam ort (S. 76). Here after agur supply "muna ndéanrair."

5°. Ir iongna linne anoir nár iompuigeadar láitreac ⁊ an Slánuigteoir ad' admáil (Ser. 79). Supply nár deineadar.

(b).
1°. Má tagann aon cómurra irteac, ⁊ go ruiprid ré ra cataoir, ní rulair duit aontigear do tabairt raor ó cíor dó (S. 15). Here, after agur, we may supply "má ráinigeann."

2°. Dá mbead beirt ban ag troid, ⁊ go breicridír ag teact í, do rtadraidír (S. 82). Here supply "dá ráinigead," or dá mba . . .

3°. Dá neorfí dí é, ⁊ annran go brórrad rí Séadna, do birread a mactnam a ráinte (S. 96). Supply "dá ráinigead."

4°. Má cuireann (aoinne aon ceirt air) ⁊ go bréacraid reirean inr na rúilib air, bain an cluar díom má cuireann ré an tarna ceirt (S. 103). Here supply "má ráinigeann"; "már rud," or some similar expression.

The change of construction occurs mostly when introducing some *unexpected, undesired* or *heterogeneous* event. Cf. above examples.

5°. Má tógann sé páirt le Concubar ⁊ an cloideam ran
  d'iompáil n-ar gcoinnib bpirrar cat láitreac
  orainn (TBC. 26). Supply "má deineann sé."
6°. Dead Cire níor raidbre go mór ná atá rí dá mba ná
  dead aon cogad ann, ac na daoine go léir d'ḟan-
  maint ra baile (TBC. 35). Supply after ac " gurb
  ḟéidir " (in construction with dá mba).
7°. The following sentence from (MSF. 26) is hardly an
  example of this ellipsis :—Nuair a bí oiread amuic
  aige ⁊ gur dóic leo go ndiúltócad an cuid eile
  d'é díol tar a ceann do comáinead ar an oliġe ar
  riúbal. Here " ⁊ gur " follows oiread, and is not
  a *new clause* in elliptic construction with nuair.
  In " agur gur " we have a contamination of two
  separate constructions after oiread :—Bí oiread ran
  aige gur dóic leo . . . and ní raib oiread aige
  agur ba dóic leo a bí.
8°. Dá bfeicead Suaire ag teact é ⁊ go mbead ḟior aige
  cad é an fuadar a bí ré, do cuirfead sé corg leir
  an ndíogaltar (5. 145). Supply after agur—
  " dá mba."
9°. Igcómnuide riam nuair a bínn féin ⁊ buacaillí eile
  ag gabáil an bótair . . . agur go n-éirigead
  aigneár nó díorpóireact eadrainn . . . (SG. 93).
  Supply " nuair a ráinigead." after agur.
10°. D'ḟeadrad muinntir na hÉireann féin é déanam
  láitreac dá gcuimnigdír air, agur cur cuige. Supply
  after agur, " dá ndeimdír."
  Sometimes there is no ellipsis and no change of construction :
  S. 43.—Nuair a tabarfá leatrgéal dó, ⁊ ba dóic leat go
  mberófá féid leir, ir amlaid dead sé in-acrann
  ionat níor daingne. Here the construction of nuair
  is carried on.

Similarly— S. 55.—Nuair a ḃíoḋar uile imṫiġṫe aḃaile
iscóir na h-oiḋċe, ⁊ ḃí ré in'aonar na ruiḋe ra
cataoir ṗúgáin ḃí an rġéal aġ ruiṫ ṫré n-a aiġne
ar an ġcuma ro.

Another probable explanation of ġo in the second clause
after nuair, is suggested by

S. 47.—Nuair a ċaġaḋ an cáirḋe
aġur ná ḋíoltí na riaca ní ḃioḋ ré ḋian ran
éiliom.

Here the second clause is negative, and so ná occurs ; as
ġo is the affirmative correlative of ná, such sentences might
lead to ġo being used in an affirmative clause.

Certain other kinds of ellipsis will be treated of in the next
chapter.

Exercise LXIX.

(Change of Construction.)

1°. What doth it avail thee to discourse profoundly of the
Trinity if thou be void of humility, and *consequently*[1]
displeasing to the Trinity ?

2°. What will become of us in the end, *seeing that*[2] we grow
lukewarm[3] so very soon ?

3°. It would be very needful that we should be sent into
the Novitiate[4] again, and be instructed in all good
behaviour.

4°. If thou standest well with God and lookest to His judgment thou wilt more easily bear to see thyself overcome.

5°. I will no longer remember his sins, but forgive them all
to him.

1. aġur ġo.   2. aġur a ṗáḋ . . .   3. faillighṫeaċ.
4. Scoil na nóḃíreaċ.

6°. We ought to be satisfied with little as though it were much, and with what is rough as though it were smooth.

7°. If thou offer thy gift at the altar *and there*[1] remember that thy brother hath anything against thee leave there thy offering before the altar, and go first to be reconciled to thy brother.

8°. What man is there among you, of whom if his son shall ask bread, *will he*[2] reach him a stone?

9° Beware of false prophets who come to you in *the clothing of sheep*,[3] *but*[2] inwardly they are ravening wolves.

10°. We have no more than five loaves and two fishes, unless *perhaps*[4] we should go and buy bread for all this multitude.

11°. As the living Father sent me *and I*[1] live *by*[5] the Father so he that eateth Me, the same also shall live *by Me* [6]

12°. For this same was about to betray Him, *whereas*[2] he was one of the twelve.

13°. Neither Me do you know *nor*[7] my Father.

14° If I shall go and *prepare*[8] a place for you, I will come again, and will take you to myself; that where I am you also may be.

---

1. Ꭺꞅuꞅ ꞅo.   2. Insert ꭺꞅuꞅ ꞅuꝓ . . . (there is *emphasis* on "stone" and (in 9°) "wolves").   3. Ctúꞃo na ꞅcaoꝓaċ.   4. Aṁlaiꝺ.   5. Ó.   6. 'Oem' báꝓꞃ-ꞃa.   7. Ní luꞡa ná maꞃ atá . . .   8. Use verbal noun.

CHAPTER IX.

Contamination and other phenomena.

A.—The term "contamination" is used technically in Grammar to denote the admixture or amalgamation of separate elements in a word or a construction. Here we confine ourselves to contamination of construction or syntax.

1° Such a sentence as cad ba ṡáḋ a leiṫéid a ċur ann? cannot be explained on the ordinary principles of construction. It *means* of course cad é an ruḋ gur ṡáḋ a leiṫéid a ċur ann mar ġeall air?

Various explanations suggest themselves:—

(a) It might be a contamination of *question* and *answer*, such as is not unknown in other languages.[1] Cad ba ṡáḋ? (This is intelligible, and easily parsed) A leiṫéid a ċur ann,—(an eaḋ)?

(b) It might be taken as a survival (with ellipsis) of the old construction in which the gen. of *the personal pronoun* was made to do duty for the gen. *relative*. It would then mean:—Cad (é an ruḋ)—ba ṡáḋ, etc? What is the thing—the like of WHICH ought to be sent?—this coming to mean in the course of time—what would be the *need* of sending such a thing?

(c) It may be modelled on such sentences as—
Cad ba ṡáḋ a ḋéanaṁ? Cad ba ṡáḋ a ċur ann?
This is quite regular and easily parsed. Familiarity with such questions might lead to the more complex question under discussion.

---

1. Cf. the syntactical development of car in French (because) from the Latin quare (why?) Il ne viendra pas, car il est malade; Ille non veniet. Quare? Non valet.

(d) One might perhaps treat "ᴀ ʟeιcéιᴅ ᴀ ċuᴘ ᴀnn" as a gen. phrase noun depending on ᵹáᴅ, and = "the necessity *of sending* such a thing." If one could feel that this is so, the question could then be parsed directly.

(e) Possibly influenced by the logical equivalent (which also is quite regular) cᴀᴅ ꝼé nᴅéᴀᴘ ᴀ ʟeιcéιᴅ ᴀ ċuᴘ ᴀnn?

It is useless (as far as *explanation* goes) to say that cᴀᴅ is used adverbially. The question is—*how did it come to be so used?* Cf. Cᴀᴅ ᴀb áιʟ ʟeᴀc é ᴅéᴀnᴀṁ? For this however we can find a simple explanation in such sentences as:—Cᴀᴅ ᴀb áιʟ ʟeᴀc ᴀᵹ ꝼéᴀċᴀιnc ᴀᴘ nιᴅ nᴀċ ᴅʟeᴀᵹcᴀċ ᴅuιc ᴀ beιc ᴀᵹᴀc? Here, if we supply "ᴀᵹuᴘ cu" before "ᴀᵹ ꝼéᴀċᴀιnc" the sentence is quite easy. So (Im. 44) Cᴀᴅ ᴀb áιʟ ʟeᴀc ᴀᵹ cuᴘ ᴅo ᴅeᴀᵹ-ᴘúιn ᴀᴘ cáιᴘᴅe?

2°. Mᴀᴘbuιᵹᴅᴀᴘ ᴀn uιʟe ᴘuᴅ ι bꝼuιᴘṁ ᴅuιne ᴅe ꝼʟιoċc Ᵹᴀeᴅeᴀʟ ᴅÁR ꝼéᴀᴅᴀᴅᴀᴘ ceᴀċc ᴘuᴀᴘ ʟeιp (SG. 54).

This is a *contamination* of two distinct constructions:

(a) Mᴀᴘbuιᵹᴅᴀᴘ . . . ᴅÁR ꝼéᴀᴅᴀᴅᴀᴘ (Compound Relative; antecedent element governed by ᴅe, relative part by ꝼéᴀᴅᴀᴅᴀᴘ).

(b) Mᴀᴘbuιᵹᴅᴀᴘ . . . Ᵹᴜᴘ ꝼéᴀᴅᴀᴅᴀᴘ ceᴀċc ᴘuᴀᴘ ʟeιp (Oblique relative governed by ʟe in ʟeιp). Ċáιnιᵹ ᴀmᴀċ ᴀᴘ ᴀn ʟoċ ᴀn cᴀᴘᴀʟʟ ᴅob' áιʟne ᴅ'áᴘ ʟeoᵹᴀᴘ mo ꝼúιʟ ᴘιᴀṁ ᴀιᴘ. (bᴘ. 33).

3°. Má cᴀιceᴀnn cu ᵹᴀċ ᴀᴅbenc ᴅÁ bꝼÁᵹꝼᴀᴘ ᴀᴘ ᴀn ᴘᴀoᵹᴀʟ ᴘo ċu . . .

This is a contamination of—

(a) . . . ᴅÁ bꝼáᵹꝼᴀᴘ ᴀᴘ ᴀn ᴘᴀoᵹᴀʟ ᴘo ᴀᵹᴀc, and

(b) . . . Ᵹo bꝼáᵹꝼᴀᴘ ᴀᴘ ᴀn ᴘᴀoᵹᴀʟ ᴘo ċu.

Dá goes naturally with ᴀᵹᴀc, but ᵹo (or n-ᴀ)

with cu. Dá (earlier Di a) was originally used in the sense of WHEN, but one can scarcely see a survival of this meaning here.

4° Double, treble, quadruple, quintuple relative construction, may be looked upon as a kind of contamination :—

Iṟ iad iṟ tṟéine atá ag déanaṁ na hoibṟe is a blending of the two statements (with dependence in thought of one upon the other) :—
(a) Iṟ iad atá ag déanaṁ na hoibṟe ; and
(b) Iṟ iad iṟ tṟéine.

5° The use of ná and aċ in type II (b and c) of Identification sentences involves a sort of contamination also. The sentence :—Sé ṟud iṟ ṟeaṟṟ duit a déanaṁ ná dul a ċodlad duit ṟéin, is a blending of—
(a) Sé ṟud iṟ ṟeaṟṟa duit a déanaṁ—dul a ċodlad ; and
(b) Nioṟ ḃṟeaṟṟa duit ṟud a déanṟá ná dul a ċodlad ;

6°. Níl leigeaṟ aṟ an meaċlú aċ muinntiṟ na hÉiṟeann do dul aguṟ eolur a ċuṟ aṟ a gcainnt ṟéin aiṟiṟ (SG. 84).

Here of course, if the construction were uniform we should have in the latter part—do dul, aguṟ do ċuṟ eoluiṟ (Subject and Object of verbal expressed [see pp. 147-148]), aṟ a gcainnt ṟéin aiṟiṟ. In the sentence as it actually occurs there is a reminiscence of some such construction as—níl leigeaṟ . . aċ go ndéanṟad muinntiṟ na hÉiṟeann dul aguṟ eoluṟ a ċuṟ, etc. Of these two uniform constructions a mixed blend is made, with the above result. It is needless to say that such constructions are not wrong ; only one must study the psychology of the language in order to appreciate them.

7°. ᴀ ꜰeᴀbᴀꞃ 1S ᴅo ḃein ꞃé ᴀn ᵹnó, is a contamination of—cóṁ ᴍᴀɪṫ ɪꞃ ᴅo ḃein ꞃé é and ᴀ ꜰeᴀbᴀꞃ ᴅo ḃein ꞃé é.

8°. Ṫá ᴀ́ṫᴀꞃ oꞃm ṫú ḃeiṫ cóṁ mᴀiṫ iꞃ'ṫᴀoi, may be looked upon as a contamination of—

(a) iꞃ ᴀṫᴀꞃ liom ṫu ḃeiṫ cóṁ mᴀiṫ iꞃ ṫᴀoi, and
(b) cuiꞃeᴀnn ꞃé ᴀ́ṫᴀꞃ oꞃm . . .

B.—Certain other irregularities of expression arise from other causes :—

1°. E.g. in the sentence—

" Iꞃ **cumᴀ nó** muc ᴅuine ᵹᴀn ꞃeiꞃṫ."

the words " cumᴀ nó " have taken on the meaning of " the same AS." This is due merely to a change in the collocation of the words. The elementary form of the statement would be—

Iꞃ cumᴀ $\begin{cases} \text{ᴅuine ᵹᴀn ꞃeiꞃṫ} \\ \text{nó muc} \end{cases}$

where " nó " has its ordinary meaning. The proverb was originated however for the benefit of the " ᴅuine ᵹᴀn ꞃeiꞃṫ," and so the language was changed in such a way as to have " ᴅuine ᵹᴀn ꞃeiꞃṫ " alone as the formal subject ; " cumᴀ **nó muc** " then became predicate (not merely cumᴀ), and so " no " developed the meaning of " AS."

2°. In a similar way " bꞃeiꞃ ᴀᵹuꞃ " develops the meaning of " more THAN " by a change in the collocation of the words. ᴅo ḃeineᴀᴅᴀꞃ bꞃeiꞃ iꞃ ᴀ nᴅóṫᴀin = " They did *more than* enough " goes back to " ᴅo ɹeıneaɒaɲ a nɒótaın ⁊ **bɲeıɲ**" " they did enough, and more "; when the change is made " bɲeıɲ ıɲ " lit. " more and," naturally develops into " more *than*."

3°. Cf. the expression " ıonann aȝuɲ " = the same AS. The sentence—

" Iɲ ıonann aȝuɲ báɲ an beata ɲo "

goes back to a simple form—

    P   S

    ⌒ ⌢

Iɲ ıonann **an beata ɲo** ⁊ báɲ

lit. = This life, *and death*, are the same thing. *But as one wishes to make the statement formally about* " *this life,*" " an beata ɲo " becomes the subject and the words " aȝuɲ báɲ " go over to the predicate and in so doing " aȝuɲ " develops its new meaning. In an analogous way ' aȝuɲ ' developed its meaning of " as " with cóṁ. Notice that the language with " ıonann ıɲ " is frequently elliptical :—

Táım ɲéıɒ anoıɲ munaɒ ıonann ıɲ ɲıaṁ.

" I'm done for *now if ever* I was "; lit. it means,— " I'm done for now, *unless* NOW AND *any other time are the same* " (the insinuation of course being that they are *not* the same, but VERY DIFFERENT.) Here we have an ellipsis of **anoıɲ**: munaɒ ıonann (**anoıɲ**) ıɲ ɲıaṁ. With this " munaɒ ıonann " phrase in this sense there is always such ellipsis. Cf. Ċ.S. 19.— " Ɒo beın ɲé an ceaȝaɲȝ maɲ a ɒéanɲaɒ ɒuıne ȝo ɲaıɒ cóṁact aıȝe, muɲaɲɒ ıonann ⁊ na Sȝɲıɒneoıɲı ⁊ na Faıɲıɲınıȝ." Here we have an ellipsis of eıɲean (or ɒuıne ȝo ɲaıɒ cóṁact aıȝe)—unless he and the

S. and Ph. were the same; they were not, but very different. *He* had "power," *they* had none. So ꝼᴀṡᴀᴅ ᴀ ċoᴅlᴀ ꝣo luᴀċ ᴀnoċċ munᴀb ıonᴀnn ıꝛ ᴀꝛ- éıꝛ—means munᴀb ıonᴀnn ᴀнoċċ ıꝛ ᴀꝛéıꝛ,—if to-night and last night are not the same; I mean them to be very different. In such sentences the phrase often means—as contrasted with. "I'll go to bed early to-night THOUGH I DIDN'T last night."

4°. Somewhat akin to this new meaning developed in a word by a change of position is the phenomenon we have in—ní ꝼıú bıoꝛán ıꝛ é, "it is quite insignificant." Lit.—it *and a pin* (a pin and it) are not worth (much). The peculiarity is that instead of saying ní ꝼıú bıoꝛán é, "it (the thing in question) is not worth a pin (a type of insignificance), we put it *and the pin* on the same level, and say that neither (or the combination) is worth much. This peculiarity may in origin be due to the collocation " bıoꝛán ıꝛ é " in a sentence with ıꝛ ıonᴀnn,—ıꝛ ıonᴀnn bıoꝛán ıꝛ é, which is logically almost equivalent to ní ꝼıú bıoꝛán ıꝛ é, the latter however being more vivid and rhetorical. Cf. S. 221.
—níoꝛb ꝼıú tco bıoꝛán ᴀꝣuꝛ ᴀnᴀm ᴅuıne ꝛeᴀċᴀꝛ ꝣꝛeım ꝼᴀꝣáıl ᴀꝛ ᴀ teıċéıᴅ ꝛın.

Cf. also the use of ᴀꝣuꝛ in—

ḃeıᴅ coꝛ ċᴀm ᴀıꝛ ᴀn ᴅá lá **ıꝛ ᴀn ꝼᴀıᴅ ᴀ ṁᴀıꝛꝼıṙ ꝛé.** (The "two days" may be the day on which the thing in question began, and the day of death).

5°. We have a somewhat unusual collocation (outside questions) in the proverb—" ᴀn cé leıꝛ ꝣuꝛ cumᴀnꝣ ꝼáꝣᴀb." This of course is equivalent to—ᴀn cé ꝣuꝛ cumᴀnꝣ leıꝛ (ᴀn áıc)—ꝼáꝣᴀb (ꝛé é). It may

have been influenced by ᵹibé, (cibé, pé) leir . . . .
The collocation was fairly common in early Irish :—
Cach nech leis narb 'áil trina pecad (GM.—ZCP. II, 12)

C.—Besides the cases of ellipsis (explaining change of construction) mentioned in the last chapter, we have other cases which must not be neglected :—

1°. Sentences like ní neaṗc ᵹo cuṗ le céile are elliptical. This one means ní neaṗc **ceaṗc aon neaṗc** ᵹo (nɔeineam) cuṗ le céile.
So ní h-aiceancaṗ ᵹo h-aonciᵹeaṗ.
níoṗ ṗóɔluiṗcí ᵹo ɔcí iaɔ.
ní cailín maic ᵹo ɔcí í.

2°. Ní luᵹa ná maṗ a ḃíonn aon ṗoṗmaɔ aiᵹe le h-aoinne. (Im. 26). Such sentences are puzzling to the learner, especially as in English they run " *no more* does he envy any man." In Irish they are elliptical. The above sentence, with the thought fully expressed would be—ní luᵹa (a ḃíonn aonniɔ eile uaiɔ—this must be supplied from the previous sentence), ná maṗ a ḃíonn, etc.—I.e., The way in which he wants anything else is not less than the way in which he envies any man. Now as we were told previously that he wanted nothing else (but God's glory), this is equivalent to saying—" *no more* does he envy any man." With this use of luᵹa cf. the use of móiɔe in the phrase ní móiɔe.

An ɔóic leac an nɔéanṗaiɔ ṗé ḃáiṗceaċ? Ní móiɔe ᵹo nɔéanṗaiɔ. " *Probably not.*" Lit. " that it *will* (rain) *is not more likely* (than that it *won't* ").

CS.—215.—" Ní ḃṗuaṗaṗ cionncaċ in-aon niɔ é ɔe ṗna neiciɔ acá aᵹaiḃ á cuṗ na leic aᵹuṗ ní luᵹa ná maṗ a ṗuaiṗ héṗóɔ." " *No, nor Herod, neither.*'

1.e. ní luġa (ꝼuaꞃaꞃ-ꞃa cionncac é) ná maꞃ a ꝼuaiꞃ hénóꞅ.

The sentence preceding the "ní luġa" is negative in form, but it is the *affirmative* form of that sentence that is understood as the subject of the verb 'iꞃ' in ní luġa. . Hence in English ní luġa frequently appears as No MORE. English takes it in connection with the previous *negative*. MSF. 97.—Níoꞃꞃ ꝼéiꝺiꞃ aon loct ꝼaġáil uiꞃci. Ní lúġa ná maꞃ ab'ꝼéiꝺiꞃ aon loct ꝼaġáil aꞃ an aꞃán a cuġcí ꝺúinn.

3°. **Ní ꝼuláiꞃ nó** is frequently used to express logical (as distinct from physical or moral) necessity. Ní ꝼuláiꞃ nó tá tuiꞃꞃe oꞃt tꞃéiꞃ an tuꞃuiꞃ. You must be tired—not that it is your *duty* to be tired, but it is a logical necessity from the circumstances : it must be *true* that you are tired. The idiom is explained by an ellipsis : there is part of the thought suppressed, as being comparatively unimportant, and in any case not to the point for our purpose. We might here fill in the lacuna thus :—

Ní ꝼuláiꞃ [ġuꞃ ꝺuine ana láiꝺiꞃ tu]
nó tá tuiꞃꞃe oꞃt.

i.e., you must be a strong man *or else* you are tired. Then the "nó" is kept even when the first part is suppressed. One may say also—ní ꝼuláiꞃ nó ġo ꞗꝼuil tuiꞃꞃe oꞃt ; here the second alternative is brought under the influence of ní ꝼuláiꞃ ; two alternative necessities (logical) are spoken of—

(*a*) ní ꝼuláiꞃ (ġuꞃ ꝺuine ana láiꝺiꞃ tu ;) nó—
(*b*) ġo ꞗꝼuil tuiꞃꞃe oꞃt.

When we say ní ꝼuláiꞃ nó ġo ꞗꝼuil tuiꞃꞃe oꞃt we

reject the first and accept the second, keeping however the ní ó of the disjunctive proposition.

Some people say (and write) ní ḟuláiṗ ná ɼo ḃruil cuiṗre oṗc, in imitation of the ná in type II b. Identification. But this is *false* analogy, as the ná there is developed naturally before the PREDICATE, while the ná here would be before the *subject* of ir. Nor can it be justified on the ground of changing nó to ná after the negative ní. When that is done the ná has a negative force ; here the nó has an *affirmative* meaning.

Some people also say—ní ḟuláiṗ ḋuic ḃeiṫ cuiṗreaċ, meaning " you must be tired " (*logical* necessity). This is not good. It is better to reserve ní ḟuláiṗ ḋo . . . for obligation, or duty ; ní ḟuláiṗ nó . . . for logical necessity ; ní ḟuláiṗ alone sometimes expresses logical necessity—ní ḟuláiṗ ɼuṗ ḋuine ana láiḋiṗ ṫu ; ní ḟuláiṗ cu ḃeiṫ cuiRseaċ ; sometimes obligation, duty—ní ḟuláiṗ ḋul a ḃaile but here the action in question is connected in the mind with some responsible agent. Ḟuláiṗ here means excess ; it is the word ḟuṗóil, which has gone through the changes, ḟuṗáil influenced perhaps by the word ḟuṗáil = ORDER, COMMAND, ḟuláiṗ. Ní ḟuláiṗ ḋom ḋul aḃaile, therefore, means much the same thing as ní móṗ ḋom ḋul a ḃaile ; it is not " excessive " not " a big thing," not " too much " ; it is *demanded* by the circumstances, it is my *duty*,—I *must*. In practice however ní ḟuláiṗ is stronger than ní móṗ.

TBC. 131.—Ḃa móṗ an oḃaiṗ ḋo Ċú Ċulainn é maṗḃú. Ní ḟuláiṗ nó ir ḟeaṗ ana-láiḋiṗ é.

S. 121.—Ceaṗaim ḟéin ná ḟéaḋraḋ Seaġán Ceaṫaċ

STUDIES IN MODERN IRISH

ná an ragart a n-aigne do focrú ar aon puo eile ać air reo. nárb fuláir (we may supply— go raib oul amúóa ar ouine éigin) nó go raib an geallmaint ann.
Cf. TBC.—17.—Ní mait í do ciall nó níor múinir a gceact go cruinn dod' teactairib.
n. 43.—Ní fuláir nó tá coolad ort 7 tuirre tréir an lae.
S. 105.—Ceapaim nać foláir nó bíor ar mo meadair puo éigin.

4°. Nó go has for a long time been used in the sense of go = until. Pedersen, in his "Vergleichende Grammatik der Keltischen Sprachen," B. II, T. I., p. 319, takes the Middle Irish 'noco' to be a development of na-con used with the subjunctive after negative sentences. We think it at least equally probable that the use arose, somewhat in the same way as the nó in ní fuláir nó . E.g., one might say—

Dubairt ré go bfanfad ré ann go bfagad ré bár, nó go dtiocfad duine éigin ćun é fuargailt. Then, by omission of the first go clause—go bfanfad ré ann nó go . . . Or again,—dubairt ré go bfanfad ré ann nó go dtiocfad . . . where nó go at first means *or else that ;* but this meaning would easily pass into that of UNTIL. Cf. n. 137.—Bí fior aige go mait go gcaillfead rí an tanam, nó go mbead droć obair éigin toir lámaib aici.

5°. Ná glac páram mar geall ar t'éirim aigne ná ar do géar-ćúir, le h-eagla go gcuirfeá mí-fáram ar Dia, 7 gURbé Dia a tug duit pé deag-tréite

atá ionnat (Im. 12). Here the clause beginning—
agus gurb é . . . is elliptical : the gur is not in
construction with te heagla of course, but with some
words like a ráḋ understood after agur. Notice that
" a ráḋ " would also be elliptical as in the next
example.

6°. Caḋ é an ḋeipe a ḃéarfaiḋ rinn in aon ċor **agus
a ráḋ go ḃfuilimiḋ ċom failliġteaċ ċom luat
ra tá** ? (Im. 45). Here something like " ir fíor "
may be supplied after agur. Or the phrase has
been developed out of another context, where agur
was quite regular.

7°. Tá ruil agam anoir go ḋtuillfiḋ Míċeál an t-
airgead ċom macánta **agur dá mba** ná ḃeaḋ ré
fagálta roim ré aige (S. 67). Here after agur we
must supply—do tuillfeaḋ ré é. So—ḃí ré ag
gáiriḋe ċom mait **agur dá mbeaḋ a ċuir aige.**
We must supply—" do ḃeaḋ ré " after agur.

8°. irt'oiḋċe = at night. This phrase has probably
come into being from the combination " de ló ir
d'oiḋċe," by day" and " by night ;" de ló means
by day ; and the remainder of the phrase " ird'oiḋċe"
was taken to mean 'by night '; then the pronun-
ciation, and folk-etymology affected the spelling.

CHAPTER X.

Miscellaneous.

A.—Prepositional pronoun instead of Genitive or Nominative.

1°. Instead of genitive :—

(a) P.H. 156.—ro-shói fuil do chnáim dó = His blood turned to bone.

(b) Im. 20.—ba ṁait leir ɡo ᴅtiocfaḋ an bár air, ⁊ ɡo rɡarfaḋ anam le colainn aiɡe (that *his* soul should separate from his body).

(c) Im. 49.—Caḋ a bfuil ᴅe ḋaoiniḃ ᴅo mealtaḋ ⁊ ɡur rtracaḋ anam a colainn acu ɡan ċoinne!

(d) S. 226.—Annran ᴅo bfir ar an bfoiḋne acu. Their patience.

(e) Ċ.S. 249.—Má fanann riḃ ar mo ḃriatar ir fior-ḋeirɡioḃuil aɡam riḃ fearᴅa.

(f) Ċ.S. 268.—1 ᴅtrco ɡo mbeaḋ riḃ inḃur ɡclann aɡ an rolur. (children of light).

(g) Ċ.S. 270.—Siḃ a ḃeit inḃur n-ᴅeirɡioḃuil aɡamra (My disciples).

(h) ᴅo neartuiɡ ré aimṁianta acu (Ser. 179).

(i) S. 13.—" Ní fuláir nó ní hé feo an ċéaᴅ uair aɡat (your first time) aɡ aireaċtainc teaċt táirri riaḋ."

2°. Instead of nominative :—

(a) Im. 21—An faiᴅ ir beo ar an raoɡal ro ḋo.

(b) S. 73—ᴅo ḋuḃaiɡ ⁊ ᴅo ɡormaiɡ aiɡe.

(c) Im. 17—Nuair a ṫaḃann aon riuᴅ beaɡ ´nár ɡcoinniḃ tuiteann an luɡ ar an laɡ aɡainn láitreaċ (We collapse).

B.— Introductory " tá."

In English we say—" A man who had several sons was dying." This sudden way of presenting several facts in one sentence is not consonant with Irish clearness of expression. The Irish will be—bí fear ann, ⁊ bí cúigear nó reirear mac aige, ⁊ bí sé ag dul cun báir.

Similarly—"Some resign themselves, but with some exception. Some also at the first offer all,"—will in Irish have this introductory tá:—(Im. 175) **tá daoine agur treigid riad iad féin, ac puinnte beag éigin. Tá daoine eile agur tugaid riad uata gac aon rud ioctorac bápa.**

So—"Some people would despise riches out of sheer pride" will in Irish be—tá daoine, ⁊ le neart uabair, ní cuirfidír ruim i raidbrear (Ser. 147).

Again—"Some people would like to satisfy God and at the same time they would wish to satisfy the world too," will in Irish be—"**tá daoine ⁊ ba mait leo Dia do fáram, ⁊ ra n-am gcéadna ba mait leo an raogal do fáram, leir.** (Ser. 147).

Exercise LXX.
Introductory "tá."

1°. Many people *make it more their study*[1] to *know*[2] than to live well.

2°. Some suffer great temptations in the beginning of their conversion, and some in the end.

3°. Many secretly seek *themselves*[3] in what they do, and are not sensible of it.

4° Many are found to desire *contemplation*[4]; but they care not to practise those things which are required thereunto.

5°. Some are carried by a zeal of love towards these or those with greater affection, but the affection is rather human than divine.

---

1. Ir mó acu.   2. Colur a cruinniú.   3. A dtoil féin (emphatic).   4. Dlút-maccnam a déanam.

6°. When some people are preparing themselves for a noble action they feel all the greater inclination to selfishness.
7°. Many seek to fly temptations *and fall*[1] the more greivously into them.
8. I observed that some of the lads possessed *ability*[2] and *clearness of judgment*[3] and *mental capacity*[4] beyond the *common*,[5]—in some cases, far beyond *it*.[6]
9°. Some people are never satisfied unless they see a chance of getting some of other people's property.
10°. A certain class of people are always looking out for an opportunity of self-aggrandisement.
11°. Some people, out of sheer pride, would fast from food *till they died*.[7]

C.—ꙅuṗ with the verb ip after ip minic :—

We should naturally expect the *direct* temporal relative clause (instead of oblique) after ip minc. As a matter of fact this is the form which is used *with all verbs, except* ip. E.g.,

Iꜱ minic a ṫaꙅaḋ an ꙅlaoḋaċ ola i láp na hoiḋċe.

But when we emphasise the words "i láp na h-oiḋċe" by bringing them forward in the sentence by means of the verb "iꜱ," they will be preceded by ꙅup :—

1°. Iꜱ minic ꙅUR i láp na h-oiḋċe a ṫaꙅaḋ an ꙅlaoḋaċ ola (MSF. 139).

So—Iꜱ minic a ḋeiꞑ ꜱé an clear pan i láp an lae.

But—2°. Iꜱ minic ꙅup i láp a lae a ḋeiꞑ ꜱé an clear pan.

Sometimes we meet an apparent exception :—

Im. 227.—Iꜱ minic ꙅo ḋtaꙅann ceann-pé opm péiꞑ ꜇ ꙅo lapaim le náipe map ꙅeall ap mé ḃeiṫ cóṁ puap ionam péiꞑ, ꜇ cóṁ ḃeaꙅ ꙅpaḋ ḋuiṫ. This we can easily explain by an

---

1. Use ip aṁlaiḋ. 2. Ciꜱim aiꙅne. 3. Soluꜱ ḃpeiṫeaṁntaip.
4. Cúil-péiṫ. 5. coitċiantaċṫ. 6. Repeat noun. 7. ꙅo báp.

ellipsis of "ᴀ ᴘáɪɴɪɢeᴀɴɴ" or some such words after ɪꜱ mɪɴɪc.

3°. Iꜱ mɪɴɪc ɢᴜɴb ᴀɴ ɴᴀ Cɴɪoꜱᴛᴀɪðᴛɪb ɪꜱ ꜱeᴀꜱꜱ ᴀ ᴛᴀɢᴀɪð ɴᴀ ᴛɴɪobᴛðɪðɪ ɪꜱ ᴛɴuɪme (Ser. 52).

Exercise LXXI.

"Iꜱ mɪɴɪc ɢuꜱ ..."

1°. We like to think and discourse on the things that please us well, but oftentimes that is a vain and foolish *proceeding*.[1]

2° Such is our weakness that we often *more readily*[2] believe and speak of another that which is evil than that which is good.

3°. I have often been in company and would prefer that I had not, and often talking and had rather I had been silent.

4° Oftentimes we had more *sanctity*[3] the first day of our *conversion*[4] than we find ourselves possessed of after many years spent in *the profession of piety*.[5]

5° Oftentimes we prefer what is hurtful, and reject what is beneficial.

6°. A man often feels *late at night*[6] that he has the capacity for doing quite a lot of work.

7°. *Least said*[7] is frequently soonest mended.

8°. People say—"*the more*[7] *the merrier*," but it is often "*the more*[7] the sadder."

9°. A merry evening frequently makes a sad morning.

10°. Oftentimes *the longer*[7] a man is in a certain place the more he wishes that he had never gone there.

1. ɢɴó. 2. ᴛúɪꜱɢe ʟɪɴɴ. 3. beᴀɴɴuɪɢᴛeᴀᴛᴛ. 4. Use ompuɪɢ ᴀɴ ðɪᴀ. 5. ɢᴀɪɴm cꜱᴀɪbᴛeᴀᴛᴛᴀ. 6. Emphatic. 7. Put the "ðá" clause *before* ɢuꜱ.

D.—Accusative of Specification :—

We have already seen that in Old Irish there was a difficulty about expressing the genitive of the relative. Sentences like—

(a) intí as énirt iress
(b) réte ní réid a mbrith

show that sometimes, as in (a), the *relative* was expressed and the *genitive* relation left to be inferred from the context ; at other times, as in (b), that the genitive (of the *personal* pronoun) was expressed, and the *relative* nature of the sentence left to inference. We have also seen that modern Irish has simplified the problem by using a special form of relative, and showing the genitive relation by the genitive of the personal pronoun. The sentence (a) e.g., is expressed in modern Irish thus—

(c) ᴀn τé ʒuɾ Lᴀʒ ᴀ ċpeɾoeᴀṁ.

But there is another very common way of expressing the thought—

(d) ᴀn τé ɩɾ Lᴀʒ cpeɾoeᴀṁ.

This is sometimes equiparated with the Old Irish construction, but wrongly. The form of the word " iress " in the Old Irish sentence shows that it is nom. ; the only satisfactory explanation of (d) is to say that cpeɾoeᴀṁ is *accusative* of respect, or specification. It points out the thing *in respect of which* the person is said to be weak. The construction occurs also with comparative and superlative adjectives :—

(e) ní pᴀɩb ouɩne bᴀ ṁó ᴀ́τᴀs nᴀ́ nɩᴀṁ.
(f) ᴀn τé ɩɾ Luʒᴀ eoLᴀs ɩɾ é ɩɾ mó cᴀɩnnτ.

In Old Irish the accusative was used after (a) the equative form of the adjective :— sonartaidir *slébe* " cóṁ Lᴀ́ɩoɩɾ Le ɾLéɩbτe" ; and (b) after certain positive adjectives :- bá tualang cách FORCITAL alaili " o'ɾéᴀoɾᴀo ʒᴀċ ᴀoɩnne múɩne ᴀo ᴀ céɩLe (ᴀ céɩLe ou ṁúɩneᴀo). The construction has spread considerably in modern Irish.

Exercise LXXII.

Accusative of Specification.

1°. They felt that they had the best right TO[1] all that wealth.
2°. I never knew a doctor *of such*[2] knowledge and intelligence.
3°. The women and children *are just as*[2] wildly anxious to come as the men,—and more so.
4°. *Personally*[3] I never saw two persons so affectionate and *devoted*[4] to each other.
5°. There is scarcely another man of as keen intellect in Ireland.
6° *It seems to me*[5] we ought to remember that misdeed, it was so far out of the common, and at the same time so fraught with danger.
7°. Did you ever listen to a woman with so little control over her tongue?
8°. The most intelligent persons make the least *faux pas.*[6]
9°. The least sensible persons make the most mistakes.[7]
10°. I never saw a man *so little able to*[8] keep his money from melting away.

E.—Accusative of Space and Time :—

The accusative is also used (though not exclusively) to denote the length of time and the direction of movement or the extent of space traversed. The accusative of time was very common in the early Irish period—e.g., in n-aidchi sin ; the accusative of space is equally common in the modern language. In the modern phrase ' ⱂn oiⱃeⱥⱃ ⱃⱥn ' we have probably an old accus. of time, though it is now applied to

---

1. Ċun.   2. Use cóṁ móⱃ ⱃⱥn, Repeat with ' intelligence.'
3. Ⱥm' ⱃúiliƀ cinn.   4. Cóṁ móⱃ uⱃⱥim ⱃo . . .   5. Use ⱃⱥⱃ liom.
6. Use cuicim. The sentence should be an Identification, type 4.
7. Type IV.   8. Cóṁ beⱥs ⱃⱥn cumⱥⱃ ⱥⱃ . . .

express other relations as well. So—ꞡᴀċ n-oıḃċe. The accusative of space occurs in such sentences as—

(a) Ꙗo ꝼluᴀıꞃ ꞃé ᴀn bóċᴀꞃ ó ċuᴀıḋ
(b) Ꙗ'ımṫıꞡ ꞃé ᴀn cnoc ꞃuᴀꞃ
(c) Ꙗo ꝼluᴀıꞃ ᴀn ḃeᴀṫᴀċ ᴀn ꞃımné ᴀmᴀċ
(d) Comáıneᴀmᴀıꞃ lınn ıᴀḋ ḃᴀınꞡeᴀn nᴀ Sᴀıleᴀċ ꞃıᴀꞃ (MSF. 77).

Exercise LXXIII.

(Accusative of Space and Time.)

1°. There they were in front of me—horses and dogs, men and attendants; all of them proceeding along the roads towards the north-east.
2°. Just as I reached the shore the boat left the harbour.
3°. They proceeded along the road in a south-westerly direction *towards*[1] Kincora.
4°. He kept watch so carefully that not even a[2] crow could have come down the hill unknown to him.
5°. When he was going out OF[3] the door, she remarked—"upon my word it's hard to satisfy some people."
6°. Is that your mother that I see coming up the field?
7°. I remained a day and a night, and thought that was quite enough.
8°. I had been there a whole week before I *even*[4] thought of writing to you.
9°. *I fancied*[5] I heard a child's voice going out the chimney.
10°. After meeting the poor man *I proceeded on my way*[6] along the western road.

1. ꞃé ḃéın.   2. Use the vivid *definite* article.   3. Accusative.
4. ınᴀon ċoꞃ.   5. Ꙗo ꞃᴀṁluıꞡeᴀꞃ.   6. ċıománeᴀꞃ lıom.

F.—ᴀb not inserted after ᵹup before a predicate beginning with a vowel—

The rule is generally given that in dependent 'ıꞃ' sentences ᴀb is inserted after ᵹup, when the predicate begins with a vowel. This rule is by no means universal. We find the ᴀb NOT inserted:—

(a) With verbal noun phrases beginning with a pronoun
ll. 251.—'Ouḃapc ꞃéın ᵹup í coıméᴀ'ᴅ annꞃo ḃᴀ ċeapc.

(b) With prepositional pronouns beginning with a vowel: mᴀp ᴅ'eᴀ'ᴅ ᵹup ORCᴀḃí ꞃí ᴀᵹ ꞃéᴀċᴀınc.

(c) With prepositional phrases beginning with a vowel: 'ᴅ'ᴀ'ᴅṁuıᵹeᴀ'ᴅᴀp ᵹup AR mᴀıṁ ᴀ ḃí ᴀ ḃuı'ᴅeᴀċᴀp ᴀcu 'Oıᴀ 'ᴅo cᴀḃᴀıꞃc ᴀn cᴀḃᴀpcᴀıꞃ pın 'ᴅóıḃ. But see sentence 3°, p. 212.

(d) With adverbs, beginning with a vowel :—
S. 78.—Ceᴀpᴀp ᴌᴀıcꞃeᴀċ ᵹup ANNSO ᴀ ḃí ꞃí, ᴐ 'ᴅo leᴀnᴀp í.

(e) Even with ordinary nouns, beginning with a vowel: S. 77.—Nᴀ ḃí 'ᴀ leoᵹᴀınc opc ᵹup amᴀ'ᴅán cu, mᴀp ní neᴀ'ᴅ.—mᴀp ᵹup OḂAIR í nᴀċ ꞃéı'ᴅıp ᴀ 'ᴅéᴀnᴀṁ.

Especially when the following syllable contains a *labial* (as in the last two examples) there seems to be a preference for OMITTING ᴀb. Also in the first four cases the general tendency is perhaps in favour of the OMISSION.

G.—Aspiration after the genitive ᴀ independently of the gender and number of the noun to which it logically refers :—

It has been noted already that proleptic ᴀ causes aspiration independently of the gender and number of the noun to which

it logically refers. The usage is not confined to *proleptic* a :—
1°. Bí cuipp na mban ip na leanb aici **á caiceaṁ** ipteac ap an otpáiġ (n. 338).
2°. Tá poinnt neite aṡam '**á tabaipt** ré n'oeapa le oéioeannaiġe (n. 313).
3°. Tá an punann aici **á ceanġal**.
4°. Ip í (an éaṡcóip) atá acu **á ṿéanaṁ** piaṁ (SĠ. 93).
5°. Puaip ré ṙa teampul oaoine 7 ba acu '**á ṿíol** 7 caoipe 7 colúip (ĊS. 228).
6°. Do ċpeio a lán oaoine in a ainm nuaip a ċonacaoap na mípbúiltí a bí aiġe '**á ṿéanaṁ** (ĊS. 228).

It is difficult to explain this construction. The following considerations may be of use :—

(a) In enumerations the attention is sometimes fixed on the individuals. Hence such usages as tpí **capall**. This would explain aspiration with plurals.

(b) With 2° above we may compare the sentence with proleptic a :—Tá ré á tabaipt ré n'oeapa aṡam le oéioeannaiġe **poinnt neite do beit bun or cionn le céile annpo**.

Some have maintained that a here (and in 2° above) is equivalent to DO, comparing such sentences as—Ip iomoa pompla do ṗéaopaimíp DO tabaipt anuap. But this is an entirely different construction, and *equally common in modern Irish*. To confuse them is to show complete lack of appreciation of the point at issue. The modern Irish—Ip mó pompla o'ṗéaopaimíp a tabaipt anuap, is, even to the tyro, quite different from—tá a lán pomplaí aṡainn á tabaipt anuap.

(c) Generalisation of one form frequently takes place :—
1°. E.g., "ip" is now used for all three persons, and

both numbers, though originally it is 3RD person SING.

2° Aipir—originally only of *3rd* person *sing. masc.* is now used of all persons, both numbers, and both genders. In Middle Irish the 2nd pers. sing. form was frequently used in a general sense (doridisi).

3° It seems likely that the form ré noeapa is due (in its construction with cabaip) to a *3rd* pers. *sing. masc.* form—cugad an téigceoip ré n-aipe. In this theory ré n'-aipe became ré noeapa, and was used for both numbers and genders, and all three persons.

4°. That " a " aspirates where the noun is feminine may be explained on the principle that one is thinking of THE THING rather than of THE NAME of the thing. In such cases the masculine is naturally used (inasmuch as we have no neuter at present). De facto the " a " is probably often neuter. For the masculine use, cf. ir bpeag an áic é. Cad é an pud é riúd call ? (*when we don't know* what it is).

II.—Sense Constructions :—

(*a*) Dob'uapal an cpeirean iad (TBC. 2).

Ordinarily peirean is a masculine noun. Here, when referring to females, natural gender is made subservient to sex, peirean being treated as if it were feminine. This is "sense construction."

(*b*) ba ROGA liom cómnuide ar an paogal ro 7 cura am'rocair ná reilb na bflaicear a d'ragáil gan cu (Im. 232).

Here again we have sense construction, the word ná following roga because roga is equivalent to the comparative reapr.

(c) a Coim. When addressing a nun of this name we treat the word as if it were a feminine. So such invocations as "a Sólár na n'oubrónac" in the Litany of the B.V.M., can be explained as instances of " sense construction." They can also be explained of course, on the *phrase-noun* principle. In our opinion "a rólár" is much better in such cases than "a rólair." So—a cumann mo cléib ar a péiltean marcalac (FS., V., 28). " eiblín a pún" (heard in Ballyvourney) not a púin (as frequently sung). In any case pún was *originally* feminine.

I.—Absolute Constructions.

Different cases have been used *absolutely* in the different Indo-Germanic Languages. Latin used the ablative ; Greek the genitive, and occasionally the accusative ; Sanskrit the locative, and sometimes the instrumental or the genitive ; Old English the dative ; Modern English the nominative. In various instances Irish uses the nominative form, where we might have expected a genitive, dative, or accusative, or where the nom. is " out of construction." We may look upon these as instances of absolute construction :—

(a) bi rear ann 7 é ar leat-rúil.

agur é ag rád na cainnte rin táinig duine cun uactaráin na rinagóige.

(b) ní fiú iad é. ní fiú rgilling an leabar ran. fiú was originally a substantive here and followed by the genitive. The genitive actually occurs as late as Keating :—Cagraid an Caerar 'r go fiú an ríog móir (K.P. VIII, 329). Even at present in such expressions as ní raib fiú na mbróg uirc the genitive is usual.

(c) In phrase nouns :—toirg (an saidbreas go léir a beit aige) ; cun (an obair a déanam) ; in some places obair is not inflected here.

(d) Ba mór an t-uabbár é, an té a cífead é.

(e) With proleptic a, including dá :—
Bí iongna opm a luigead airgead a bí aige.
D'fanair liom, dá méid deitneas a bí opt.
Dá feabar ní, bíonn opoc-duine éigin ap a tí.
Dá luigead é tu, ní leanb tu!

(f) Certain words, now used mostly in prepositional sense :—
iomtúra (concerning) ; dálta, dála (concerning), Mid. Ir. imm dala ; cum (*Kudsmen : L. ca-cumen, but now usually held to be an unstressed form of the noun coicim) ; timceall, taob leir, toirg (cf. do thoisg na h-inghiona [Z.C.P. II. 142]).

(g) féacaint in the sense " to see " (purpose) :—
Do cuadar irtead féacaint cia bí ann.

(h) Rád, in the elliptical phrase " 7 a pád " :—
Bí iongna opm 7 a pád go ndéanpá a leicéid.

(i) In such cases as ap ndóig, ap nóin; the introductory a leicéid reo.

(l) In phrases like ap táinig gac fí an líon do gealtad? (See p. 160).

L.—The Subjunctive Mood.
There are five main uses of the Subjunctive in modern Irish:

1°. The Subjunctive *of purpose:*—
(a) Ragad ann go bfeicead é.
b) Ir cuige do cupead ann é, cun go ndeinead ré dícheall ap fiotcáin a déanam eatorta.

The conditional, however, is usual with ionnur, iotreo, irlige, etc., possibly on the analogy of *consecutive* clauses introduced by these words. The conditional of tá is frequently used in cases where

STUDIES IN MODERN IRISH 221

the subjunctive of other verbs would be normal. The reason is that the form generally known as the conditional of cá is in reality the old past subjunctive, just as the future forms beiṫ, beaṗ, beiṫ (with *short* vowels) go back to the old present subjunctive (Bergin, Ériu, Vol. 2, pt. I, p. 46). It would only cause confusion, however, in the modern Grammar, to refer the *subjunctive* uses of these forms to a paradigm other than that of the *future* or *conditional*.

2°. The *optative* Subjunctive :—
   (a) ʒo mbeannuiʒiṫ Dia ṫuic.
   (b) ʒo bḟóiṗiṫ Dia oṗainn.
   (c) ʒo ʒcúiciʒceaṗ do ṗaocaṗ leac.
   (d) ʒo ṗaib maiṫ aʒac.
   (e) ʒuṗab amlaiṫ ṫuic, etc.

3°. The Subjunctive of *indefinite time* :—
   (a) ḟan ʒo dcaʒaḋ-ṗa.
   (b) Ná labaiṗ cun ʒo labaṗcaṗ leac.
   (c) Dubaiṗc ṗé ʒo ndéanḟaḋ ṗé a ḋíceall aṗ iaḋ a coiméaḋ ṗiaṗ cun ʒo dcaʒaḋ an conʒnaṁ.
   (d) Saṗ a nḋṗuiḋeaḋ níoṗ ṗia ó aimṗiṗ an Ċoláiṗḋe (MSF. 108).

4°. The Subjunctive with Dá :—
   (a) Dá dcéiʒeaḋ ṗé ann do cuiṗḟí pionóṗ aiṗ.
   (b) Dá dciʒeaḋ an lá dob' áluinn an ṗʒéal é.

   In modern Irish only the PAST subjunctive is used with this word. The *present* was quite common in early Irish. The subjunctive of cá is not usual. (See under 1°). The conditional is used instead :—
   Dá mbeinn-ṗe iḋ'ċáṗ iṗ ʒo lláṗ do ṗaʒainn-ṗe.

5°. With muna, to express uncertainty, or indefiniteness.
Outside these cases of course the indicative is used :
(a) muna ocigiú ré ir bocc an rgéal é.
The conditional, future, or habitual present of
tá are used instead of the Subjunctive (See under
1°) :—
(b) muna mbeaú ré ann ir teann a labrrainn-re.
Notice the difference between :—
(c) muna raib ré ann (supposes his absence a fact)
do ceapar-ra go breaca é.
(d) Dá mba ná beaú ré ann (supposes his presence)
cionnur do círinn é?
Similarily (e) má bí ré ann (he *was*) do connaic ré an radarc
(he did).
(f) Dá mbeaú ré ann (he wasn't) do círeaú ré an
radarc (he didn't).
The subjunctive of the copula with ro- is now used as a dependent form for the present indicative—deir ré guRb é Críort é. It is also used as a subjunctive of course :—gurb amlaiú duit ; and, without ro,—go mba hé duit (Ulster).

Exercise LXXIV.

1°. Let us go into the neighbouring towns and cities that I may preach there also ; for to this purpose I am come.
2°. No man can enter into the house of a strong man and rob him of his goods unless he first bind the strong man.
3°. Wheresoever you shall enter into an house, there abide until you leave that place.
4°. I say to thee thou shalt not go out thence until thou pay the very last *mite*.[1]

---

1. Cianóg.

5°. Unless you shall do penance you shall all likewise perish.
6°. Let it alone this year until I dig about it and dung it.
7°. Send Lazarus that he may dip the tip of his finger in water to cool my tongue.
8°. Where is the guest chamber where I may eat the Pasch with My disciples?
9°. If you did believe Moses you would perhaps believe Me also.
10°. Except you eat the flesh of the Son of Man and drink His blood you shall not have life in you.
11°. If I wash thee not thou shalt have no part with Me.
12°. As the branch cannot bear fruit of itself unless it abide in the vine so neither can you unless you abide in Me.
13°. If I go not the Paraclete will not come to you.
14°. Except I shall see in His hands the print of the nails, and put my finger into the place of the nails, and put my hand into His side, I will not believe.
15°. Who is he, Lord, that I may believe in Him?

CHAPTER XI.

Active, Passive, Autonomous, and тá Constructions.

So many mistakes have occurred, even in print, in the use (or abuse) of the forms coming under this heading, that we think it necessary to give here a bird's-eye view of the whole matter. The chief cause of the blundering was that people failed to distinguish between circumstances in which there was direct reference to the *action*, and those in which the reference was, not to the action, but to *a state of affairs previous or subsequent to the action*.

The action "orcailt."

Present Tense.—A. Direct reference to the action :—

I Habitual :—
    (*a*) *Absolute* :—
        1°. *Active* :—Orglann ouine áipite na vóipre ap a hoċt a ċlog.
        2°. *Passive and Autonomous* :—Orcailteap na vóipre ap a h-oċt a ċlog.

    (*b*) *Contemporaneous* :—
        1°. *Active* :—bíonn ré gá n-orcailt 7 rinn ag teaċt.
        2°. *Passive* :—bío riav vá n-orcailt 7 rinn ag teaċt.
        3°. *Autonomous* :—biteap gá n-orcailt 7 rinn ag teaċt.

II Actual :—
        1°. *Active* :—Tá ré gá n-orcailt anoir.
        2°. *Passive* :—Táiv riav vá n-orcailt anoir.
        3°. *Autonomous* :—Tátap gá n-orcailt anoir.

B. Direct reference to previous or subsequent state :—
  (a) Habitual :—
    1°. Bíd riaḋ ar orcailt ón-a 8 go dtí a 9 (subsequent state).
    2°. Ní bíd riaḋ ar orcailt roim a 8 (previous state).
  (b) Actual :—
    1°. Táiḋ riaḋ ar orcailt anoir (subsequent state).
    2°. Níl ré a hoċt fós; nítiḋ riaḋ ar orcailt fós (previous state).

Imperfect Tense.—A. Direct reference to *action* :—
  (a) *Absolute* :—
    1°. *Active* :—D'orglaḋ ré ar a 8 a ċlog iaḋ.
    2°. *Passive and Autonomous* :—Do h-orcailtí ar a 8 a ċlog iaḋ.
  (b) *Contemporaneous* —
    1°. *Active* :—Do bíoḋ ré ǵá n-orcailt 7 rinn ag teaċt.
    2°. *Passive* :—Do bídír ḋá n-orcailt 7 rinn ag teaċt.
    3°. *Autonomous* :—Do bicí ǵá n-orcailt 7 rinn ag teaċt.
B.—Direct reference to previous or subsequent state :—
  (a) *Previous* :—Ní bídír ar orcailt roim a h-oċt.
  (b) *Subsequent* :—Ní bímír-ne ann go dtí 8.15, 7 ḋá briġ rin do bídír ar orcailt rómainn.

Past Tense :—A.—Direct reference to Action :—
  (a) *Absolute* :—
    1°. *Active* :—D'orcail ré ar a 8 a ċlog iaḋ.
    2°. *P. and A.* :—Do h-orclaḋ ar a 8 a ċlog iaḋ.

(b) *Contemporaneous* :—
  1°. *Active ;*—Bí ré ġá n-orcailt 7 rinn aġ teact.
  2°. *Passive* :—Bíodar ġá n-orcailt 7 rinn aġ teact.
  3°. *Auton.* :—Bítear ġá n-orcailt 7 rinn aġ teact.

B.—Direct reference to previous or subsequent state,:—
  (a) *Previous* :—Ní rabadar ar orcailt ar a 7 a ċlog.
  (b) *Subsequent* :—Níor froireamar-ne an áit go dtí 8.15 7 dá brig rin bíodar ar orcailt rómainn.

Future Tense.—A.—Direct reference to Action :—
  (a) *Absolute* :—
    1°. *Active* :—Orcóċaid ré ar a 8 a ċlog iad.
    2°. *Pass. and Aut.* :—Orcórar ar a 8 a ċlog iad.

(b) *Contemporaneous* :—
  1°. *Active* :—Beid ré ġá n-orcailt 7 rinn aġ teact.
  2°. *Passive* :—Beid riad ġá n-orcailt 7 rinn aġ teact.
  3°. *Aut.* :—Beirar ġá n-orcailt 7 rinn aġ teact.

B.—Direct reference to previous or subsequent state :—
  (a) *Previous* :—Ní beid riad ar orcailt roim a hoċt.
  (b) *Subsequent* :—Má'r rud ná rroirream-na an áit go dtí 8.15 beid riad ar orcailt rómainn.

Conditional and Subjunctive :—A.—Direct reference to Action :—
  (a) *Absolute* :—
    1°. *Active* :—Dá n-orclad ré ar a 8 iad, d'féadrad na daoine go léir beit irtiġ um 8.30.

2°. *Pass. and Aut.* :—Dá n-orcailcí ap a 8 iad, d'féadfadh na daoine go léip beit ircig um 8.30.

(b) *Contemporaneous* :—
1°. *Act.* :—Dá mbeadh sé ghá n-orcailc 7 pinn ag teact do cifimir é.
2°. *Pass.* :—Dá mbeidír dá n-orcailc 7 pinn ag teact do cifimir an dóippeóir.
3°. *Aut.* :—Dá mbeirfi ghá n-orcailc 7 pinn ag teact d'féadfaimir dul irceac láitpeac.

B.—Direct reference to previous or subsequent state :—
(a) *Previous* :—Dá mbeidír ap orcailc ap a 7 . . . .
(b) *Subsequent* :—Dá mbeidír ap orcailc go dtí a 10 . . .

Imperative.—A.—Direct reference to Action :—
(a) *Absolute* :—
1°. *Active* :—Orclad sé ap a 8 iad.
2°. *Pass. and Aut.* :—Orcailceap ap a 8 iad.

(b) *Contemporaneous* :—
1°. *Active* :—Biod sé ghá n-orcailc 7 pinn ag teact.
2°. *Passive* :—Bídír dá n-orcailc 7 pinn ag teact.
3°. *Aut.* :—Biceap ghá n-orcailc 7 pinn ag teact.

B.—Direct reference to previous or subsequent state :—
(a) *Previous* :—Ná bídír ap orcailc agac fuim a 8 a clog.
(b) *Subsequent* :—Bídír ap orcailc agac go dtí a 10 a clog.

228   STUDIES IN MODERN IRISH

Verbal Noun Forms :—A.—Direct reference to action :—
  (a) *Absolute :—*

Ópouigteap (indic.), oo h-
Ópouigtí, oo h-ópouigeaó,
Ópoópap, oá n-ópouigtí
Ópouigteap (imper.)

1°. *Active :*—Dó na oóippe
  o'popcailt ap a 8 a clog.
2°. *Passive :*—ná   oóippe
  o'popcailt ap a 8 a clog
  (See p. 152).

Ópouigteap, etc.
  (b) *Contemporaneous :—*
    1°. *Active :*—Dó beit gá n-orcailt 7 pinn ag teaćt.
    2°. *Pass. :*—lao a beit óá n-orcailt 7 pinn ag teaćt.

B.—Direct reference to previous or subsequent state :—

Ópouigteap, etc.
  (a) *Previous :*—Dó gan iao a beit ap orcailt aige poim a 8.
  (b) *Subsequent :*—Dó iao a beit ap orcailt aige go otí a 10.

The Action "múineaó."

Present Indicative :—A.—Direct reference to action :—
  I. Habitual :—
    (a) *Absolute :—*
      1°. *Active :*—Múincann Seán an gaeóilg go mait.
      2°. *Pass. and Aut. :*—Múinteap an gaeóilg go mait i pcoil Seáin.
    (b) *Contemporaneous :—*
      1°. *Active :*—bíonn peipean ag múineaó na gaeóilge nuaip ip é an béapla a bíonn oá múineaó ag múinteoipib eile.
      2°. *Pass. :*—bíonn an gaeóilg oá múineaó aige pin nuaip . . .

3°. *Aut.* :—biceap ag múineaó na gaeóilge pa pcoil pin nuaip . . . i pcoileannaib eile.

II. Actual :—
1°. *Active* :—Cá pé gá múineaó anoip.
2°. *Pass.* :—Cá pí bá múineaó anoip.
3°. *Aut.* :—Cácap gá múineaó anoip.

B.—Direct reference to previous or subsequent state :—
(a) Habitual :—
Previous :—ní bíonn an ceacc múince aige nuaip a cagaim-pe.
Subsequent :—bíonn pé múince aige um a 10 a clog. ní bimpe ann pap a mbíonn pé múince aige.

(b) Actual :—
Previous state :—níl pé múince fóp aige.
Subsequent state :—Cá pé múince aige ceana.

N.B.—In dealing with the state of affairs previous or subsequent to an action which, like múineaó, takes some time, one must use more definite expressions, if one wishes to allude clearly to the state previous or subsequent to the *inception* of the act.

Imperfect Indicative—A.—Direct reference to action :—
a) Absolute :—
1°. *Active* :—**Do múineaó Seán** an gaeóilg go mait.
2° *Pass. and Aut.* :—**Do múincí** an gaeóilg go mait pa pcoil pin pao ó.
(b) *Contemporaneous* :—
1°. *Act.* :—**Do bíoó Seán ag múineaó** na gaeóilge nuaip a céiginn-pe ipceac anupaió.

230   STUDIES IN MODERN IRISH

2°. *Passive* :—ᴅo ḃíoḃ an ṡaeḃilʒ ḋá ṁúineaḋ
ṙa ṙcoil ṙin nuaiṙ a ḃ'é an ḃéaṙla a ḃíoḃ ḋá
ṁúineaḋ i ṙcoileanaiḃ eile.

3°. *Aut.* :—ᴅo ḃicí aʒ múineaḋ na ʒaeḃilʒe
annṙo nuaiṙ aḃé an ḃéaṙla a ḃíoḃ aṙ ṙiúḃal
i ṙcoileanaiḃ eile.

B.— Direct reference to previous or subsequent state :—

(*a*) *Previous* :—ní ḃíoḃ an ceaċc múince aiʒe ʒo
ḋcí a 10 a ċloʒ.

If one wishes to refer to a state previous to the
inception of the act one must say :—ní ḃíoḃ coṙnuiʒċe
aṙ an múineaḋ aiʒe ṙoiṁ a 9 a ċloʒ.

(*b*) *Subsequent* :—niop ḋeaʒaṙ iṙceaċ ʒo ḋcí 10.30,
η ḋá ḃṙíʒ ṙin ḃíoṙ ṙó-ḃéiḋeanaċ ḋo'n ceaċc,
ḃíoḃ ṙé múince an uaiṙ úḋ aiʒe um a ḋeiċ a ċloʒ.

Here again if the state in question is subsequent
to the inception (not the completion) of the act
one says :—ḃíoḃ coṙnuiʒċe áṙ an múineaḋ aiʒe
aṙ a 9 a ċloʒ.

Past Indicative—A.—Direct reference to action :—

(*a*) Absolute :—

1°. *Active* :—ᴅo ṁúin Seán ceaċc maiṫ inḋé.

2°. *Pass. and Aut.* :—ᴅo múineaḋ ceaċc maiṫ
annṙo inḋiu muṙaṙḃ ionann iṙ inḋé.

(*b*) *Contemporaneous* :—

1°. *Active* :—ḃí Seán aʒ múineaḋ na ʒaeḃilʒe
nuaiṙ a ċuaḋaṙ-ṙa iṙceaċ.

2°. *Pass.* :—ḃí an ṡaeḃilʒ ḋá múineaḋ aiʒe
nuaiṙ a ċuaḋaṙ-ṙa iṙceaċ.

STUDIES IN MODERN IRISH 231

3°. *Aut.* :—**do ḃíṫeaṙ ag múineaḋ** na Gaeḋilge nuaiṙ a ċuaḋaṙ-ṙa iṙteaċ.

B.—Direct reference to previous or subsequent state :—
(a) *Previous to inception* :—**ní ṙaiḃ toṙnuiġṫe aṙ an múineaḋ aige** aṙ 8.30.
Previous to completion :—**ní ṙaiḃ an ċeaċt múinte aige ag ceaṫṙaṁaḋ ċum a ḃeiṫ.**

(b) *Subsequent to inception* :—**nuaiṙ a ḃí toṙnuiġṫe aṙ an múineaḋ aige ṫáinig an cigiṙe iṙteaċ.**
Subsequent to completion :—**nioṙ ṫáinig an cigiṙe go dtí go raiḃ an ċeaċt múinte ag Seán.**

Future Indicative :—A.—Direct reference to action :—
(a) Absolute :—
1°. *Active* :—**múinfiḋ ṙé ceaċt maiṫ inḋiu, le congnaṁ Ḋé.**
2°. *Passive and Aut.* :—**múinfaṙ ceaċt maiṫ inḋiu má múineaḋ ṙiaṁ é.**

(b) *Contemporaneous* :—
1°. *Active* :—**beiḋ ṙé ag múineaḋ na Gaeḋilge nuaiṙ a ṙagmíḋ iṙteaċ.**
2°. *Passive* :—**beiḋ an Gaeḋilg ḋá múineaḋ aige 7 ṙinn ag dul iṙteaċ.**
3°. *Autonomous* :—**beifaṙ ag múineaḋ na Gaeḋilge ṙa ṙcoil ṙin nuaiṙ iṙ é an Béaṙla a beiḋ aṙ ṙiúḃal i ṙcoileanaiḃ eile.**

B.—Direct reference to previous or subsequent state :—
(a) *Previous to inception* :—**ní ḃeiḋ toṙnuiġṫe aṙ an múineaḋ aige ṙoiṁ a 9 a ċlog.**

232   STUDIES IN MODERN IRISH

Previous to completion :—ní ḃeiḋ an ceaċt múinte aige ap ceaṫpaṁaḋ ċun a ḋeiċ.

(b) Subsequent to inception :—ḃeiḋ topnuiġṫe ap an múineaḋ aige a ḃpaḋ poiṁ 9.30.

Subsequent to completion :—ḃeiḋ an ceaċt múinte aige uaip an ċlinġ pul a ṫpoippeam-ne an pcoil.

Conditional and Subjunctive :—
A.—Direct reference to action :—
(a) Absolute :—
 1°. Active :—ḋá ṁúineaḋ pé an ġaeḋilġ ġo maiṫ ḋ'ṗoġluimeoċaḋ na pcoláiptí ġo pupupḋa í.
 2°. Pass. and Aut. :—ḋá ṁúintí ġo maiṫ í ḋo poġluimeopí ġ pupupḋa í.

(b) Contemporancous :—
 1°. Active :—ḋá mbeaḋ Seán aġ múineaḋ, ⁊ mipe ann, ḋ'éipṫpinn ġo ṅaipeaċ leip an ġceaċt.
 2°. Pass. :— ḋa mbeaḋ an ġaeḋilġ ḃá múineaḋ ⁊ mé aġ ḋul ap pcoil ḋ'ṗoġluimeoċainn ġo ponnṁap í.
 3°. Aut. :—ḋá mbeipí aġ múineaḋ na ġaeḋilġe ⁊ mé aġ ḋul ap pcoil ḋo ḃeaḋ a pían opm inḋiu.

B. Direct reference to previous or subsequent state :—
(a) Previous to inception :—ḋá mbeaḋ topnuiġṫe ap an múineaḋ aige ap 8.30 (aċ ní paiḃ) ḋo ḃeaḋ cuiḋ ṁaiṫ poġlumṫa aġam um a 9.

Previous to completion :—ḋá mbeaḋ an ceaċt múinte aige ap 9,30 (aċ ní paiḃ) ḋ'ṗéaḋpainn é ṁeap.

(b) Subsequent to inception :—ḋá mba ná ḃeaḋ

STUDIES IN MODERN IRISH 233

ʀo ʋe ᴛnuıɢᴛe ᴀʀ ᴀn múıneᴀʋ ᴀıge ᴀʀ 9.30 ní ʋeınn ıʋeᴀnᴀċ ʋo'n ċeᴀċᴛ.
Subsequent to completion :—ʋá mbᴀ **ná beᴀʋ ᴀn ceᴀċᴛ múınᴛe** ᴀıge ʀoıṁ 10.30 ʋo ġeoʋᴀınn cuıʋ ʋe, pé 'n-éıʀınn é.

Imperative :—A.—Direct reference to action :—
 (a) Absolute :—
    1°. *Active* :—**múıneᴀʋ ʀé** ᴀn ceᴀċᴛ, nó éıʀıġeᴀʋ ʀé ᴀʀ.
    2°. *Pass. and Aut.* :—**múınᴛeᴀʀ** ᴀn ceᴀċᴛ, nó ní ᴛᴀʋᴀʀʀᴀʀ ᴀon ᴛuᴀʀᴀʀᴛᴀl.
 (b) *Contemporaneous* :—
    1° *Active* :—**bíoʋ ʀé ᴀġ múıneᴀʋ** nuᴀıʀ ᴀ ᴛéıġım-ʀe ıʀᴛeᴀċ, nó ıʀ ʋó ıʀ meᴀʀᴀ.
    2°. *Passive* :—**bíoʋ ᴀn ġᴀeʋılġ ʋá múıneᴀʋ** nuᴀıʀ ᴀ ᴛéıġım-ʀe ıʀᴛeᴀċ, nó ní beᴀʋ ʀᴀʀᴛᴀ ın ın ᴀon ċoʀ.
    3°. *Aut.* :—**bíᴛeᴀʀ ᴀġ múıneᴀʋ** nᴀ ġᴀeʋılġe nuᴀıʀ ᴀ ᴛéıġım-ʀe ıʀᴛeᴀċ, nó beıʀᴀʀ ᴀġ ġeᴀʀán mᴀʀ ġeᴀll ᴀıʀ.

B.—Direct reference to previous or subsequent state :—
 (a) *Previous to inception* :—**ná bíoʋ ᴛoʀnuıġᴛe ᴀʀ ᴀn múıneᴀʋ** ᴀıge ʀoıṁ ᴀ 9 ᴀ ċloġ.
    Previous to completion :—**ná bíoʋ ᴀn ceᴀċᴛ múınᴛe** ᴀıge ʀoıṁ ᴀ 10.
 (b) *Subsequent to inception* :—**bíoʋ ᴛoʀnuıġᴛe ᴀʀ ᴀn múıneᴀʋ** ᴀġᴀᴛ leᴀᴛ-uᴀıʀ ᴀ ċluıġ ʀul ᴀ ʋᴛıocʀᴀʋ-ʀᴀ.
    Subsequent to completion :—**bíoʋ ᴀn ceᴀċᴛ**

múinte agat ꝑul a dtiocꝼad-ꞅa, nó iꞅ duit iꞅ meaꞅa.

Verbal Noun Forms :—A.—Direct reference to action :—

Óꞅouiġteaꞅ (indic.), do h-óꞅouiġtead, óꞅóꞅan, do h-óꞅouiġti, dá n-óꞅouiġti, óꞅouiġteaꞅ (imper.).

(a) Absolute :—
  1°. *Active* :—Dó an ġaedilg do múineaḋ indiu.
  2°. *Passive* :—An ġaedilg do múineaḋ iꞅ gaċ ꞅcoil aꞅ ꝼuid na tíꞃe (see p. 152).

(b) *Contemporaneous* :—
  1°. *Active* :—Dó beit ag múineaḋ na ġaedilge nuaiꞃ a tiocꝼaiḋ an eigiꞃe. (The nuaiꞃ clause will change according to the form of the introductory verb).
  2°. *Passive* :—An ġaedilg a beit dá múineaḋ 7 ꞅinn ag teaċt iꞅteaċ.

B.—Direct reference to previous or subsequent state :—

Óꞅouiġteaꞅ, etc.—(a) *Previous to inception* :—Dó gan beit toꞅnuiġte aꞅ an múineaḋ aige ꞅoiṁ a 9 a ċlog.

Previous to completion :—Dó gan an ceaċt a beit múinte aige ꞅoiṁ a 10.

(b) *Subsequent to inception* :—Dó beit toꞅnuiġte aꞅ an múineaḋ aige ꞅoiṁ a 9 ċlog, nó ná tiocꞅaimíd in aon ċoꞅ.

Subsequent to completion :—Dó an ceaċt a beit múinte aige ꞅoiṁ a 10.

Exercise LXXV.
Active, Passive, Autonomous, and tá Constructions.

1°. I will strike the shepherd, and the sheep of the flock shall be dispersed.

2°. The veil of the Tabernacle was rent *in two*[1] from the top even to the bottom.
3°. All this *has been done*[2] that the Scriptures of the prophets might be fulfilled.
4°. He laid it in his own new monument which *he had hewed*[2] out in a rock.
5°. And Jesus coming spoke to them, saying :—All power is given to Me in heaven and in earth.
6°. The Sabbath was made for man and not men for the Sabbath.
7°. No one putteth new wine into old *bottles* ;[3] *otherwise*[4] the wine will *burst*[5] the bottles and both the wine will be spilled and the bottles will be lost.
8°. All sins shall be forgiven to *the sons of men*,[6] and the blasphemies wherewith they shall blaspheme.
9°. There is nothing hid which shall not be *made manifest* ;[7] neither was it made secret but that it may *come abroad*.[8]
10°. In what *measure*[9] you shall mete it shall be measured *to*[10] you again and more shall be given to you.
11°. He that *believeth*[11] and *is baptized*[11] shall be saved ; but he that believeth not shall be condemned.
12°. On the eighth day they came to circumcise the child and they were about to call him by his father's name, Zachary.
13°. Every valley shall be filled, and every mountain and hill shall be brought low and *the crooked*[12] shall be made straight and *the rough ways*[13] plain.

1. 'n-a ḃá ċuiṽ. 2. Tá construction. 3. Áṗċáí leaċaiṗ.
4. nó má . . . 5. ḃṗṗ. 6. An cine ṽaonna. 7. Taḃaiṗ ċun ṗoluiṗ. 8. noċt. 9. Cóṁaṗ. 10. Ċun. 11. Future tense.
12. Saċ cam. 13. Saċ ṡaṗḃ.

14°. Everyone that exalteth himself shall be humbled; and he that humbleth himself shall be exalted.
15°. He shall be delivered to the Gentiles, and shall be *mocked*,[1] and scourged and spit upon.
16°. Six and forty years *was*[2] this temple *in building*[2]; and wilt thou raise it up in three days?

---

[1] Ꞇᴀɪꞅᴄᴜɪᴘɴɪᵹɪᴍ.   [2] Autonomous.

CHAPTER XII.

Repetition of words for sake of clearness.

Modern Irish avoids all clumsy constructions which would at once obscure the sense and interfere with the harmonious flow of the language. Hence we find certain repetitions which are worthy of note :—

(*a*) When the subject (of the principal or a subordinate clause) is somewhat complex, it is frequently put first in the sentence, and repeated afterwards (in pronominal form) with the verb :—

MSF. 206.—ᴀn té ṁactnoċaḋ ᴀiṗ iṗ ḋóiċ liom ɡo ḋtuiɡḟeaḋ ṗé . . .

(*b*) Both the verb and the subject (in pronominal form) are repeated, when a clause or phrase qualifying the subject intervenes—

1°. Between a transitive verb and its object.

2ᵁ Between an intransitive verb and the complement of the predicate.

1°. MSF. 28.—Do ċaiṫ an ḟeaṗ n-a ṗaiḃ an ɡunna na láiṁ aiɡe DO ĊAIṪ SÉ é ḟéin aṗ ɡealacán a ḋá ɡlún aṗ an mḃótaṗ.

MSF 27.—Do tóɡ an ḟeaṗ n-a ṗaiḃ an ɡunna n-a láiṁ aiɡe ᴅo tóɡ ṗé an ɡunna le ṗṗóiṫ.

MSF. 208.—Tuɡ an t-Aṫaiṗ Seámuṗ (an Canónaċ anoiṗ) TUɡ SÉ ḋinnéaṗ ḃṗeaɡ ḃṗotalaċ ḋúinn.

2°. MSF. 34.—Ḃioḋ ṗé leaḃaṗ aḃ' ḟeaṗṗ a taiṫnḟeaḋ liom, ḂÍOḊ SÉ aɡam amuiċ coiṗ claiḋe.

Ser. 56.—Ḃí ḟeaḃaṗ ⁊ taiṗḃe an ḃaiṗte a ḃí aɡ Coin 'á ḋéanaṁ, ḂÍ SÉ ɡan aṁṗaṗ ḋo ṗéiṗ ḟeaḃaṗa an ḋuine a ḃeaḋ aɡ ḋéanaṁ na h-aitṗiɡe.

238 STUDIES IN MODERN IRISH

MSF. 50.—Bí an clór a bí ar ağaid tiğe na feoile amac bí sé lán de caraiğreacaib móra cloc.

MSF. 143.—Dá eağmuir rin bí an ğaeluinn a labartaí bí sí ar ailleact.

MSF. 165.—Do léim ğac rağart, ré mar a táinig ré, do léim sé ruar ar an árdán.

MSF. 210.—ğo raib an rağart raróirte a bí anro i brarróirte Cairleáin ua liatáin, ğo raib sé ağ dul cun báir.

MSF. 199.—Bí na daoine a froir an áit pómainn bíodar imtiğte amac ar an rráid.

(c) When the subject consists of several nouns, one (or more) of which is qualified by a clause, the *verb* is repeated in the plural :—

MSF. 46.—D'imtiğ Miceál 7 Caitlín, 7 an méid a bí beo de'n clainn, d'imtiğeadar ar an mbotán. (An alternative device for avoiding clumsiness is *to put the whole of the predicate together at the beginning*, thus :—

d'imtiğeadar as an mbotán m. 7 c. 7 etc.)

(d) The *verb* (and preceding particle) are repeated, when its predicative complement, somewhat long and complex, intervenes before *the object*:—

MSF. 170.—Dá n-abrainn-re leir na fearaib ud a táinig cuğam an oidce úd 'á iaraid orm beit am' rtiúrtóir orta, dá n-abrainn ná feadrainn é ...

CHAPTER XIII.

Miscellaneous.

A.—Feminine adjective not inflected in the dative singular: Feminine adjectives frequently resist inflexion in the dative singular, especially those in -ac. In many cases the phenomenon may be explained as coming under the phrase-noun principle (p. 159).

1°. Ní toil le núp n-ataip atá inp na flaitip go gcaillpí duine de'n muinntip beag pan (CS. 50).
2°. Ag péideað pé gac taob (MSF. 3). Cf. iotaob, etc.
3°. Bímíp ag obaip pan lae ap an bpeipm beag (MSF. 48).
4°. Ap an dtaob toip d'n tpáid beag (MSF. 57).
5°. Bí pé in' oidce dub (MSF. 71).
6°. Ap péid bpeag leatan (MSF. 86).
7°. Deineann an cnucán poitin móp do'n inpe beag (MSF. 127).
8°. San Abainn móp (MSF. 129).
9°. Ap úráid eigin tairbeac a déanam de'n éipim pin (MSF. 149).
10°. Sa coip bacac (S.).
11°. Leip an gcainnt uatbásac (Ser. 10).
13°. Sa mípbúilt móp pan (Ser. 66).
14°. See Ex. a., p. 110 (S. 97).
15°. Fear ip eað Catal go bpuil gpeóip ana-móp aige ı pgéalaideact Sultmar (CD. 51).

B.—Apposition.

Apposition in Irish is either—
   1°. Logical, but not grammatical:—
      (a) Tá bpeit tabpta aip ceana péin toipg náp cpeire pé in ainm míc Dé, an t-aon gein (CS. 230).

(b) Díomair tamall mait ag feiceaṁ leo ag doraṡ tiġe an atar TOMÁS MAC MUIRIS (TITLE ONLY inflected).
(c) Leaḃair an atar PEADAR Ó LAOGAIRE, taitnid riaḋ ar aiteaṡ na cuimne liom (TITLE ONLY inflected).
(d) So in the vocative :—a ataiṙ PEADAR; a ataiṙ SÉAMUS. But—a ḋeaḋair uí Laoġaire a Séamuir uí Ceallaċáin. See 2°. c. below.
(e) Tré iṁroḋ na maiġdine Muiṙe, MÁTAIR DÉ (Ser. 4).
(f) I n-éagmuiṙ lóreḃ ⁊ Muiṙe iṁátair (Ser. III).
or—2°. Logical and grammatical :—
(a) D'é rin ataiṙ céile Cáiṗair, ÁRD-SAGAIRT na bliaḋna rain (CS 277).
(b) D'fin é ataiṙ tomáir UÍ NUALLÁIN (The usual construction).
(c) So in vocative :—a Seáin UÍ Śuilliobáin (usual).
(d) Setantae macc Sualtaim atoinchomnicc-se, ocus
(e)macc Dechtire DO FETHAR-SU (S.T. 4).
Frequently in O.I.—after proleptic a :—a uathmaire. IND FIR (S.T.) ; a masse IN CHUIRP (Gl.).
(f) Corp Sant Anna MATHAR Muire (GM.-ZCP. II.,14)

C.—Dative, Genitive or Locative form now used instead of old Nom.—

Some reformers of Irish indulge in heroics occasionally about the corruption of Gaeḋealg into Gaeḋilg (not to speak of Gaoluinn !) forgetting (apparently) that the same thing has happened in hundreds of other words. It is inconsistent, not to say stupid, to be continually writing Gaeḋealg, and allowing, at the same time, the dative form to serve, instead of the nominative, in dozens of other words. The following list will help the student to realise how widely spread this change is, and when he remembers that the change in some cases had begun in the old Irish period, he will be content to accept these FACTS of language, and admit that there is nothing specially sacred about a Nom. case. The list of course is by no means complete :—

1°. Dative for older Nominative :— uíb laoṡaire (the name of the parish in which Ballingeary is situated); úir (the virgin soil ; Lat. pura (adj.) ; old nom. úr) ; ṡaebtiṫ ; scoil ; tabairt (old nom. tabart) ; ṡabáil (old nom. gabál) and so all verbals in -áil ; maidin ; min (meal ; Mid. I. men) ; triúr (triar) ; vís (as well as older viar = a pair) ; muinntir ; namaid (as well as nama) ; sometimes also carad (as well as cara) ; nádúir (natura).; toil (O.I. tol) ; Middle I. NIT (nest) for O.I. net (mod. nead, nid) ; peín (as well as pian) ; peist (as well as piart) ; óiṡ (virgin) as well as oṡ ; réir (as well as riar) ; ríoṡain (as well as riogan) ; bainríoṡain (also -an) [Here, however, we may have two original modes of declension] ; sceim (and ceiam) ; cribinn (old nom. cribeann : Keating has both forms as vocative in the same poem) seaċtmain (septimana) ; seanmóin (for reanmóir (with assimilation), which again is for rearmóin (with metathesis) from L. sermo) ; sín (as well as rion) ; snáthaid (Mid. I. snathat) ; tiṡ (Munster ; O.I. tech) ; toit, smoke (Mid. I. tutt) ; uaiṡ, grave (Mid. I. uag) ; gluais, gloss, commentary (O.I. gluas (s)) ; uair (O.I. uar, ór ; cf. fó ceaduóir) ; uaim, cave (as well as uam) ; uaim, seam, sewing (uṡaim, also uam) ; uillinn, elbow (also uille) ; urcóid (O.I. erchót) ; orṡain (O.I. orcun) ; tuarṡain ; feircint (with prothetic f- and suffixed-t ;

O.I. aicsiu, dat. aicsin) ; ꝼᴀoıꞃᴅın ; O.I. foisitiu, d. foisitin ; ꞅuᴀıꞃ, danger ; earlier ꞅuᴀꞃ.

2°. Genitive for old nom.—ꞅᴀeᴅıʟꞅe (Connaught) ; oıᴅċe (O.I. nom. adaig).

3⁰ Locative now used as nom.—cıoıııı ᴛSᴀıʟe (Kinsale).

D.— Change in parts of speech :—

In dealing with the development of ꞅo as a relative particle (pp. 109-111) we saw that both the prep. ᴀꞅ and the conjunction ꞅo had some influence. Similarly the oblique relative ᴀ (ᴀꞃ) is in origin a demonstrative (san), just as the relative THAT and the conjunction THAT in English are connected with the demonstrative that. So negative "nᴀ" and comparative "nᴀ" are transformed into the affirmative "nᴀ" of Identification sentences (Type II. b). Shakespeare's "but me no buts" shows how far the process may go. In Irish there are some interesting cases of verbs becoming substantives (nouns or adjectives) :—

1°. ꝼéıᴅıꞃ is now an adjective, but in origin it has been held to be the 3rd sing. present indic. pass. (prototonic form) of the verb ad- cota, éta he obtains. From this verb also comes the modern ꝼéᴀᴅᴀım (Mid. I. étaim) with prothetic ꝼ-. Corresponding to the negative statement ní étir (lit., it is not obtained) an affirmative statement was coined with the verb ıꞅ, viz. is étir (ıꞅ ꝼéıᴅıꞃ), and étir (ꝼéıᴅıꞃ) thus took up the functions of a substantive. Thurneysen, however, has recently maintained that ꝼéıᴅıꞃ is to be referred rather to ꝼéıᴅıꞃ, ꝼéıᴅꞃeᴀċ. Keating has ᴛıꞅ ꝼéıᴅeᴀᴅ ꝼéıᴛꞃeᴀċ (noisy, powerful) ᴅo ꞅᴀoıᴛ nᴀ n-ᴀꞃᴅ (K.P. 553), Dineen has ꝼeıᴛꞃeᴀċ, strong, stout. I can find no trace of ꝼéıᴅꞃeᴀċ in the modern language.

2°. In a similar way the O.I. perfect passive of the verb ro fitir (modern ꞅeaꞅáꞃ), namely, fess, became a noun or adjective, ní fess gave rise to ıꞅ fess (ıꞅ ꞅeaꞅ ꞇom, etc.) on the analogy of ní fiss : ıꞅ fiss, and so ꞅeaꞅ became a noun or adjective.

3°. There was in O.I. a verb fo-fuapair, fópair (fo-od-ber) meaning he attacks, makes for. From this comes the modern verb ꞅóbꞃaım, I begin, attack, meditate, happen by accident, etc. But, furthermore from saying ꞇ'ꞅóbaıꞃ ꞇom é ꞇéanaṁ (an impersonal use of the verb in the sense of " I almost did it ") we come to say also ba ꞇóbaıꞃ ꞇom é ꞇéanaṁ, where out of the impersonal ꞅóbaıꞃ, preceded by ꞇo we form a new substantive (adjective) ꞇóbaıR.

Words beginning with a vowel are liable to take on accretions from the previous word. Cf. the frequent occurrence of prothetic ꞅ-, e.g., ꞅuıꞃeoꞅ, ꞅaıꞃe, ꞅuaꞃ, ꞅaıll, ꞅaıꞃnéıꞃ, ꞅanaım, ꞅıaꞅꞃaıꞅ, etc., and the variation between p and ꞅ in words like pꞃéaṁ, ꞅꞃéaṁ ; paıꞃċe (parochia), ꞅaıꞃċe ; ꞅıll, pıll, ꞇıll ; pꞃoṁaꞇ, ꞅꞃoṁaꞇ ; paılm, ꞅaılm (ꞇoṁnaċ na ꞅaılme) ; Mid. I. petarlaicc for older fetarlaic (vetere lege) ; pıꞇıbín : ꞅıꞇıbín. Cf. also the confusion of initial n- with final -n of the article, in—uıṁıꞃ (number : = nuıṁıꞃ), eaꞅ (O.I. ness) eaꞅcóıꞇ ; neaꞅcóıꞇ (boil, sore ; O.I. nescóit).

E.—Some words in which Indo-Germanic "p" has been lost.
  1. -arc in immchomarc = questioning. Cf. L. posco < †pr̥k-sco ; procus (suitor), precor = I pray.
  2. The prep. aꞃ (in relative construction are -ara- ; cf. Gall. Are-morici) Gr. περὶ, etc.
  3. alꞇ = joint. Cf. Gk. ꞇı-πλάσιος, double.

4. -ᴀon in ꝼıoꞃᴀon < †epōno, †epno ; cf. Eng. even (Pedersen).
5. ᴀn-uıꞃıꝋ (last year) ; Gk. πέρυτι, πέρυσι.
6. άṫ = ford. Gk. πάτος a trodden or beaten way ; L. pons.
7. as-ren ; Gk. πέρυμηι I sell.
8. all (rock ; ᴀıʟʟ, ꝼᴀıʟʟ) ; †palsos. Cf. Germ. Fels (rock), Eng. fell.
9. ᴀıṫıꞃne (calf) < †pathre-nıo. Root-pa = feed. L. pascor, pabulum (Z.C.P. VII, 2).
10. άıʟ (fitting, desired) < †pak-li. (Cf. L. pango, paciscor). (Or possibly †ad-li ; cf. adas, comadas).
11. ᴀṫᴀıꞃ ; L. pater.
12. céᴀċꝋᴀ (plough) ; Gk. καμπτός = bent. (I.G. pt > cht).
13. cꞃeᴀꝋᴀꞃ = wood-cock, barn-owl, patridge, barnacle ; immediately from †Kreb-ro, but cf. L. crepo (screpo), (Marstr).
14. coʟ (sin, impediment, prohibition ; blood relationship) ; L. culpa.
15. cᴀoꞃ (berry) ; Gk. καρπός = fruit.
16. cᴀoꞃᴀ (sheep) ; L. caper.
17. coꞃꞃάn (carrán) ; L. carpo ; Gk. καρπός.
18. cᴀċṫ (O.I.) = a female slave ; L. capta. (pt > cht).
19. cꞃō ; †Krapos ; Eng. roof = hroof.
20. cuᴀn (harbour) ; cf. Eng. haven (†Kopn-) ; Kjöbenhavn.
21. cʟuᴀın (meadow) < †klopni—(Thurn.).
22. cᴀm (crooked) ; Gk. κάμπτειν = to bend, bow.
23. cúıꞅ (five). I.G. penque ; L. quinque ; Gk. πέντε ; cf. L. pugnus (fist).
24. eᴀꝋ (in ꞃe h-eᴀꝋ ⁊ ꞃe h-ᴀımꞃıꞃ ꝼᴀꝋᴀ), time, space ; †pedo- ; Gk. πέδον ground, earth, land, soil. L. oppid-um. Possibly the same root is to be found in ıomᴀꝋ, ıonᴀꝋ (in both of which the ꝋ was originally aspirated).

25. eapc = speckled ; Gk. περκνός. Unless it belongs to the root erc- (shining, radiant) found in ruaipc, ou-aipc. Cf. L. arguo, argentum, argilla (white-clay).
26. ad-ella (v.n. aüall ; cf. caüall, üiall, cpiall) < †pelna. Gk. πίλναμαι pass. of πιλνάω, I bring near to ; L. appellere. " Germanici triremis Chaucorum terram adpulit" (Tac. Ann. 2, 24).
27. éiceac (falsehood) < †peiti-ka (Marstr. Z.C.P. VII, 2). Pedersen, on the other hand, derives either from 1° epi-togh (tongid, he swears) comparing Gk. ἐπι-ορκέω (swear FALSELY) ; or 2° from I.G. †eito- O.I. oeth, Eng. oath, comparing, for the change of meaning, the word luige (used as vb. n. of tongid) which means etymologically " lying."
28. éan (bird) ; †pet-no- ; cf. L. peto, penna, petulans (diminutive).
29. eicpe (= tail, end ; lit. feather) ; †pet-rio. Cf. éan.
30. po (pó, pé, pá, paoi) ; Gk. ὕπο; Sk. upa.
31. pop :—Gk. ὕπερ, L. super, Sk. upari. 31° puaim < upo-vok-smen (Marstr.) ; L. vox. Cf. pocpom, pocponn (po-copann).
32. il (iol) (many) ; Gk. πολύς ; Goth. filu.
33. ic (corn), iotlainn (haggard) ; Sk. pitus ; L. pituita, phlegm ; a gummy exudation from trees.
34. iü (drink) ; Sk. pibati ; L. bibit (for pibit).
35. íp, íop (prep. and adv.—down) ; †pēd-su (If not from prep. in).
36. O.I. iress, hiress. Still extant in the negative compound ampar (doubt). Originally vb. n. of ar-sissedar. ir- is one of the stressed forms of the prep. ar (q.v.). For the meaning (faith) cf. Gk. ἐπίσταμαι = I know (Attic), believe (Herodotus).

37. ιαμ (τιαμ, ριαμ ανιαμ, ιαρταμ, etc.); apparently a neuter -μο extension of the I.G. epi- found in Gk. ἐπί.
38. ιαρš; piscis?
39. ιάμ : †plāμ—; Eng. floor ; cf. Sc. G. blàr.
40. ιάn :—Either from †plānus (level, with the unevennesses *filled up*) directly, or a form of the root plē (L. plenus, Gk. πλήρης).
41. cuṁ-αιι (handmaid ; lit. praegnans) -αιι < †paln (cf. 40).
42. ιion : plenus.
43. ιáṁ : palma (with lengthening).
44. ιeac ; cf. πλάξ, anything flat or broad : planus < placnus.
45. ιuαṁ : pilot ; Root †pleu = sail. Gk. πλέω, πλεύσομαι.
46. ιucταμ (boat) ; cf. Eng. sloop?
47. μοι: Gk. μολπή (song) dancing to music; Melpomene.
48. neacτ (niece) ; L. neptis.
49. nια : L. nepos.
50. oμc : L. porcus.
51. όμ, uαμ †oup-su (uαcταμ †oup-tero ; τuαμ, μuαμ, αnuαμ) ; Goth. iup = upwards (Pedersen). Thurn. on the other hand sees -ks in the μ of όμ, comparing uαcταμ and the Gall. Uxellodunum (Hightown).
52. μeó (frost) ; L. pru-ina.
53. prep. μe : cf. L. prin-cipium ; Gk. πρίν.
54. μιαṁ : L. primus < †pris-mos, μιαṁ < †prisam-.
55. μαιτ-neac (fern) : †prati-.
56. άιτ : †pothni ; Sk. pathas = place (Pedersen).
57. μuαn : L. somnus < sopnos †svepnos. Cf. L. sopor ; Gk. ὕπνος (with labial infection from π or the lost digamma ? Or υ represents an ablaut grade of υε-).
58. μeαμμ (sickle) ; L. sarpo ; Gk. ἁρπη, kind of falcon ; sickle, scimitar.
59. μeacτ : septem : ἑπτά
60. μαομ : †sapero- ; L. sapio.

61. O.I. soud, in ιompóʊ, cιonncóʊ :—Root svap, sup; cf. Lat. dis-sip-are.
62. ɼpón : Root pster ? L. sternuo.
63. ɼιne (teat, nipple, pap); aspirated in O.I. bó tri-phne (cow with udder of three teats). Lithuanian spenys.
64. ɼeιp, ɼeιpιʊ (now = heel; orig. = ankle) aspirated in dual (O.I.) dí pherid ; Gk. σφυρόν = ankle.
65. O.I. selg (spleen); Gk. σπλήν, σπλάγχνα. Mod. I. ɼeaιʒ.
66. ce (warm ; O.I. tee) : L. tepent-es.
67. cɑn (time ; but compare Eng. then); L. tem-pus.
68. cuιle (flood) : < to-li-n (Root plé).
69. ʊíleɑnn, ʊílιnn, ʊíle :—dí-li-n (Root plé).
70. úp : L. purus.
71. uɩɑɩʊ : cf. Gk. πύλιγγες (curled hair). So uɩċɑ (beard); uɩɑɩʊ (uɩ-ɼɑʊɑ = long-bearded ?).
72. upɼɑ : prep. ɑp+root of L. postis (Pedersen).
73. pιoċc : < †pɼptu : Gk. πρέπω (Pedersen). But Marstr. (Z.C.P. VII, 2, 361) derives from r̥kta, a weak form of the root in ɼu-ɑιpc, ʊuɑιpc (also ɼo-pċɑ, ʊo-pċɑ).
74. pɑnn : †parsna ; L. pars.
75. ɼo : L. pro.
76. en = water; englas (milk and water) < †pino (cf. ιʊ L. bibo) (Z.C.P. II, 306).

CHAPTER XIV.
Word-formation.

A.—Verbal Nouns :—

1°. -o stems :—cúṁoac, cuiṁpeac, (cuibpeac), copc, polac (po-laiᵹim), pulanᵹ (pulaᵹ) tópmac (oo-for-maig), tapann, tatant (act of driving,' barking at, etc., do-seinn), aoall, taoall, oiall, tpiall (the last four from the root ell-, cf. Lat. appellere = to come to land (Tacitus).

Notice that in cúṁoac, cuibpeac, polac, tópmac, the final -ac is not a suffix but part of the verbal root itself.

2°. io- stems :—cf. Latin gaudium puioe (†sodium from the o grade of the root -sed, Lat. sedere ; solium. For the interchange of l and d cf. old Latin impelimentum for impedimentum ; lacrima for the older dacrima, Gk. δάκρυ, I. dér, oeop ; lingua, Ir. teanᵹa (for oeanᵹa) ; Ir. cuileactain for cuioeactain ; cf. ceioṁ (plague) for oeioṁ (Root ded- = evanescere, tabescere).

éipᵹe, eipeipᵹe ; eaᵹna (no longer a *verbal* noun ; wisdom) ; ppeaᵹpa (frith-gaire) ; poba (fubae from fo-ben) ; luiᵹe ; taipbe (torbe from torban, dororban) ; tuile (do-lin). poba, taipbe, tuile no longer *verbal* nouns.

3°. ia- stems :—claioe, ᵹuioe, ite, pliᵹe (no longer *verbal*). Cf. L. invid-ia.

4°. Different stems but with -t (th, o, or o, or ?) ending in modern Irish :—beit (buith), bpeit, beannact, mallact (no longer *verbal*), bpat (mrath from mairnid, betrays) cleit (later ceilt), oútpact (no longer *verbal*), oeapṁao, formad (root men- in L. mens,

STUDIES IN MODERN IRISH 249

E. mind) oui̇ge (ouigeað where th in unstressed syllable has become oh. In ꝺeaṗṁaꝺ, ꝼoṗmaꝺ, final c has been eclipsed by preceding -n). ꝼiaꝼꝼaiꝺe (early I. iarfaigid, from †-sagitus) atċuinge, atċuingiꝺ ; ceaċt, ꝑat (no longer *verbal*).
The verbal noun form is (frequently) different in compounds as compared with the simple noun. E.g., bꝑeit, but in compounds bert :—caḃaiꝑt, aḃaiꝑt (O.I. epert) ioḃaiꝑt ; ḃéim, but in compounds -ḃe, -ḃae,—ꝼoḃa (O.I. fubae) caiṗḃe (O.I. torbe).

5°. -tu suffix :—meaꝑ, ꝼioꝑ, coiṁéaꝺ. Sometimes the old verb has become obsolete, and a new verb has been formed from the old verbal noun, e.g., meaꝑaim, coiṁéaꝺaim ; so téimim side by side with the older lingim ; céimnigim as compared with elder cingim (obs.).

6°. With -tiu suffix in old nom. :—ꝺíꝺean, ꝺíoin (protection. O.I. dítiu) ꝼoigꝺe (patience. O.I. foditiu), ꝼeiꝑcin, ꝼeiꝑcint (ꝼaicꝑin, ꝼaicꝑint) O.I. aicsiu (†ad-ces-tio). In ꝼaoiꝑoin (O.I. fóisitiu, from fo-sissedar), we have analogy, on the model of foditiu, airitiu, etc. The old dative is frequently used in the modern language as nominative—a thing not unknown in the Old Irish period—e.g., tabairt, gabáil instead of tabart, gabál. In ꝼeiꝑcint we have the old dative, with prothetic ꝼ-, change of ai to ei, metathesis of ꝑ and c, and the addition of a final -t. For the change from ai to ei, cf. mac, gen. mic for earlier meic, maic. In speech one frequently hears ꝼicim (not ꝼeicim).

7°. With mu- suffix (masc.) :—gníoṁ, ꝺéanaṁ, ꝼógnaṁ coꝑnaṁ (now frequently coꝑaint), ꝑníoṁ. But imꝑeaꝑán (from same root. The earlier form was imbressan. The a has been lengthened on the

250 STUDIES IN MODERN IRISH

analogy of diminutives in -án). cuilleam, caipipe (loyalty, for earlier tairissem).

8°. With ma- suffix (fem.) :—cpeipoeam (no longer verbal; cpeipoeamainc is used instead); maoiroeam, agallam. cpeipoeam and maoiroeam are now masculine.

9°. With mn- smen- suffix :—béim, céim opéim (opings-), léim, péim, pogluim, cuicim (O.I. tothaim), gaipm. Notice that béim, céim, péim are no longer *verbals*. Also that, as in the case of bpeit, the verbals béim, gaipm take a different form in compounds :—poba (O.I. fubae), ppeagpa, cagpa, pógpa, agpa (also ppeagpad, ppeagaipc, etc.); nairom (now pnaróm) from napc-; peinnm; maróm (this last on the analogy of naróm). Gaipm occurs in the compound cogaipm = summoning, invitation, etc.

10°. With suffix -ni, (fem.) :—buain (bong-) (now frequently buainc, and by confusion with verb bain, bainc); áin (root ag- to drive) cáin iomáin(c), ciomáin(c), comáin(c).

11°. Miscellaneous :—alcpam; anacal, aónacal (suffix lo- ?) gabáil (suffix -dla) gein, peic, cpeic (these two on the model of ioc), éipic (from peic) leanamain(c) (early lenamon), panamain(c) (Mid. I. anad) leagan, péacain(c), pic, cimcipeacc (from root reth- with ending modelled on ceacc). Other forms of the noun corresponding to pic are :—1°. ress, seen in Mid. I. esraiss = way, passage; 2° rithin in póipicin, help. Coga (or used formally as verbal cogad), poga (both from root gus-; cf. Augustus (Avi-gustus), Eng. cost); rcpíbeann (rcpíbinn) léigeann, aippeann (from Latin gerundial forms); ippeann (earlier iffern) on the analogy of these;

STUDIES IN MODERN IRISH 251

céaval, poipceaval (suffix -tlo). Many of the above are no longer used as *verbals*.

12°. Sometimes the verbal noun is from a different root to that of the verb :—E.g. gal is used as the vb. noun of the old verb fichid = fights. With ֍al cf. Gk. χολή· and with ficnιo, Latin vi-n-co. ֍al survives in certain compounds :—víoֆal, toֆail, poֆail, poֆluive ; ap poֆail = outlawed ; eaֆal (ek + gal) pionֆal (murder of a tribesman < fine) ; peapc used as verbal to capavo (obs. or nearly so) ; ól : ιvιv (obs.—c.f. L. bibo, for pibo). A new verb ólaim is now used. Similarly the verbs corresponding to tavovpe (O.I. taidbsiu) aipnéip, paipnéip (O.I. aisndís), pcéal (ad-fét) are now obsolete, and these nouns are no longer VERBALS. A new verb aipnéipim has been formed from the verbal noun aipnéip.

13°. -av (atus) :—molav, bualav, etc.

14°. -uֆav, iuֆav for verbs in uiֆ, iֆ :—beannúֆav, ípliúֆav.

15°. -acc : éipteacc.

16° buaccainc, aipeaccainc, maipeaccainc. These seem to be modelled on the old dat. sing. of mallacc, beannacc, viz. mallaccain, beannaccain (O.I. bendachtin, maldachtin) with the addition of a final -c. So acnuacainc, aicbeuvcainc.

17°. Intensive or iterative forms in -úcán (from verbals in -uֆav, iuֆav) and -acán (from others) :—ceipciúcán, pֆpúvácán, ollmúcán, cpuinniúcán, piappaiveacán, luiֆeacán, ֆeappacán. These may have originated with diminutives from verbals in -ac like cúmvac, cumvacán. The transition from the diminutive to the iterative and intensive meaning is easy enough The " petty" questioner is generally insistent.

18°. -ċın, ċaın :—fóıpıċın (fóıp<fo+peth) ; feapċaın (pour <feapaım ; then downpour, *rain*).

19°. -ɀal, -ɀaıl, -uíol :—puruíol, feaoɀaıl, ḃpúċtɀaıl, ɀnúrɀaıl (quiet lowing), etc.

B.—Composition :—
1°. First element a *noun*, second element *adjective :—*
folċ-ḃuıḋe, uċt-leaċan. When an ADJ. is made up of a noun and an adj. the adjective must come second. If, however, the compound is a noun, the adj. may come first : móp-ċúṁaċt, móp-luaċ ; but as an adj. luaċṁap, lóɀṁap (the termination -ṁap is in origin the adj. móp). Words like fıonn-ḃappa are really nouns, whereas ḃáıpp-fıonn is an adjective. Notice that the initial consonant of the second element is aspirated. This is because the STEM of the first element is used ; where these stems ended in a consonant -o was added or, in some cases, substituted (e.g., teɀlaċ < †tego-slogus) ; aspiration in Irish shows this ; in Gallic words the vowel appears, e.g., Ir. eaċpaḋ, Gall. Epo-redia, Dago-(Ir. ḋeaɀ-)-vassus, Dumno-rix, Vergo- bretus (name of magistrate amongst the Ædui, and = cuius iudicium efficax est. Vergo- = feapɀ, Bitu- (Ir. ḃıċ, cf. ḃıċ·ḃeo) riges. Cf. Gk. μονο-γενής only-begotten. Gall. Cingetorix, Carent-o-magus.

2°. First element a noun, second also a noun :—
talaṁ (-n stem)—ċúṁrcuɀaḋ (earthquake) : muıp (-i stem)—ḃpan (sea-raven) ; pıɀ (-g stem)—ṫeaċ ; teaɀ (-s stem)—laċ (2nd element = plóɀ pluaɀ ; when the vowel is shortened (through loss of stress)

final gh broad becomes ch) : fioṫ-ċat (lit. wood-cat,
i.e., mouse-trap) ; ioṫal-aṫraṫ (idolatry) ; marc-
fluaġ (cavalcade) ; briatar-ċat (battle of words) ;
ḋún-ṁarḃaṫ (homicide; the first element is equivalent
to ḋuine) ; ban-ċara (ban is the composition form
of bean), bainrioġain, croḃang = bunch, cluster
(quantity held in hand) (also croḃaing) < croḃ =
claw, the hand from wrist to fingers, +ang (cf. Gk.
ἄγγos, pail, bowl, bucket—Z.C.P. VII. 2, 397).

3°. 1st element an adj., second a noun :—
ápṫ-rí, ceart-láṙ, cruaḋ-ċáṙ, ḋeaġ-ḋuine, ṫroċ-
teangaḃálaiḋe, reanaċair, nua-fiaḋnaire (all *nouns*).

4°. 1st element an adj., second also an adj. :—
uileċúṁaċtaċ, ḋeaġ-ḃlarta, ṫroċ-fuaḋmaċ,
ḋuḃġlar, fionn-ruaḋ.

5°. 1st element an adj., 2nd a verb :—
céaḋ-ċuir, uile-ṁairḃ.

6°. 1st element an indeclinable particle (other than a preposition), 2nd element a noun :—It is worthy of
note that when an ADJ. is made up of an indeclinable
particle and a n**o**un, the adj. becomes an -i stem
in Irish (as in Gk. and Latin) though the noun was
an -o or a- stem :—E.g., ronairt (so + neart) énirt
(O.I. < ess + nert) raiḋḃir (so + aḋḃar) ; ḋaiḋḃir
(ḋo + aḋḃar) ; ionnuaċair (in + nuaċar) ; ḋeiḋḃir
(fitting ḋi + aitḃéar, i.e. without reproach) ; rutain =
everlasting (ro + tan) ; oirḋirc, = illustrious (ar +
dearc). The change takes place also sometimes
when the resulting compound is a NOUN :—ḋeoġair
= a diphthong (ḋe, composition form of ḋó, ḋá +
foġar), inċinn (in + ceann), Ḋiarmuiḋ (ḋi + formaḋ)
But on the other hand ḋoċar, roċar ; foitin =

shelter, may be from ɼo+ɼíon. Cf. the Latin adjectives imbellis, imberbis, inermis, exsomnis, exanimis, bicornis, multiformis, etc. (from o- u- and a- stems). With u, io, ıᴀ stems the phenomenon is not so general. ıonnɼᴀıc (worthy) is probably from ın+ɼeıcc (sell); ɼoıʟɓıɼ and ɓoıʟɓıɼ come probably from ʟᴀɓɼᴀ (ʟᴀɓᴀıɼ, speak).

Further exx. of indeclinable particle + noun:—

The Indo-Germanic negative particle n̥ (appearing in Latin as in, in Gk. as a- in Teutonic languages as un-) becomes in Irish

(a) ın- before ᴅ, ꜱ :—ınᴅʟıꜱe, ıonꜱnᴀɓ (in+ꜱnᴀċ).

(b) en- before c, c :—éᴀꜱcóıɼ, éᴀꜱɼᴀɱʟᴀċc (i.e. en + coɼᴀɱʟᴀċc).

(c) an- before vowels, labials, and other explosives than those mentioned in (a) and (b)); ᴀıneoʟᴀɼ, ᴀınɓɼıoɼ, ᴀınɱíne; ᴀn- irregularly before c in ᴀınċɼeıɓeᴀɱ.

The neg. particle ᴀɱ—in ᴀɱɼᴀɼ (ᴀɱ+ıɼeɼɼ, faith). ᴀımɼıɓ (barren) < Early I. birit == a sow. SK. bharanti = bearing; Root-bher.

The neg. particle ɓí—in. ɓíċɼeᴀɓ (cɼeᴀɓ = Eng. thorp, O.H.G. Dorf, village).

The neg. particle mí—in mí-ɼᴀɼᴀɱ, etc.

The neg. particle ɓo—in ɓombʟᴀɼ, ɓoċᴀɼ (aspirating, on analogy of ɼo-).

The neg. particle neᴀɱ—in neᴀɱ-ᴀıɼe, neᴀɱ-ɓʟᴀɼcᴀċc.

7°. 1st element indeclinable particle, 2nd an adj. —

éᴀꜱcóıɼ (en + cóıɼ); ᴀnnɼᴀ (difficult; an + asse, easy). From this word comes ᴀnnɼᴀċc = love, affection; cf. the change of meaning in meᴀɼᴀ, in—

ir meara liom Seán ná Séamar ; indeanb ; eantrom ; eagramail (en + cormail). Superlative particle an (ana-) in—ana-mait, etc. ; aindpiorac. In ruaicnid (well-known, illustrious) we have the change from an o- to an i- stem, though the last element is an adjective, not a noun : (†su-aith-gnáth) doраіd, роpaid may be from either péid, or the noun Rat. neamrшmeamail, mí-párta, amulcac.

8°. First element *preposition*, second element noun, adj., pronoun, or verb :—

(*a*) The preposition ad (Latin ad) :—

1° Before vowels and old u > ad:—
adnacal (ad + anacul) ; taidbre (with initial to-) (from do-adbat).

2°. Is assimilated to t, d, c, g, b, m, and s :—aitpead (ad+tread ; the a is lengthened because of the noun ait). Aduigim (ad+dógaim ?) ; aierin (mod. feierin feircint = †ad - ces - tio agallam (ad-gládathar). aibid ripe (O.I. abaig from bo(n)g-). Amur (ad+mess). Hence verb aimrigim ; atá (root stá).

3° Before l, r, n it becomes á :—áil (<ad-li ; cf. adas, comadas O.I.). Áram (ad + ríom), áinrid (ad + ness + id).

4°. Before the prep. od (syncopated) it became aud, ed, id, and in mod. Irish, iod, íd :—iodbairt, íobirt (ad + od + beir).

(b) The preposition ar (er, ir, air, ur, oir, úr) :—(cf. L. AR-biter, agi-ER). Oirdirc (oirdeirc, oirdearc) pron. uirirc in South Munster ; urnaige, urnaigte. (Also úr- ; from ar-ini-guide) ; syncopated in aitrige (ad-eir-rige) ; úrlabra, úrlár, ullam (O.I. erlam, irlam ; Sc. G. ùrlaim, expert. Cf. Gall. Aremorici = people living before the sea ; Are - brig - nu - s =

(village) lying on a hill (brig = O.I. bpí (gen. bpeʒ) = hill).

(c) aic,-aið :—aicne ; aiceapʒ (aithe+sc<Root-seq Thurn. I, 453) ; aicpiʒe, cacaoip. So accuinʒe, ac-lá, aicbliaðain (the New Year). Cf. Latin at,=*but*. In modern Irish three meanings are distinguishable :—
    1°. iterative :—aicbeoðaim, aic-bpipim.
    2°. negative :—aiccpeiðeam = apostacy.
    3°. back :—aiciompáil, aicbéim.

(d) céað (O.I. ceta-, cita- cét-). Only in céaðfaið (sense) from cét+buith. In W. Cornish, and Breton it means 'with' and is probably the same as the Gk. κατά (†Kn̥ta). Thurn. I, 455.

(e) cóm Latin (cum, con-) :—
    1°. Before vowels and l, n, r :—cóm :—cómaiple, coimðeacc, cómlionað. In cómnápo, cómnaoip, the nasal m causes insertion of n-before vowel.
    2°. Before i, e or u, sometimes cúm :—cúmpanað (com+uð) cuimpeac.
    3°. Before d, g, written con, but with ʒ = conʒ :— conʒnam (com+ʒniom) conʒaðáil (coinneáil) ; coinðeatʒ (contention, comparison). But cómnʒap.
    4°. Eclipses t, c and > coð- coʒ- :—coðlað (†contulud). (In speech of course the d is assimilated to l) ; coʒap (con + cop) coʒað (con + cac).
    5°. Before s>co (with original doubling of s) copnam (com + pniom) copmail (com + samail).
    6°. Before old v the m of com disappears in :—ðo cuaið (cum-ved). Similarly before m in cuimin

STUDIES IN MODERN IRISH 257

(com-men). On the other hand cumarg (cum+mearg), cuimil (com+meil).

7°. In other cases before v, the m becomes v and the resultant is b :—cubur (†cum+vissus), coguabar, cubaid (mod. cuibe) (com+fid = a letter of the alphabet); cf. cuibear, cuibearaċ, for earlier cuidbear, etc.; coibċe (com+ fiaċa) = hire, debt, dowry. Coiblige (com + fo + luige), coibnear (com+fine+ar) coibneartha. But cf. coimneara (next) and O.I. com-nessam. Coimeartan (com+fearcar = vesper).

8°. In borrowed words coin- often represents Latin con- and eclipses f: coinbliocc (con-flictus), cointinn (con-tentio). Coinriar (conscience; cf. cubar, coguabar).

9°. Before i m disappears in cuing, coingir, if these are to be derived from com+iung (Lat. jungo, jugum).

10°. In later compounds the ante-vocalic form cóm is used before all consonants and aspirates on the analogy of rem- remi- (ream-) :—cóm-ċionól, cóm-gluaireaċc, cóm-molaim, cóm brúgad. In cómbaid and its compounds the m and b are both unaspirated. In cumaoin the two m's apparently give an unaspirated m.

(f) di, de :—(Latin de).

1°. Before most consonants, and vowels—di :—díogbáil, dítreab, díreaċ; diall, dí-áirme (innumerable).

2°. Before c broad, fo, and possibly b (broad)—de- :— deaċor (O.I. de-chor) dearmad (†de-ro-ment), deabaid (de-buith). In déanam there is com-

K

pensatory lengthening. So víðeʌn (O.I. dítiu from di étiu).

3°. Before ꝟo->ꝺu in ꝺúꞇꝛʌċꞇ; cundubart (com-difo-bert) doubt, now conncʌƀʌıꝛꞇ = danger.

4°. Before old v in other cases, ꝺı and ꝺe appear: O.I. diad and dead = end; cf. ꝺeo, ꝼʌ́ ꝺeoıꝺ; mod. I. ꝺéıꝺeʌnʌċ, ınꝺıʌıꝺ. Welsh—diwedd.

5°. Before ꝼ it appears both as ꝺe and ꝺı (ꝺí?):— ın-ꝺeʒʌıꝺ, ınꝺíʒʌıꝺ (de-śaigid). The latter possibly on the analogy of ınꝺıʌꝺ (from ꝺıʌꝺ the end; mod. ınꝺıʌıꝺ). ꝺe is the form to be expected on account of the *a* in saigid.

(g) eʌċꞇʌꝛ :—eʌċꞇꝛʌnnʌċ; eʌċꞇꝛʌ (expedition, adventure). Cf. L. extra.

(h) ess, as (L. ex) :—

1°. Before vowels, and c, t, s,—eʌꝛ, eıꝛ :—eʌꝛonóıꝛ, eıꝛeıꝛʒe, eʌꝛcʌꝼʌ, ꞇeʌꝛꞇuıʒ (to-ess-ta), eʌꝛꞇʌ́n.

2° Sometimes ʌıꝛ—ʌıꝛeıꝛʒe. Here possibly owing to wrong connection with the ʌıꝛ of ꞇʌꝛ n-ʌıꝛ, ʌıꝛnéıꝛ (O I. aisndís < as-ind-fét).

3°. Before l, m, n, r, é appears :—éʌıóꝺ (ess-lud; cf. Gk. ἤ-λυθ-ον, ἐ-λεύ-σομαι), éıꝛıc, éımım (ċımıʒım), I refuse (cf. early I. for-énıd = he cannot), énıꝛꞇ (ess+nert). Mod. ınıꝛꞇe (weakness (Anal. of INERTIA?

4°. Before b, g, d it occurs in the form ek- (with -s lost) and the k assimilates :— ʌƀʌıꝛ (O.I. epir < ek + beir) eʌʒʌl (ek+gal : cf. ꝺíoʒʌl, ꞇoʒʌıl, ꝼóʒʌıl) etrocht (shining).

5°. Later on we find ess- (instead of this ek-), in mod. I. eʌꝛ :—eʌꝛƀʌ (ess + bae = good), ꞇeʌꝛꝛʌċ (with

STUDIES IN MODERN IRISH 259

το-). The modern Irish ⱭⳠⲀⲒⲢ for O.I. epir is due to confusion between ⲀS and Ⲁⱱ, or to phonetic development from s + d (infixed pronoun). Cf. neⲀⱱ (O.I. net) < ni-zd-os (root SED) L. nidus ⲦⲀⱱS (Tasgus).

(i). Ᵹⲁn (O.I. cen) :—ceⲀnⲀ, ceⲀnnⲦⲀⲢ (= the district *on this side*, as opposed to ⲀⲒⲒⲦⲀⲢ). The original meaning was "on this side." Cf. L. cis, citra; Gk. ἐ-κεῖ; Irish bith cé = this world here.

(l) ⲒⱱⲒⲢ, eⲀⱱⲀⲢ :—(L. inter) :—eⲀⱱⲀⲢᵹⲛⱱⲉ, ⲒⱱⲒⲢⲘⲉⲀⱱⲟnⲀⲦ: ⲊⲀⲢⱱⲀⲟⲚ (Thursday < (eⲀ)ⲢⱱⲀⲢ ⱱⲀ ⱵⲟⲒne?). This preposition aspirates on the analogy of ⲀⲢ. In ⲊⲀⲢⱱⲀⲟⲚ (if the derivation be correct), the second ⱱ is assimilated to the first (i.e., the aspiration is removed).

(m) ⲢⲒⲀⱱ :—(Root veid, vid. L. video. E. wit, Germ. weiss; cf. ⲢeⲀⱱⲀⲢ ⲢⲒⲟⲢ, ⲢⲀⲟⲒ (so+uid-s), ⱱⲀⲟⲒ (do+uids), ⲟⲒⲚⲘⲒⱱ (cf. un-wit-ting); ⲀⲒⲘⲒⱱ may be a participial form like ⱱⲒⲢⱱ. ⲢⲒⲀⱱⲚⲀⲒⲢe (directly from the noun ⲢⲒⲀⱱⲁ (gen. ⲢⲒⲀⱱⲀⲚ)).

(n) Ⲣⲟ (Gk. ὑπό, L. sub) :—(For to-fo- see p. 263 and for de-Ⲣⲟ p. 258.)

1° Before consonants :—Ⲣⲟ, ⲢⲀ Ⲣⲟ (with compensatory lengthening) :—ⲢⲟⲒᵹⱱⲉ (patience; O.I. fodιtiu = suffering). The Munster form ⲢⲟⲒⱱⲚⲉ probably goes back to the dative (O.I.) foditin; ⲢⲟᵹⲚⲀⲘ (Ⲣⲟ + ᵹⲚⲒⲟⲘ), ⲢⲟᵹⲀⲚⲦⲀ. In Ulster ⲢⲀⲒⱱⲉⲀⲢ we have ⲀS, (< O.I. fo-d-ɟera). Mid. I. fuba ⲁⲄⲤ ruba = hewing and killing.

2° Before o, a > Ⲣⲟ, ⲢⲀⲀ, ⲢⲀ :—ⲢⲟᵹⲢⲀ (Ⲣⲟ+ⲟⱱ+ᵹⲀⲒⲢe) ⲢⲀⲀⲢⲚⲀⱱ = tumult (fo-od-ess-anad) ⲢⲀᵹⲀⲒⲘ (Ⲣⲟ+Ⲁⱱ + gabaim); ⲢⲟⱱⲀⲒⲢ (Ⲣⲟ-ⲟⱱ-beir); **ⱱⲀ ⱱⲟⱱⲀⲒⲢ** (ⱱ'ⲢⲟⱱⲀⲒⲢ)—(see p. 243). In Mod. I. this prep. takes the forms: Ⲣⲟ, Ⲣⲉ, ⲢⲀ, ⲢⲀⲟⲒ.

260 STUDIES IN MODERN IRISH

(*o*) ꜰᴏꞃ (L. super, Gk. ὑπέρ) :—ꜰᴏꞃᴍᴀᴠ, ꜰᴏꞃꜰᴀꞃ, ꜰᴏꞃᴀɪʟ (ꜰᴜʟᴀɪꞃ, with metathesis) ; sometimes lengthened— ꜰᴏɪꞃᴄᴇᴀɴɴ, ꜰᴏꞃʟᴀᴍᴀꞃ, ꜰᴏɪꞃꞃᴇᴀꞃᴄ.

(*p*) ꜰꞃɪᴛ (Root vṛt of L. verto, *vorsus*) :—
1°; Before vowels ꜰꞃɪᴛ :—ꜰꞃɪᴛɪɴɢ = return track ; ʙᴇᴀɴ ꜰꞃɪᴏᴄᴀɪʟᴛᴇ (nurse).

2°. Before consonants :—the th of ꜰꞃɪᴛʜ assimilates :— ꜰꞃᴇᴀɢꞃᴀ (ꜰꞃɪᴛʜ-ɢᴀɪꞃᴇ ; e for ɪ in first syllable because of a following a, or o. Cf. ꜰᴇᴀꞃ ; vir(os) ; ᴏꞃᴇᴀᴄ : †dṛka, †drika ; cf. Gk. ἔδρακον (with ṛ). Other grades in δέρκομαι and δέδορκα. ꜰᴇᴀᴠᴠ : vidua ; ʙꞃᴇɢ (gen. of ʙꞃɪ hill) < brigos ; ɴᴇᴀᴠ (O.I. net < †ni-zd-os ; L. nidus, E. nest) ; ꞃᴇᴀꞃɢ (†sit-ko-s ; L. sitis thirst) ; ꞃɴᴇᴀᴄᴛᴀ (beside old verb snigiṿ = L. ninguit), ʙɪᴛ (but gen. ʙᴇᴀᴛᴀ, O.I. betho).

3ᵛ. Later compounds show ꜰꞃɪᴛ before consonants, aspirating on the model of ᴀɪᴛ :—ꜰꞃɪᴛ-ᴠᴜᴀʟᴀᴠ (re-percussion) ꜰꞃɪᴏᴄɴᴀᴍ (care, diligence) = O.I. frithgnam < ɢɴíᴏᴍ ; for meaning cf. Lat. *officium* (facio). In the modern Irish form *the th of ꜰꞃith has become h- and unvoiced the gh of* ɢɴíᴏᴍ ; ꜰꞃíᴏᴄ- instead of ꜰꞃɪᴏᴄ- possibly on the analogy of ᴄꞃíᴏᴄɴᴀᴍᴀɪʟ WHICH HAS THE SAME MEANING as the adj. form ꜰꞃíᴏᴄɴᴀᴍᴀɪʟ ; ꜰꞃɪᴛ-ʟᴇɪɢᴇᴀᴍ = reperusal. The Connaught ꜰꞃᴇɪꞃɪɴ instead of ꜰꞃɪꞃ ꞃɪɴ is on the analogy of ʟᴇɪꞃ ꞃɪɴ.

(*r*) ɪᴀꞃ, ɪᴀꞃᴍ :—ꜰɪᴀꜰꞃᴜɪɢ (with prothetic f-, metathesis of ꞃ and ꜰ, and assimilation to verbs in -ᴜɪɢ :< †iar-fo-saig) ; ɪᴀꞃᴛᴀꞃ (aspiration on analogy of ᴏɪꞃᴛᴇᴀꞃ). This preposition seems to be formed, by means of a suffix in r-, from the I.G. †epi (Gk. ἐπί) which in I. would give ᴇɪ (with loss of p) ᴇ, ɪᴀ (Thurn. I, 468).

STUDIES IN MODERN IRISH

(s) imbi, im :—

1°. Before vowels, and ŗ- ım, ıom :— ımeaȝla, ımŗeımŗe, ımŗeaŗán (Earlier imbressan ; á lengthened on analogy of diminutive -án), ıomáın (†im-ag-ni-), címċeall (with co-).

2° Before ŗ > ımp :—ıompóꞅ (†imbi-śoud), ımpíꞅe (†imbi-śuiꞅe). But later ımŗeaŗc, ımŗníom.

3° Before other consonants ım (aspirating) :—ımċeaċc, ımꞅeaŗȝaꞅ, ı n-ımıȝcéın (a contamination of ın ımcéın and ıȝcéın).

Three meanings in modern Irish :—

1°. intensive :—ımꞅeaŗȝaım (revile) ; ımeaȝlaıȝım == terrify ; ımcıȝım, ıomcuŗ.

2°. mutuality :—ıomaȝallam, ıombuaılım.

3°. literally (round about) :—címċeall, ıomáın.

(t) ın (In composition it has three forms in, en, and ini (Gk. ἐνί) and a fourth form ınꞅ is probably identical with the old Latin preposition endo, indu, seen in *ind-uere*).

1°. en, which becomes é before c, c :—éırceaċc (O.I. étsecht) ŗéaꞅaım, ŗéıvıŗ (O.I. étir < ad-cota— enta). But see p. 242 ; ꞅéıcŗın (†do-en-ci). In ceaȝaŗȝ, eaȝaŗ, eaȝna the e is short, irregularly.

2°. ind :—cıonnŗcnaım. The d appears in the O.I. perfect tindarscan (to-ind-ro-scan) ; ıonncamaıl, similitude (ind-samail) ; cıonncóꞅ (to+ind+ soud ; cf. ıompóꞅ), cıonncuıȝım ; ıonnŗaꞅ (attack. O.I. ind-red ; root "reth," run) ; indarpe, mod. ıonnaŗba(ꞅ).

3°. in-before vowels and many consonants :—ınŗıúċaꞅ, Inid (L. initium) ınıŗle (humility) cınŗeaꞅ (aspiration (to-in-fed (śvet)) ; ınbeaŗ (estuary).

4°. ini :—úpnuige, úpnuigte (< er-ini-gude : mod. guide) ingean ; Ogham inigena

(*u*) ior :—ioccap (probably on analogy of uaccap) ; ireal. Pedersen derives it from †pēd-su. It is possibly a genitive from the base of the preposition in ; cf. acc ; Gk. ἐκτός. Cf. L. in-tus ab-s. Adverbial in r-ior, t-ior, an-ior.

(*v*) ó, úa and od, uad :—

1°. iodbaipt, ibbipt (ad-od-ber) ; diomar (di-ud-mess), cúmdac (com-ud-ding).

2°. After ro, po, to > ró, pó, tó :—rógpa (ro-od-gaipe) tógáil (to-od-gabáil).
In tobap (to-od-ber) and torac (to-od-siag) we have short *o*.

3°. Before ι, p > ó, ua :—tionól (do-in-ó-la). Cf. Latin ÁU-fero.

(*w*) ór :—uaccap (cf. Gall. Uxello-dunum, i.e., Hightown. L. auxilium, Gk. αὐξάνω). We have it adverbially in r-uar, t-uar, an-uar. Pedersen derives it from †oup-su and uaccap from †oup-tero- (I.G. pt > cht). Goth. iup = upwards.

(*x*) pe- (before) :—peám-focal, peám-puidiugad (preposition) ; cf. Lat. prae, pri-mus, prin-cipium ; Gk. πρίν.

(*y*) po- (L. pro). In Mod. Irish the *o* is long, in its adverbial use with adjectives :—pó-máit, pó-fuar. It combines initially with only a few verbs—paid, pug, páinig, pinne, pigim, poicim (ro-saigim) (now usually rpoicim, rpoirim) picc (in- go picci, but mostly without the po- now, as go nuige (as far as). In most cases it is joined to a preceding particle—go, ní, muna, etc. Preceded by de > deap :—deapmad and deapmad. We have it in poga (choice) pabad (robud < ro + bud ; cf. Gk. πυ-ν-θ-άνομαι) = warning.

STUDIES IN MODERN IRISH 263

(i) reac :—reacaroim (present, bestow) ; reacavav novlag
= A Christmas box. Formed apparently from the
prep. pron. reacav = past you (2nd sing.) ; cf. L. secus.
(j) tap, vap :—toipmeapc ; taipmteact (obs.).
(k) to (pretonic vo) :—
  1°. Before consonants, mostly to, (tu), tó (with
  compensatory lengthening) :— tuitim (O.I.
  tothaim) tómap. Reduced to ti (with compensatory lengthening) in tígeact (on analogy of
  tigim, teact. In O.I. it was tuivéact (tuidecht)
  with v instead of th.
  2° ta, tá—tavaip, tápla (on analogy of -tarat, and
  because of loss of a in do-rala : -tarla (In O.I. the
  1st a was short.
  3°. te—in teilgim (do-léig) possibly from to-en-
  léig > teillgim. Thurn. I, 481.
  4°. ti—in Connaught form tiubpav, on the model of
  the old reduplicated future with i in reduplicating
  syllable.
  5°. Before vowels :—t- (except before ov- > tó, tua,
  tógáil) :—tigim, tuigim, tugap, timceall (i because of position before mbc).
  6° tó before for, od, fo :—tópmac (to-for-mag)
  tógaim (to-od-).
(q) tpé :—tpiall. Cf. avall, tavall, viall.

The following prepositions are not used in Composition :—
ag (except with pronouns), amal (except with 3rd s. pronoun
in amlaiv), le (except with pronouns), go (to) (except with
pronouns), reac (with perhaps one exception), ol. The
following only rarely :—piav, ioip, eactap, céav, gan (only
in ceanntap, ceana), iap, ip, óp, tap, tpé (except with
pronouns).

264   STUDIES IN MODERN IRISH

The following are preserved ONLY in Composition:—aḋ, aiṫ, inṅ, oḋ, fiaḋ, eaċtar, céaḋ, ír, ro, fop, cóṁ (as prep.), except in such expressions as ꝼo n-iomaḋ réaḋ (L.O.). Seaċ (outside composition) is generally followed by ir (aꝼur); re, occurs, outside composition, in the form roiṁ, and (as an adverb) in the form riaṁ. Im, outside compounds, takes the form UM (probably through loss of stress in such forms as umam-ra). The modern preposition ċum, ċun (earlier dochum, is a noun < †Kudsmen; L. cacumen; or, according to the latest derivation < toiċim) is used separately with nouns; the prepositional pronouns with which it is usually associated (ċuꝼam, etc.) are originally formed from co, ꝼo (= to).

C.   Suffixes.
I. Nominal Suffixes.
(a) Verbal Nouns. These have been already dealt with (pp. 248-252).
(b) From **Adjectives** :—
  1°. -e (Old -ia. Cf. L. sapient-ia) ꝼáilte (now = welcome; originally = joy, from ꝼáiliḋ = joyous) ruaire, ruaraiꝼe. Sometimes -i in Mod. I. for earlier -e. E.g., miniċi(ꝼe) for mid. I. *mence*. In O.I. this was the ordinary way of forming a noun from adjectives in -aċ. In modern Irish we frequently use for these also the suffix -ar. E.g., buiḋeaċ - ar, aireaċ - ar, aiṫreaċ - ar, béarlaċar. With many adjectives, however, this suffix -e is not used. E.g., mór, beaꝼ, etc, adjectives in -aṁail; those ending in a vowel, e.g., ceannra, te.
  2°. -e (neut. io- stem) ḋeire, maire. There is no distinction any longer between these and 1°.
  3°. -isse (Mod. ire) an extension of No. 2° raoiṗre

(ꞃaop), ꝺaoiꞃꞃe (ꝺaoꞃ). These of course in the modern language are fem.

4ᵘ. -tut- (O.I. nom. in -u ; cf. L. juventus) ; In Mod. I. the ending is either -a, or -e :—beaṫa (O.I. bethu) < beo, ꞃláinte (O.I. slántu).

5ᵘ. -as (old -us < essus, estus, and -as < assus) :— ionnꞃacaꞃ, binneaꞃ, coꞃṁaileaꞃ, cuibeaꞃ (earlier cuibꝺeaꞃ < cubaiꝺ) ; ꝼaicċioꞃ (O.I. faitigus) < ꝼaiteaċ, lit. fore-seeing, cauticus. This meaning is close to the modern meaning in many places—shy.

6°. -s from monosyllabic adjectives :—baoiꞃ (baoṫ) ꞅaoiꞃ (ꞅaoṫ) ꞅnáꞃ (ꞅnáṫ) ꞃcíꞃ (ꞃcíṫ, tired ; cf. éaꞃꞅaiꝺ, quick) ; teaꞃ (te) does not belong here. It is probably < †tepes-tu- cꞃioꞃ (girdle) comes from the same root as cꞃoiꝺe,—†kr̥d-su .

7ᵘ -aċt, to form abstracts :—ceannꞃaċt, ꞅtoꞃꞃaċt, coꞃṁalaċt, etc. I.G., -akta probably from root ag- drive, and therefore = that which is driven. Hence *group* ; then *nature*.

8° -a (now usually -e instead, 1°). Mid. I. boċta, now boiċte. But úꞃlabꞃa (from verb) ceannꞃa (originally *noun*, now an adjective. The old adjective was cennais).

9°. -tas, -das (= Mid. I. tu, + as) the former after consonants, the latter after vowels :—bꞃéantaꞃ (Mid. I. bréntu) ꝺoꞃċaꝺaꞃ (Mid. I. dorchatu).

10°. -aꞃ, aċaꞃ (in a few nouns). There are many numeral nouns in -aꞃ (from ꝼeaꞃ) :—aonaꞃ, tꞃiúꞃ (the old dative ; the nom. was tꞃiaꞃ), ceatꞃaꞃ, etc., iolaꞃ (iol = many). The few in aċaꞃ seem to take their origin from ꞃalaċaꞃ (ꞃalaċ)—this perhaps because of clábaꞃ, also = dirt, mud. The original meaning of ꞃalaċ (L. salax, from salio = I leap) was lustful, lecherous. The meaning, however, has broadened. On the model of ṗaṫaċaṗ, apparently, are formed—ṫaġaċaṗ (weakness, from ṫaġ), maṫṫaċaṗ (with ṗaḃaiṗc) = slowness, weakness.

11°. -ṫ from adjectives in -aċ :—ṗeaḋmannaċ-ṫ; caṗṫannaċ-ṫ.

12°. -aḋ :—uaṫaḋ = singleness, unity, singular number < root of Gk. *αὐτός* (self).

13°. -iḋe (preceded by a suffix -qo, diminutive) ṗeanaċaiḋe; also -aṗ (preceded by the same suffix) ṗeanaċaṗ; cf. Latin senex (oldish ; the suffix qo- does not appear in this word in Latin outside the nom. sing). re-*ci*-pro-*cus* = going backwards and forwards (from *re* and *pro*).

14° -ṗeaċ (fem.) Cf. L. issa ġaiṫṗeaċ = foreign woman : earwig. óinṗeaċ; ḃáinṗeaċ = a white cow (ḃán); ċéiṗṗeaċ (the female blackbird : ciaṗ = black) ; minnṗeaċ = a young she-goat (meann-án, mionn-án)

15°. -is-tero- (-ṗeaṗ); ṗinnṗeaṗ (†sen-is-tero-) " is " is the comparative suffix (iōs, ies, is) in its weakest form, seen in L. magis (for the other two, Lat. major (mag-iōs), majestas (mag-ies-tas). Tero- is the compar. suffix common in Gk. (cf. L. al-ter, in-ter. Eng. other, whether. I. alltar, ceannṫaṗ, ceaċṫaṗ, etc.).

16°. -aċ :—ṗáṗaċ (desert).

17°. -ine :—ṗiṗinne. The n is doubled in ṗiṗinne according to *MacNeill's law.*

18°. -óġ :—ġnáṫóġ (wild beast's lair).

19° án, diminutive :—beaġán, móṗán.

(c) From Nouns :—

1°. -aċṫ :—ḃiaċṫ, ḃaonnaċṫ, ṫeaċṫaiṗeaċṫ, ṗiliḋeaċṫ.

In early I. frequently from nouns in eaṁ :—
bṗeiċeaṁnaċṫ. From these the termination
-ṁnaċṫ spread. E.g., bibdamnacht. From this
noun the modern biṫeaṁnaċ seems to have been
formed.

2°. -aċṫain, aċṫainṫ -ċainṫ (the two latter for verbal
nouns) :—cuiroeaċṫain, aipeaċṫainṫ, aiṫbeoṫċainṫ
(see p. 251).

3° -as :—lánaṁnap, aṫaiṫpap (a double suffix here.
From aṫail == adultery, concupiscence, with
reminiscence of the L. adulterium, perhaps). Now
usually aṫailṫpannap from the adjective aṫal-
ṫpannaċ, which owes its suffix perhaps to the adj.
eaċṫpannaċ (which again is influenced by the Lat.
externus, extraneus).

4° isse (mod. iṗe) a neuter io- stem :—piaṫnuiṗe
(Directly from the noun piaṫu (gen. piaṫan).

5°. -paṫ, paiṫ : Collective. (There were two such
suffixes in O.I., one neuter (connected probably
with reth run), the other fem. (connected with I.
riad == journey, Gallo-Lat. rheda == chariot) :—
luaiṫpeaṫ (ashes) now luaiṫpeaċ ; oiṡpe (ice)
O.I. aig-red ; ṡnioṁpaṫ (from this comes the
strong plur. of ṡnioṁ, ṡnioṁapṫa). So ṡeiṁpeaṫ
(Gk. χιών, L. hiems), paṁpaṫ. (Cf. Saṁain ; Gk.
ἡμέρα) laoċpaṫ(m), macpaṫ(f.).

6°. -laiṫ.—Collective. Really the noun plaiṫ == kingdom :—éanlaiṫ(e).

7°. -ṫpaċṫ.—Collective—banṫpaċṫ.

8°. -aipṫ.—Collective—conaipṫ (hounds). Possibly we
may see here the word ppaiṫ (series), L. sero. For
change in compound cf. bpeiṫ : ṫabaipṫ.

268 STUDIES IN MODERN IRISH

9°. -ʟᴀċ.—Collective. (The word ʀʟóᵹ, ʀʟuᴀᵹ); ᴄᴇᴀᵹ-ʟᴀċ (household); muᴄʟᴀċ.

10°. -ɪ́ᴏe (earlier id, ith). The agent :—ʀᴄéᴀʟᴀɪ́ᴏe, ᴀɪnmnɪ́ᴏe (Nominative).

11°. ᴀṁ, eᴀṁ :—ḃʀeɪᴄeᴀṁ, ꜰéɪċeᴀṁ (debtor) ᴏúɪʟeᴀṁ (creator); (ꜰeᴀʟʟʀᴀṁ (philosopher) is a borrowing from the L. philosophus (Gk.), but has been assimilated in form to these nouns. The old form was felsub.

12°. -ᴀɪʀe (Lat. -arius) :—ᴄeᴀċᴄᴀɪʀe, ʀeᴀċᴄᴀɪʀe, ḃᴀ́ʀᴀɪʀe, áʟᴀɪʀe (a brood-mare). Cf. ꜰᴀʟᴀɪʀe, an ambling horse, and Eng. palfrey).

13° óɪʀ :—ᴄoɪnnʟeoɪʀ, ᴏ́óɪʀʀeoɪʀ.

14°. úɪʀ :—ᴏoċᴄúɪʀ (m. 3rd decl.). But CRÉATÚIR (f. 2nd decl.) is from L. creatura.

15°. -ᴄóɪʀ, -ᴏ́óɪʀ, -ᴀᴏ́óɪʀ (L. -ator), ᴄeoʟᴄóɪʀ; ʀʀeᴀʟ-ᴀᴏ́óɪʀ, ḃʀéᴀᵹᴀᴏ́óɪʀ.

16°. -ᴀ́n (masc. diminutive : < †agnus) : — ᴄnoᴄᴀ́n, ʟɪoṁᴀ́n (O.I. lem, L. ulmus).

17°. -ᴀᵹᴀ́n (dim.) :—íoʀᴀᵹᴀ́n, ᴀᴏᴏᴀᵹᴀ́n. Here we may have an accretion of the ᵹ of ḃeᴀᵹᴀ́n; or else a double suffix—the Britannic suffix óg (= I. ᴀċ) + ᴀ́n. Other varieties of this diminutive are -ᴀᴄᴀ́n, ᴀᴄᴀ́n, -ʀᴀᴄᴀ́n, ᴀᴏ́ᴀn : — méᴀʀᴀᴄᴀ́n (thimble), ʀᵹᴀᵹᴀċᴀ́n (strainer), ʀᴀṁnᴀċᴀ́n = a salmon trout (lit. a yearling trout, if from ʀᴀṁ = summer; cf. ʀᴀṁᴀɪʀᴄ = young heifer < sᴀṁ + ʀeᴀʀᵹ = unfruitful, dry; ᴄnúᴏᴀ́n = gurnet is derived, from the adj ᴄʀuᴀɪᴏ́ : also ᴄʀúᴏᴀ́n, ᴄʀuᴀᴏᴀ́n (Z.C.P. VII, 2, 405). For the converse change of ᴄn > ᴄʀ cf. Ulster ᴄʀoᴄ (ᴄnoᴄ), ᴄʀᴀ́ṁ (ᴄnᴀ́ṁ); ᴏoᵹʀᴀᴄᴀ́n, ḃɪoʀᴀ́nᴀᴏᴀ́n (pin-cushion), ḃʀéᴀᵹᴀᴏᴀ́n (toy).

18°. -naiṫ (Fem. diminutive) O.I. nat (e.g., óthathnat; uaċaḋ : pauculus). ḃláṫnaiṫ (Little Flower), also bláthnat (weasel) which *may* be the same word. Opanncaiṫ (flea) is < ṫeapṡ-naiṫ.

19°. -ín (Dim.) piṗín, ṅóiṗín. Same as I.G. suffix-ino-. Cf. Gall. Ticinos (Ir. ceiċim, I fly ?), Eng. swine; su-ine : L. sus.

20°. óṡ -ċóṡ :—óṗḋóṡ, ríḋeóṡ, ḃáḃóṡ, etc. Generally diminutive; míolċóṡ = gnat; cuaṗnóṡ (nest of honey bees).

21°. -ne, -íne :—(Dim. or Collective) : pole; poilcne (a single hair : so puainne); ṡṗán; ṡṗáinne. aintine (stormy weather; an-paḋ = storm.

22°. -lo (I. al) :— Caċal (cf. L. Catullus), Tuaċal (tuaċal = withershins). ṫeiṗeal = the turn to the right. Earlier we find tnaithbél, tuaithbil, suggesting that the second element is -ḃéal. It is however certainly -sel (svel) Irish ṗeal, turn, time, spell, space. Further ceiṁeal (darkness) ; cf. L. temere, tenebrae. néal (neb-lo) coll (hazel :—L. corylus = cosylus, Eng. haz-el).

23ᵛ anaṗ :—in cṗéaḋanaṗ, originally a period of three days, from O.I. cṗéḋe, three things, but under the influence of the Latin, triduanus. Now = abstinence.

24° ceaṗc :—in cuaiṗceaṗc, ṫeiṗceaṗc. The ṗ of cuaiṗceaṗc seems to be due to ṫeiṗceaṗc. Cf. converse influence of cuaiḋ on ceaṗ (instead of ḋeaṗ). The origin of the suffix is obscure ; could it be connected with the L. pars ?

25° lann :—the place where things or persons are kept; leaḃaṗlann, oċaṗlann, aṁaṗclann, aiṗmleann. But ann-lann = sauce contains the Welsh llyn = drink. Cf. I. linn.

26°. tar :—aiteantar : ugoaptár (In P.H. augtortas). In Mod. I. the second a is long.

27°. -ac :—coinnleac (connlac) = stubble < Middle I. condall, stalk, stubble.

28°. -apnac (a double suffix -ap (belonging originally to nouns like clagap, cogap: in this last it is not a *suffix*) + nac (the suffix -ac added to -n stems) :— cogapnac; clagapnac (the suffix is usually diminutive, but this word means *heavy* rain; so however does the simple clagap; it has perhaps an iterative force here, referring to the frequent falling drops). Then also—cnagapnac (crackling, rustling noise) < cnag; miogapnac (dozing); liacapnac < liac, (sighing); luibeapnac, lubapnac (collective : weeds in general) gnúrapnac (under-lowing of a cow); riorapnac = whispering (riora).

29°. -actac. Apparently also a double suffix from -act + ac (or ac + tac) :—gnúractac (under-lowing < gnúract); caractac (coughing).

30°. -pac, -lac (of the noises made by animals) :— amartpac (barking); géimpeac (lowing; also géimneac); gpágallac (clucking of hens); méitleac (bleating); riorapac (riotapac, neighing). -aptac in rraotaptac (sneezing) and ualltaptac (of swine).

31°. -gail, gal, uiol :—gpággail (= gpágalac), gnúrgail (lowing); puruiol (pouting); comartuiol; brúctgail (belching); reaouiol (reangail) (whistling).

32°. -sine (cf. 21) :—fáirtine (< fáio) < fáitrine. For change of o into t before r cf. cpot < cput in phrase in cput rin. Also Ulster biot ré < bioo ré.

(d) From **Adverbs** or **Prepositions of place**; and **pronouns** :—
-ṫaṗ :—oiṗṫeaṗ, iaṗṫaṗ, uaċṫaṗ, ioċṫaṗ, ceannṫaṗ, alltaṗ, eaċṫaṗ (exterior) aiṗṫeaṗ ; ceaċṫaṗ (originally, each of two ; now mostly with negative-neither) ; neaċṫaṗ (from O.I. nech), ionaṫaṗ (intestines).

(e) From **Verbs** :—
1°. -ṫ: the agent, or kindred meaning :—áiṅṗiṫ (accusative case < ad-ness-).
2°. -aċṫ : abstracts :—ṫuġṫaċṫ, beannuiġṫeaċṫ (derived directly from participle).
3°. -aṗ, -ṫaṗ :—ṫaḃaṗṫaṗ, ṗáġalṫaṗ (also directly from verbal adjective in ṫe, ṫa).
4° -nt (-aṫ) :—caṗa (caraid = he loves: still alive in Ulster). Cf. L. part. in- NT-.
5°. -uos (cf. Gk. perfect participle active in -ως) Coimṫiu (Lord) < †com-med-wōs (Root of midithir = he judges ; vb. n. meaṗ).
6°. -s :—ḃáṗ : originally vb. n. to root ba-; cf. Gk. ἔβη; Sk a-ga-t.
7°. -aṁ :—Agent. luaṁ = pilot, from root †pleu-sail.
8°. -neoiṗ (through verbal nouns in -n) -ṫóiṗ, aṫóiṗ :— ṗġṗiḃneoiṗ (ṗġṗiḃinn), molṫóiṗ, ṗíġeaṫóiṗ.
9°. -ṫaṗ :—lóṫaṗ (canal) L. lavacrum ; Gk. λουτρόν, bath ; ṫaṗaṫaṗ (gimlet) ; Gk. τέρε-τρο-ν.
10° -aiṗe :—claṫaiṗe (lit. a digger ; claiṫiġim, I dig ; claiṫe = a fence ; claġaiṗe (Dineen) = a fish after shedding its spawn, should be spelled claṫaiṗe. It is the same word, the change of meaning being sufficiently clear (Z.C.P. VII, 2, 369).

STUDIES IN MODERN IRISH

II. Adjectival Suffixes :—

(a) From **verbs** :—tio- (ce, ca, ċe, ċa) : buaiLce, moLca, beannuigċe, ragċa.

(b) from **numerals** :—

1°. -to, -eto : ṗeiṗeaḋ, cúigeaḋ, ḋeiċṁaḋ (we may look upon the ṁ here as the final *m* of †dekm̥).

2°. The double suffix m̥mo + eto :—(I. ṁaḋ, aṁaḋ) ceaċṗaṁaḋ, cṗioṁaḋ, etc. In the I.G. period apparently sometimes the -mo suffix, and sometimes the -to suffix was used. Hence L. decimus (†dek-m̥mo-s), Gk. δέκατος (†dekm̥-to-s). The combination in Irish was helped by ṗeaċċṁaḋ, ḋeiċṁaḋ (where *m* belonged to the cardinal) and naoṁaḋ where ṁ may represent the original final *m* of novem (cf. Gk. ἐνενήκοντα).

(c) From **Nouns** :—

1°. -d(a)e :—(Mod. ḋa, ċa):—ḋa is often pronounced -ga : —maoṗḋa, ṗíoxḋa, cṗóḋa (cṗú, blood ; L. cruor, cruentus), ḋaonna (O.I. doínde, from plur. of ḋuine), banḋa ; muinnceaṗca, neaṁċa (heavenly), coiḋneaṗca. This suffix denotes—quality, mode, belonging to, material, time, origin.

2°. -aċ :—uileċóṁaċcaċ, peaċcaċ, onóṗaċ, éiṗeannaċ, inṁeaḋonaċ, buiḋeaċ, ḋleagċaċ (M.I. dlighthech).

3°. aṁail :—ṗeaṗaṁail, ṗLaiceaṁail. English -ly.

4°. ineaċ (From -n stems with addition of -aċ) :— anaċ | ainmneaċ, aLbanaċ, maṗcanaċ, ḋéiṗcineaċ (cf. Sc.G. déistinn, teeth on edge, disgust < dét ? Or Mid. I. déistiu = refuse of everything) ; ṗiaċcanaċ, inncinneaċ ; then added to words which did not end in -n :—coiLċeanaċ, ḋéiḋeanaċ, ḋuiṗcineaċ. Words like eaċcṗannaċ may have

STUDIES IN MODERN IRISH 273

had some influence also ; cf. L. externus, extraneus
aḋaltṗannaċ.

5°. -iḋe :—colnaiḋe, uṁaiḋe, ḃiṫ-céillṫiḋe, eaġnaiḋe (wise).

6°. -aṁnaċ :—(From nouns in -aṁain(t)) :—creiḋeaṁnaċ, oiṗeaṁnaċ, leanaṁnaċ.

7° -ṁaṗ :—(= the adjective móṗ) :—ciallṁaṗ, éaḋṁaṗ, ṗonnṁaṗ.

(d) From **prepositions** :—-lo :—uaṗal (óṗ), íṗeal (ioṗ).

(e) From **adjectives** :—

-ḋa :—beoḋa, móṗḋa.

-aċ :—bléiteaċ = a mullet (< †bhleiti-ko- (Z.C.P. VII, 2, 389) lit. the sparkling one ; cf. Eng. blithe).

D. Miscellaneous :—

1°. ionann (equal to, all one, the same) is derived by Pedersen from the def. article + aon.

2°. éiġin seems to be gen. of the noun éiġean (m. and f. Cf. the phrases aṗ éiġin, and luċt éiġin). In earlier I. we frequently find what seems to be the fem. dat. used adverbially (without a preposition) : E.g., P.H. 3506 co ro-b ann écin (there especially) ; 3758, is doig écin, it is quite likely ; 3855 is demin écin, it is absolutely certain ; 7898, acht induind fén écin, but in our own selves ; 7934, acht is indíu écin, on this very day ; 3095, co mad he Ísu écin. But we also find the adjectival use :— 344, oen bliadain écin, one year anyhow ; 2504, eirc co locc écin, go to some place or other. éiġin is sometimes used wrongly by learners instead of áiṗiṫe. Speaking generally ḋuine éiġin = Lat.

aliquis, but ᴅuine áιpιċe = Lat. quidam; so ꝼuᴅ éιɢin = aliquid; ꝼuᴅ áιpιċe = quiddam.

3°. ιᴀꝛᴀċᴛᴀ seems to be gen. of ιᴀꝛᴀċᴛ. Distinguish cᴀpᴀll ιᴀꝛᴀċᴛᴀ and ιᴀꝛᴀċᴛ cᴀpᴀιll.

CHAPTER XV.

Change of Meaning in Words.

Words change their meaning in two ways :—
   I. By association with different prepositions, particles etc., in composition.
   II. By the broadening or narrowing of their connotation owing to various psychological or other causes.
I. (a) ᴀnᴀcᴀl, by itself means *protection, deliverance*. When combined with the preposition ad- it means *burial :* ᴀᴅnᴀcᴀl. Also, with metathesis of n and l, and lengthening of -ᴀn to -án :—ᴀᴅlᴀcán. Then further by assimilation of ending to that of verbals in -ᴀᴅ, ᴀᴅlᴀcᴀᴅ, the usual form in Munster at the present day.

Combined with to- and ino- it means the act of *bestowing*, O.I. tindnacul. But the word has undergone similar changes to those of ᴀᴅnᴀcᴀl > ᴀᴅlᴀcᴀᴅ, its modern form being tioᴅlᴀcᴀᴅ (with loss of n before first ᴅ (now aspirated) and compensatory lengthening of l). The plural tioᴅlᴀicte, tioᴅlᴀicti = benefits received.

(b) There was an old verb caraid = he loves (cf. L. carus, caritas, Fr. chère). It survives still, but is not much used. We find the root in several compounds, however, with more or less change of meaning : With oᴅ- prefixed, and -ᴀr suffix > ocrᴀr = hunger (oᴅ-cᴀr-ᴀr). With the preposition ᴀᴅ- > accur (O.I.) = joy. The mod. I. ᴀcᴀr = profit, loan, use of a thing ; also tool, instrument, may be the same word. At all events we have it in a compound with the negative an-, viz.: anacair = affliction. Ciocar = ravenous hunger > cioc + car- (two c's coming together > unaspirated c). So trócaire = mercy < trógcaire, lit. loving pity.

(c) ciall = sense, understanding. With vi- it means "one's best effort" viceall. With fio (wood; a letter of the alphabet) it means a chess-board, the game of chess fioceall (now often spelled ficceall).

(d) O.I. fed- v.n. fedan (†vedhna) = lead. With ar- and com- v.n. erchót it means *hinder*. With root and meaning, cf. Eng. wed; and for meaning the L. duco (in matrimonium).

(e) O.I. gal (cf. Gk. χολή) v.n. of O.I. fichid (cf. L. vi-n-co), he fights.
There are various compounds in mod. Irish:—
With ar- iorgail = contention, attack, battle.
,, vi- viogal = vengeance.
,, fo- fogail = robbery, depredation.
fogluive = robber.
,, to- togail = destruction. With finefiongal = slaughter of a tribesman.
,, ek(s)- eagal = fear.

(f) fiaca = debt, obligation. With com- coibce = dowry.

(g) The verb gab (L. hab-eo) occurs in many compounds:
With fo-ao- fágaim; cf. L adhibeo.
,, con- congbaim, coinnigim; cf. L. co-hib-eo.
,, vi- viogbáil; cf. L. debeo < de-hib-eo.
,, to-for-ess- tuarargbáil (account); cf. L. ex-hib-eo.
,, fo- fagáil.

With di- in- :—diongḃáil (equal, match) ; cf. Eng. a great " *take.*"

,, to-od- :—tógáil.

,, suffix -la :—gaḃal = fork ; estuary ; land enclosed at confluence of two rivers ; the groin ; prop, pillar. The diminutives gaiḃlín, góilín are common in place-names.

(*h*) -gaire = the act of calling (simple, gairm) ; cf. L. garrulus. The root gar- occurs in many compounds. With ad- agra (also agraḋ, agairt) = challenge, revenge, dispute.

,, to-ad- tagra (also -aḋ, -airt) = pleading, alluding to. The forms in -airt are due to taḃair, taḃairt.

,, in- :—inguire (feeding of cattle) ; cf. inġior.

,, to :—togairm = summons, invitation, petition.

,, fo- od- :—fógra = proclamation.

,, frith :—freagra = answer ; freagairt = answering.

,, fo- :—foġar = sound, noise.

,, de- fo- :—deoġair (diphthong : de- is here the composition form of dó, dá (2).

(*i*) gním = I do, make. (Root gen. gne, gn (L. gigno, Gk. γίγνομαι). Vb.n. gníoṁ. In many compounds: With di- :—déanaṁ = do, make.

,, fo- :—fóġnaṁ = service. Adj. fóġanta = serviceable.

,, com :—congnaṁ = help. Cf. caḃair.

,, ad- and suffix -tom :—aigneaḋ (†ad-gni-tom). For meaning cf. L. natura (nascor) with gigno, γίγνομαι, genus, γένος.

(*j*) Root gus : Eng. cost. L. Au-gus-tus.

With ɼo- :—ɼoʃɑ (choice ; usually *subjective ;* ᴅein ᴅo ɼoʃɑ ɼuᴅ.
ᴛo- :—ᴛoʃɑ (choice ; usually objective ; ᴛoʃɑ ꜰiɼ iɼeɑᴅ é.
Sometimes, however combined, ᴛá ᴛoʃɑ ⁊ ɼoʃɑ nɑ ʒɑeᴅiᴛʒe ɑnn.
With imbi- ɼo- :—iomoɼɼo (O.I. immurgu) = however, indeed, moreover ; also, but, now. Lit. the opposite choice.

(k) ᴛéiʒ, leave, let, lay (cf. L. linquo) : In Mod. I. the e is usually short (M. ᴛeoʒ). With ɑɼ : ᴛeiʒ ɑɼ = pretend.
With od-ess > oɼcɑiᴛ (oɼᴛɑiʒ) = open.
,, to-od-ess (to being dropped in mod. I. and ꜰo inserted before oᴅ) > ꜰuɑɼʒɑiᴛ = redeem, rescue.
,, ᴛo-en- > ᴛeiᴛʒim = throw away.

(*l*) From the root plé (L. plé-nus, Gk. πλή-ρης) in its weakest form. pl- we get ᴛuiᴛe (flood), ᴅiᴛe (deluge), ꜰuɼóiᴛ (excess < fo-ro-oᴅ-) ; ᴅeɑɼóiᴛ (insignificant, as adj.) < di-ro-od-.

(*m*) From the root ᴛo-n-ʒ :—
With ꜰo- > ꜰuᴛɑnʒ = suffering.
,, in > v.n. ellach, originally = union. The modern eɑᴛᴛɑć = household goods, furniture, cattle, is probably the same word. Ceɑᴛᴛɑć = hearth is from ᴛeme.

(*n*) The root lu- = move, energize, v.n. luud, gives probably the modern ᴛúᴛ, vigour, energy ; and possibly ᴛuɑᴅ (mention, discourse, betroth) with narrowing of meaning. Thurn. derives this word from root of L. laus, laudo (au > ua). With ess- > éɑᴛóᴅ = escape, slip away.

(o) From meaṙ (O.I. mess, v.n. of midithir, he judges) we get—
    With ʋi- oʋ- > ʋíomaṙ = pride.
    ,, co- > cómaṙ = measure; a riddle; cuiṙe (cómaiṙe), measure for clothes.
    ,, com- > cumuṙ (proportion: then *power*), cumaṙaċ = lit. well-proportioned, then powerful.

(p) From the root rig- bind :—
    With com- > cuiṁpeaċ (cuiḃpeaċ) = a binder; the act of binding.
    ,, ʋi- > ʋipeaċ (or it may be < L. directus with change of suffix.
    ,, ḟo- > ḟuipeaċ = act of delaying, keeping (transitive).
    ,, aʋ- > áṗaċ = act of binding; buaṗaċ = tying of cattle.

(q) ṗeicc = act of selling :—
    With in- > ionnṗaic = worthy, (fit to be sold).
    ,, ess- > éiṗic = fine, compensation, "eric."

(r) reth- run :—
    With ess- éiṗim.
    ,, co- imbi- di > cimcipeaċc (with suffix assimilated to ceaċc).
    ,, ḟo > ḟóiṗ = help, v.n. ḟóiṗicin. Cf. L. suc-curro.
    ,, co > cóiṗ? pursuit. Also coṗaʋ = fruit, result ; cf. L. eventus.
    ,, inʋ > ionnṗaʋ = attack.
    ,, co (and different form of v.n.) > cuṗuṙ (cf. Mid. I. esraiss (passage way).
    ,, di- oʋ- > O.I. diúrad, what's left over.

Here perhaps we should connect mod. I.
oıúıp = drop, with reminiscence of ʋeop.

(s) From saig-, v.n. saigid = act of seeking, going to :—
With ad- > ascid, ɑıpce = boon, request. Hence
ın-ɑıpce = gratis, for nothing, for the *mere asking*.
  ,, to- ad- > caıpce (safe-keeping).
  ,, aith-com-di- > (O.I. cuindchid, without aith-) modern ɑccuınʒe, ɑccuınʒe (request, beseeching).
  ,, ıɑp- po- (and prothetic p-) > pıɑppɑıʋe. (Earlier iarfaigid).
  ,, ın- > ıonnpɑıʋe = attacking, approach. (Earlier insaigid).
  ,, po- > poıcım = I reach. (Now usually ppoıcım).

(t) seq- say :—Cf. L. inseque : Gk. ἔννεπε.
  With to- ad- > cɑpc =- account, rumour.
  ,, di- oʋ- > ʋúıpıʒım (awake), O.I. ní diúschi.
  , to- en- com- > ceɑʒɑpʒ (irregular short e).
  ,, in- > ınnpce (speech, gender).
  ,, suffix -tlo- > pcéɑl (< †sqe-tlo-m).
  ,, ɑıce- > ɑıceɑpc (Thurn.). Is this ɑpʒ in "ɑp ɑn ʒcéɑʋ ɑpʒ"?

(u) pní- (L. nī-tor) v.n. pníom :—
  With com- copnɑṁ = 1° defending, 2° contending.
  ,, po- puınneɑṁ = energy, vigour, momentum.
  ,, co- ess- ro- céɑpnɑṁ (also céɑpnóʋ) = return, recover, steal away, depart, die, etc.

(v) pıocc = race, stock, posterity. With ʋı-ʋılleɑcc = orphan, and with addition of personal suffix -ıʋe > ʋılleɑccɑıʋe.

(w) cumɑ = shape < com-bɑe (v.n. of benɑıʋ).

cumᴀ = all one, the same < †com- smiio (root *sem* (one) of Latin *semel*, Gk. εἶς, μία, ἕν (i.e. †sems, †sm̩iia, †sem).

(x) cLé (cLi) = left. With ᵽo > ᵽoċLᴀ = the North. Cf. ᴛuᴀiᴅ (North) and ᴛuᴀᴛᴀL (cᴀᵽᴀᴅ ᴛuᴀᴛᴀiL = the left turn).

II. 1°. connᴛᴀᴅᴀiᵽᴛ = danger: in Mid. I. doubt.

2°. ᴅᵽonnᴀim = I bestow. Originally I *spoil*, *damage*; then *spend*, *consume*; and finally *bestow*. A good example of specialisation in meaning.

3°. connᵽᴀᴅ = *contract*; then *league*. There is no reason to get angry with **connᵽᴀᴅ** nᴀ ᵹᴀeᴅiLᵹe.

4°. ᴀṁᵽᴀᵽ = 1° want of faith, 2° doubt in general.

5°. cLᴀᴅᴀiᵽe = 1° a digger, 2° thief, rogue, scoundrel, etc. The word cLᴀᵹᴀiᵽe (Din.) = a fish after shedding its spawn, is probably the same word and should be spelled with ᴅ (instead of ᵹ) (Z.C.P. VII, 2).

6°. O.I. foditiu (v.n. of fo-daim) = suffering: The Connaught I. ᵽoiᵹᴅe (patience) looks very like the same word syncopated (but cf. O.I. foigde < fo + gude = begging. The change of meaning is intelligible in either case), and with ᵹ substituted for the ᴅ of the O.I.; the ᴅ of ᵽoiᵹᴅe would represent the O.I. t. The d of O.I. foigde is, of course, aspirated. The Munster ᵽoiᴅne may go back to the dative form foditiN.

7°. O.I. ad-etha = attacks (for the root, cf. L. ita-re, frequentative from ire) has for vb.n. ᴀiᴅeᴀᴅ; modern oiᴅeᴀᴅ = tragic fate, death. Also iᵽ móᵽ ᴀn oiᴅeᴀᴅ ᵽLᴀice ᴛú = you deserve to be beaten with a rod.

8°. O.I. dringid, steps, advances, has vb.n. ᴅᵽéim (cf. céim, Léim, etc.). In Ulster it means *expectation*, *emulation*, etc. Ópéimıpe = ladder.

9°. O.I. erchót, v.n. of ar-com-fed-, is in modern I. uṗcóıv. The old word meant *hindrance*; uṗcóıv = evil, damage, iniquity. P.H. 7734 : urchóit na spréide = the lust of wealth.

10°. ꝼeıꝛ is old v.n. of ꝼoᴀım = I sleep (cf. German Wesen.) It meant however, not physiological sleep, but 'passing the night'; then a night *festival;* then festival in general; then the particular kind of festival which it now denotes. Derivative— ꝼeıꝛıpe.

11°. ꝼuıne nᴀ ꝣṗéıne : the setting, going down of the sun. Perhaps from root- ne with ꝼo- prefixed and -io suffix; cf. Gk. νέομαι = go or come (Pedersen). ꝼuın, knead, bake, is a different word. Pedersen proposes ꝼo + ꝣní, but this seems unlikely, as one would expect a long vowel. Possibly from the root snī- (cf. ꝼuınneᴀṁ and the L. subnixus), though we should expect -nn. The double n, however, would not be such a serious obstacle, as the short vowel in Pedersen's derivation.

12° ᴀṗᴀċ = the tying of cattle ; now = security, guarantee, help, hope, opportunity.

13°. ꝼuıṗeᴀċ (ꝼo + rig) originally transitive, retain, delay; now intransitive, delay.

14° ċúıṗeᴀṁ (to + rím) originally = act of recounting; now in specialised meaning—elegy.

15°. mᴀıċeᴀṁ = pardon (cf. W. madden, I. made = vain). Lit = make nothing of Its form is affected by mᴀıċ, with which it has nothing to do etymologically.

16°. ʟᴇɪᴄᴇɪʀ, kind, sort, the like of ; earlier lethet (mod. ʟᴇɪᴄᴇᴀᴅ = breadth). Cf. P.H. 3091, tria tharmcruthugad a letheti, lit. through a transfiguration of its sort (size). Hence we sometimes find ᴀ ʟᴇɪᴄᴇɪʀᴅᴇ. In the special meaning of " kind, sort," the word is kept as a fem. and e is long (perhaps by association with ᴍᴇɪʀᴅ), whereas ʟᴇɪᴄᴇᴀᴅ in the sense of " breadth " is masc. An early example with é is found in Gm. Z.C.P II, 30 :—a lethét sin d'aráu. Cf. No. 17ᵇ

17°. ʀᴀsᴀʀ (lit. " size " from the English) ; then kind, sort. Cf. 16° and the English " to *size* up " a person (i.e., tell what *sort* he is).

18°. ɴíʟ ᴇ́ɪɴɴᴇ ɪs ᴀɴɴʀᴀ ʟɪᴏᴍ ɴᴀ́ ᴄᴜʀᴀ. Aɴɴʀᴀ is comparative of ᴀɴɴʀᴀ (difficult), earlier annsu ; positive annse (< an + asse, easy). In the idiom quoted it is used somewhat like ᴍᴇᴀʀᴀ, and like ᴍᴇᴀʀᴀ, takes on the meaning " dearer." So the derivative ᴀɴɴʀᴀᴄᴄ means *love, affection*.

19°. ᴘᴜᴀᴅᴀɴ ᴀʟʟᴀ : In Arran, means a " sparrow hawk," but in W. Munster is used in the sense of ᴅᴜᴅᴀ́ɴ ᴀʟʟᴀ (also ᴅᴀɪɴᴀ́ɴ) = a spider. We find at Ml. 59d as a gloss on " Aranearum " innan *damán n-allaid*. This is a diminutive from the existing word ᴅᴀᴍ ᴀʟʟᴀɪᴅ = a stag. Dᴀᴍ originally signifies a domesticated quadruped (from same root as Lat. domo ; domitus, subdued) and in particular, the cow (a common standard of value in ancient Ireland). Then, with the addition of ᴀʟʟᴀɪᴅ (wild : silvaticus ; Fr. sauvage) it means *a stag*. The diminutive ᴅᴀᴍᴀ́ɴ ᴀʟʟᴀɪᴅ was applied to the spider, because of its swift, vigorous movements, and its precipitate flight at the approach of man. Marstrander (Z.C.P.

VII, 2, 409) sees a difficulty in deriving from ᴅᴀṁ (in the sense of 'deer') and suggests ᴅᴀṁ a worm, reptile, louse (D.I.L.R.I.A., p. 59). In ᴅᴜʙáɴ ᴀʟʟᴀ we see folk-etymology at work. It literally means "the little black thing of the wall (ꜰᴀʟʟᴀ, ᴀʟʟᴀ) or of the rock, cliff (ᴀɪʟʟ, ᴀɪʟʟᴇ)," ꜰᴜᴀᴅáɴ ᴀʟʟᴀ is a further contortion of the original meaning. A common word for spider in Ulster at the present day is ꝼíɢᴇᴀᴅóɪꝼ (weaver).
20°. ʙéᴀꝼʟᴀ : the English language ; originally bélre = any language (< bél mouth).
21° ʙɪᴄᴇᴀṁɴᴀċ, if I am right in deriving from O.I. bibdu (guilty, a guilty person) through the abstract bibdamnacht, shows considerable change of meaning in the modern language :—thief, beggar, rogue, rascal ; padding in the sole of a shoe.
22°. ᴄᴇᴀᴅ (permission). Kuno Meyer holds that this is simply -cet of the Latin word licet Irishised. From meaning "it is permitted" it has come to signify *permission*.
23°. ᴄéᴀꝼᴀᴅ : Originally, to *suffer ;* now generally, to CRUCIFY, crucifixion, from its frequent use in ᴄéᴀꝼᴀᴅ ᴀꝼ ᴏᴛɪɢᴇᴀꝼɴᴀ íoꝼᴀ Cꝼíoꝼᴛ.
24°. ᴅáɴ (L. donum). Originally gift ; Wb. 28ᶜ2 : ní riat na *dánu* diadi ara n-indeb domunde, they shall not sell the divine GIFTS for worldly gain ; then gift of *poetry* ; then a poem ; and specially a poem in syllabic, as distinguished from accentual, metre. In Mid. I. business, trade, occupation.
25°. ᴅéɪꝼᴄ : originally love of *God* (ᴅé + ꝼᴇᴀꝼᴄ) ; now generally love *of the neighbour ;* charity, alms.
26°. ᴅᴇᴀʟʟꝼᴀṁ :—flash, blaze, shining ; then appearance, likelihood.

27°. ċaicneaṁ :—shining ; to please ; love (cuġaŗ caicneaṁ ꝺo'n ainniŗ).

28°. ꝺeoŗaiꝺe :—exile : probably from earlier ꝺeoŗaꝺ, ꝺeoŗaiꝺ = outlaw, stranger, exile (from di + urrad = a native freeman with full rights). The word also means at present- fugitive, beggar, pilgrim, penitent (with reminiscence of ꝺeoŗ, a tear). In its present form the word is assimilated to personal nouns in -iꝺe.

29°. ꝺíoġḃáil (from di + gabáil), lit., taking away from ; now loss, harm, injury ; want (like eaŗḃa) in Donegal; also slight inclination to one side or other ; cuiŗ inꝺíoġḃáil é.

30°. ꝺóċa now means likely, probable, rather. It is really the comparative of ꝺóiċ (often written ꝺóiġ ; cf. Gk. δοκέω, L. doceo). The o was originally short, as in Gk. and Lat. When the comparative meaning of ꝺóċa (O.I. dochu) was no longer felt, a new comparative ꝺóiċiġe (ꝺóċaiġe) was formed.

31° ꝺualġuŗ : originally, one's *right*, what is due TO one. Now, one's *duty*, what is due FROM one. The first sense is also found.

32°. ḟéaꝺaim : originally, I obtain, get. Now, I can, am able (with accus.) ní ḟéaꝺŗainn é. I couldn't. Cf. ní ḃḟuiġinn ꝺul ann, and provincial English " I couldn't GET going."

33°. malaiŗc : destruction, perdition. Now merely, change, something else, different ; a ṁalaiŗc ꝺe ġnó. Is it a collective from L. malus ?

34°. miaŗ : < L. mensa :—table ; plate ;dish.

35°. ŗŗṕéiꝺ :—(L. praeda < prae-heda < hendo in praehendo, prendo) = cattle driven as spoil. Then, fortune, wealth, worldly goods ; then dowry, wife's portion.

36°. meᴀr : vb.n. of midithir, he judges ; hence judgment ; then favourable judgment ; esteem.

37° cρéᴀdanᴀr, now = abstinence (as distinct from fasting, croρsᴀd). In Mid. I. = a space of three days (O.I. tréde = 3 things ; but also through L. triduanus) ; then three days' fast or abstinence ; then abstinence in general.

38°. cρéιte = qualities ; good qualities ; accomplishments, shows a generalisation in meaning from O.I. tréde = three things. "Accomplishments" in Irish storytelling were often enumerated in *"threes."* Cf. Meᴀdb's requirements in her husband—" fer cen neoit, cen ét, cen oman " ; and Déirdre's desire for a husband who should have " duibhe an fhich, dirrce na fcla, ⁊ gile an tsneachta." The Irish " Triads " are well-known.

STUDIES IN MODERN IRISH

ABBREVIATIONS.

In addition to the usual Grammatical contractions :—
V = verb.
P = (material) predicate.
S = (,,   ) subject.
p = pronominal (formal) predicate.
s = pronominal (formal) subject.

1. Acts (ξníoṁapṫa na n-Appol), Canon O Leary.
2. Aep. (Aepop a ṫáinig go héipinn), Canon O Leary.
3. A.M.C. (Aislinge Meic Conglinne : The Vision of Mac Conglinne), Ed. Kuno Meyer.
4. B.K. (Stories from Keating).—Bergin.
5. Ḃp. (Ḃpicpiu).—Canon O Leary.
6. C.Ḋ. (An Cpaop Ḋeaṁan).—Canon O Leary.
7. Ċ.S. (na Ceiṫpe Soipgéil).—Canon O Leary.
8. Caṫ. (Caṫilína).—Canon O Leary.
9. C. na nζ. (Capaiḋ nan ζaiḋheal).—Norman Mac Leod, D.D.
10. Cl. (An Cleapaiḋe).—Canon O Leary.
11. Don. (Donlevy's Catechism, 1848).
12. D. (Manuel d'Irlandais Moyen).—G. Dottin (Paris).
13. D.S. (Na Daoine Sidhe is Uirsgeulan eile).—Celtic Press, Glasgow.
14. Ḋonnċ. R. (Ḋonnċaḋ Ruaḋ Mac Conmapa).
15. D.I.L. (R.I.A.).—Dictionary of the Irish Language (Pub. by Royal Irish Academy).
16. eip. (eipipṫ).—By Canon O Leary.
17. F.A. (Finnpgéalṫa na h-Apaibe).—Feappgup Finn-ḃéil.
18. F.S. (Fuinn na Smól).
19. ζ. (ζuaipe).—Canon O Leary.
20. Gl. (Old Irish Glosses).
21. Im. (Aiṫpip ap Ċpíopṫ).—Canon O Leary.
22. K.T.B. (Keating's Cpí ḃiop-ġaoiṫe an Ḃáip).
23. K.H.—Keating's History.
24. K.P.—Keating's Poems.

STUDIES IN MODERN IRISH

25. Luke (Gospel of St. Luke in na Ceitre Soirséil).—Canon O Leary
26. L.O. (Laoi Oirín ar Tír na n-Óg).—Ed. Flannery.
27. MS.F. (Mo Sséal féin).—Canon O Leary.
28. Ml. (The Milan Glosses).
29. n. (niam).—Canon O Leary.
30. n. ng. (naoi ngábad an giolla Óinb).—Míceál ó Máille.
31. PH. (Passions and Homilies from the Leabar breac).—Ed. Atkinson.
32. PB. (Poetry of Badenoch).—Sinton.
33. Ser (Seanmóin ir trí pició).—Canon O Leary.
34. S.T. (Stories from the Táin).—Strachan.
35. S. (Séadna).—Canon O Leary.
36. Sg. (Sgot-buala).—Canon O Leary.
37. TBC (Táin bó Cuailgne).—Canon O Leary.
38. T.g. (Tadg gaba).—Doyle.
39. Thurn (Thurneysen). Th. Hb. (Thurneysen's Handbuch des Alt-Irischen).
40. John (Gospel of St. John in na Ceitre Soirséil).
41. Wb. (The Würzburg Glosses).
42. Z.C.P. (Zeitschrift für Celtische Philologie).

Lightning Source UK Ltd.
Milton Keynes UK
UKHW011251230920
370396UK00002B/776